Before I was married I had six theories about bringing up children. Now I have six children and no theories!
— Lord Rochester
(1647-1680)

Excerpts from "Brain" ©1982 University of Oregon, Department of Education and
Mildred C. Robeck. Inquiries should be addressed to College of Education, University
of Oregon, Eugene, Oregon 97403.

Research results from the study by Sister M. Vivian Skluzacek, S.S.N.D. ©1972 Sister
M. Vivian Skuzacek S.S.N.D. Inquiries should be addressed to Sister Maureen Murray,
School Sisters of Notre Dame, Inc., Good Counsel Hill, Mankato, Minnesota 56001.

Excerpts from "Child Behavior" rev. ed. from the Gesell Institute of Human
Development © by Louise Bates Ames, Francis L. Ilg, Sidney M. Baker and Gesell
Institute for Human Development.

"How to Test for Hypoglycemia" ©1980 Alexander G. Schauss, published by Parker
House, 2340 Parker Street, Berkely, California.

Excerpts from "No Miracles" in press, Academic Therapy, ©1985 Svea J. Gold and
Academic Therapy Publications.

Cartoons "Hi Mom! Hi Dad!" ©1977 by Lynn Johnston, Meadowbrook Press,
Deephaven, Minnesota 55391.

Cartoons "Do They Ever Grow Up?" ©1978 by Lynn Johnston, Meadowbrook Press,
Deephaven, Minnesota 55391.

When Children Invite Child Abuse

a search for answers when love is not enough

by
Svea J. Gold

In consultation with:
Louise Bates Ames, Ph.D.
Carl H. Delacato, Ed.D.
Lendon H. Smith, M.D.
Alexander G. Schauss, M.A.
Florence Scott, R.N.
Ray C. Wunderlich Jr., M.D.

Fern Ridge Press
Eugene, Oregon
London

To
my husband
LARRY GOLD

With much thanks ...
To Bonnie Bergonin, Bruce Berglund, Ann Breslauer, Larry Burr, Ron Lechnyr, Ray Lowe, Don Mihaloew, Jeannie Morris, Dr. Janice Phelps, Mark Souther, Peter Springall, and Wil Willhite, all of whom have freely shared of their time and their professional knowledge with me. And, especially, to Jessica Kline.

Also to Sister Maureen Murray (SSND) who has given permission to use the graphs of Sister Vivian Skluzacek. To Mildred C. Robeck and Dean Robert D. Gilberts of the University of Oregon Department of Education for permission to use the material on the brain. To John Unruh for sharing his chart on testing for functional neurological development.

With special thanks to Sarah Coleman for her enthusiasm for this project, and the help of Wilma Simonsen and Jennifer Stevenson in editing.

To my family: my great-uncle Kurt Goldstein, one of the great pioneers in brain research; my father graphologist Frank Victor (Grunfeld), who believed, before it was fashionable, that psychotherapy worked better if you gave the patient some needed vitamins; to my mother, E. Eva Grunfeld, who kept us all alive. And to Regina Lautenschlager, who was family by choice.

And to all the libraries and their staffs — from shelver to library director, to all the indexers and computer searchers — and, of course, the authors willing to share their knowledge, without whom this kind of research could not exist.

But most thanks of all to Sean, my son, who, in growing up with two imperfect parents, seems to have learned the patience to cope in an imperfect world, and of whom I am so inordinately proud that I dared write this book!

WHEN CHILDREN INVITE CHILD ABUSE

CONTENTS

THE EARLY SCHOOL YEARS

THE TEEN YEARS: JUVENILE DELINQUENCY

The ideas, procedures and suggestions contained in this book are not intended as a substitute for consulting with your physician. All matters regarding your health require medical supervision.

The masculine pronoun for the infant and child is used throughout much of this book, although this presents a sexual bias which I would rather not reinforce. The he/she escape from such bias is too distracting. Also, for convenience sake, the word "mother" is used though in many situations the father might be equally involved.

i. Introduction

No Miracles: A day in the life of an Abused Child

Miracles do not happen. There are no miracles, only connections between cause and effect. If "miracles" are reported in magazines and newspapers, they always happen in some big city at some famous hospital, or are created by some scientist who is about to win a Nobel prize.

Miracles certainly would not happen in a quiet Oregon community called Woodburn, just a few miles off I-5 freeway, on the stretch between Portland and Salem. It was a hot summer day, and two boys, about 14 years old, were coming home from the swimming pool. They wore swimming trunks and T-shirts and carried their wet towels around the neck to keep cool. Because it was hot, they took a shortcut and slowly ambled down Arthur Street. At the corner of Arthur and First Street there stood a strange-looking building, more like a showroom with enormous glass windows. For a moment the boys pressed their noses against the window to see what was happening inside. Shading their eyes, they could see that inside, there was some strange equipment. Attached horizontally between two pillars was a ladder. There was a metal frame about eight feet high and three feet wide, from which, at two-foot intervals, hung knotted ropes. A little further was a long mat and next to it, a huge plastic pipe which was mounted on a horizontal wheel. Still, further in the back, as the boys' eyes adjusted from the glare of the sun, they could see several waist-high tables, and around them stood a bunch of teenagers engaged in some kind of rhythmic activity.

Inside the building, Florence Scott watched carefully as the three teenage volunteers moved the arms, legs, and head of a three-year-old boy who had cerebral palsy. When she was convinced the rhythm was smooth and the boys' good-natured chatter was keeping the child in a cooperative mood, she turned away.

A woman was helping a four-year-old little girl swing by her hands, monkey fashion, from the ladder which was attached between the two pillars holding up the roof. "Wait," said Florence Scott. "I think it will be easier if you make the ladder a little higher." And she adjusted the mechanism which lowered or raised the ladder. It was at that moment that she noticed the two boys who had walked in through the doors, which were wide open because of the heat.

One of the boys was fairly tall for his age, dark-haired and unusually handsome. The other was red-haired and freckle-faced with a friendly, alive expression.

"What's going on in here?" the redhead wanted to know. Florence Scott explained that this was a place where people who had children with brain injuries, or with learning problems, or people who had had an accident or a stroke, could come and use the equipment to help them get well. While she was talking, the dark-haired boy had moved between two waist-high tables and, bracing himself on either side, was swinging his body, pendulum fashion, in a curiously obsessive rhythm. Florence looked up from her conversation with the other boy: The dark-haired one was making strange sounds — sounds that, she said later, were impossible to describe.

"What's the matter with your friend?" she asked the redhead. "You mean Randy?" replied the boy. "Nothing. He's always like that."

But Florence Scott had become alert. While she showed the redhead the different equipment, how it worked and why it was used, she kept an eye on the boy called Randy, who was making those strange noises.

By now the woman had lifted the little girl down from the ladder. Giggling, on hands and knees, the little girl crept at great speed in the direction of Randy and sat there with complete fascination, watching him swing. Randy stopped and stared at her. She reached out her little hand and touched his leg. Randy pulled back as if she had touched him with a red-hot poker and withdrew to the other side of the table.

"Do you go to school together?" Florence Scott asked Randy's friend. "He doesn't go to school," the redhead said casually, as if it were the most normal thing in the world. "He lives with his grandparents, here on the next block. His mother beat him up when he was little, or something, so he's not allowed to live with her." And the boy mentioned the name of the people with whom Randy was living.

Long after the two boys had left, after all the patients and all the volunteers had gone, Florence Scott sat in her office and leafed through the telephone book. So that strange, handsome Randy, who was so afraid of being touched, was an abused child! That would account for his pulling away like that — but from a little girl? And that strange, rhythmic swinging, those weird noises! Florence Scott had seen other children like that. They did strange things for no apparent reason. Sometimes, they almost seemed as if they were possessed by an alien spirit. Occasionally, you read in the papers that they had been murdered by their parents in some strange rite of exorcism. "We didn't mean to kill him, Your Honor!" the parents would say later in court. "We were just trying to exorcise the evil spirit that was in him."

Florence Scott looked at the empty therapy room she could survey from her modest little office. The building had been bought with donated funds. The center was run with the proceeds from a thrift shop in the back, and its services were free to anyone who needed to come there. There had been many over the years, some badly injured, some so slightly that no one would suspect there was anything wrong at all. Some of the injured became completely normal. With others, there was always some remnant of the problem, but there was always some improvement. Florence Scott did not believe in miracles, only in ever-increasing knowledge and in application of that knowledge.

She slid her fingers down the columns of the phone book. Randy's grandparents should not be hard to find in such a small town. But there was an unwritten law among the people who work with the brain-injured: Even if you think you can help someone, you do not volunteer the information. Usually, people consider their child's handicap their private burden, and they get very angry if anyone tries to talk about it. Florence Scott's finger rested on the name and the address, but Florence hesitated, her other hand on the receiver.

In the meantime, Randy's grandmother was calling Randy to

dinner. It was a problem getting that child to do anything. Here again, the boy was swinging between two chairs and making those ridiculous noises. The grandmother shook her head. That child was so difficult, so unapproachable. She loved him. He was so good-looking; even so, without schooling, he was a child without a future. Randy's grandmother did not believe in miracles, either.

And yet, if just for a moment she could have glimpsed the future, if just for a moment she could have seen herself, four years later, giving him a last hug as she put him on the plane to go to college, she might have sensed what was about to happen — here, in one of the most unlikely places in the world, a sleepy little town called Woodburn — there was about to happen a miracle. Because just at that moment the phone rang, and a voice said, "My name is Florence Scott, and I work with an organization called 'Oregon Hope and Help.' We work with people who have neurological problems. I just met your grandson this afternoon, and I think we could help him. Do you think you might be interested in coming to talk to me about that?"

ii. Introduction

How
To Use
This Book

This book is not about one child or one method of treatment. This book explores connections between many interrelated factors which will affect children to behave in such a way that the adults will get angry and abuse them. It is from treating the Randys, the truly incomprehensible children of this world, that we are beginning to learn how to help difficult children. If all the answers are not in this book, never cease looking, because there is new research done every day and you might find the answers in tomorrow's newspaper.

Now, those who have never had a child, never had to live with a child for any length of time, will find it incomprehensible that anyone could even dream of abusing, much less could actually murder a child. Anyone who has had a child (or almost anyone — I do know of some supermothers with marvelous children), in fact, anyone who has ever dealt with children for any length of time, may begin to wonder how so many do escape unharmed and somehow manage to survive.

This book, then, is dedicated to all the parents and all the teachers who have ever entertained the joyful thought of strangling their charges — and to giving them the information they need to cope without having to entertain such thoughts for more than a fleeting moment.

The factual information in this book belongs to the consultants listed on the title page: Louise Bates Ames, Carl H. Delacato, Alexander G. Schauss, Florence Scott and Ray C. Wunderlich, Jr. (Billing in alphabetical order.) They have allowed me to use their research, provided new ideas and checked the final version so there would be no errors. Others who have personally conferred with me or whose research I have incorporated are mentioned separately throughout.

The passionate conviction that there are answers — and all the wisecracks — are mine.

I feel we are all capable of abusing our children: All it takes is to shake a child under four years of age, and you can cause brain damage! Most people do not know that. And so the book contains all the material, much of it new, some of it known for years, that I wish I had known before raising my own child.

It is not the kind of book that suggests that if you did everything right with your child, all would be well and you could live in harmony with your offspring for the rest of your life. (If that were possible, very few people would ever leave home!) It is a book which brings together much information that can be found, but only after much searching and in many different books and articles. And, if somewhere along the line, you recognize a child, your own or one that somehow touches your life, and can find in these pages an approach which might help protect that child, then the book has done its work.

By all means start with the part of the book that covers your prime concern at the moment. But do read all the chapters in Section I and Section II — no one chapter is independent of any of the others. Each one is meant to open new doors and suggest solutions which will make children easier to live with. Each one is essentially only an introduction, simply because it is impossible to cover so many concepts exhaustively in one single book.

Specific techniques are listed in the Appendix, and need be read only if their use seems to be indicated in a specific case. The book is divided into 3 sections. Section I deals with the 70% of the abused children who, statistics show, have some medical or developmental problem. Whether the problem started before the abuse and led to it directly, or whether it was caused by the abuse does not matter. It must be remedied.

Section I is divided into three parts, because the incidence of child abuse changes in severity and type with the age of the child.

Part 1: The Early Years.

Children with a mild problem are often abused during the early years. They cry more, fuss more, and generally cause more trouble than healthy infants. If the problem becomes severe enough, parent and child may get help from a doctor or agency. However, especially if there is a borderline handicap, one which is not readily diagnosed, they often get abused and may even get murdered.

Part 2: The Early School Years.

The more subtle the handicap, the less likely it is to show up until the child reaches school. Here, again, the child with the obvious disability, at least in most schools, will get some help. Those with subtle learning problems get abused by their teachers, their parents, and worst of all, by their classmates.

Part 3: The Teen Years: Juvenile Delinquency.

There are some whose problems remain undetected until they reach the teen years. In those cases, the earlier experience of years of failure and frustration tends to have pushed the child into an antisocial subculture, and he may end up in trouble with the law.

Section II may be the section you wish to read first. It deals with the normal developmental phases which any healthy child will go through. Since normal child development is worth an entire book by itself, it only covers those behaviors which have been shown to have been the trigger in an enormous number of child abuse statistics. They are the kind of things a child does which a parent feels honor-bound to change, and which usually will disappear as the child grows a few months older — if the parent does not lose his patience or his mind first.

Section III is the Appendix and contains information you will need if you wish to test some of the techniques mentioned in the earlier sections.

If your concerns are with a teenager, start with Section I, part 3 and reading backwards, so to speak, you may then recognize some of the child's earlier symptoms and the causes of his present problem in the chapters on the earlier years.

If you are interested in the younger years, reading the latter parts of the book will emphasize how important it is to take action early, for it will show what can happen if no action is taken.

And if there is a touch of levity here and there, remember Noel Coward's philosophy: For God's sake, don't be serious, the situation is far too desperate! Also, if you can't wait to see how Florence Scott and Randy's grandparents, not by that one miracle, but by hard work, got Randy ready to go to college, the rest of his case history is in Part 1 of the Appendix.

iii. Introduction

Connections: A Justification For The Existence Of This Book

Child abuse is as old as mankind. It was never called child abuse, because it was almost taken for granted. If we have no actual facts or figures, we do have legends and stories:

Abraham was quite willing to sacrifice his son to God, and the fact that God sent him a ram to sacrifice instead was a step toward a new understanding: Children are more than just a piece of parental property.

Nobody seemed particularly upset that when the oracle prophesied that the little baby Oedipus would some day kill his father and marry his mother, the mother slit the infant's heels, put a thong through the slit, and had the baby hung from a tree to die.

In Roman times, if not earlier, the philosophy was "spare the rod and spoil the child."

During medieval times, six-year-olds were taken from their doting mothers and made to help the men in the fields and in the stables.

During the later, more enlightened period, some attempts were made to treat children in a more benign fashion, but infants were sent to live on a farm, presumably for their health, and there, more often than not, they died — conveniently for the parents — from one disease or another.

Since even in loving families it was rare to have more than two or three survive out of a brood of ten, who would know which ones died of abuse or neglect?

During the Victorian period, children were sent off to work — under the most appalling conditions — in the factories and mines, and it took 50 to 100 years to write legislation to protect them from such abuse.

Those parents who did not have to send their children off to work protected themselves from the realities of child rearing by having a "Nanny." Often she was a young, ignorant girl, anxious to live her own life, and it is hard to tell just what idiocies were perpetrated in the nursery.

At six years of age, many boys were sent off to school. There, in the name of making them hardy gentlemen, they were beaten at the slightest provocation and, if nothing else, endured the most awful homesickness.

The result of these apparently unbearable conditions was that, for the most part, only the hardiest of children survived. It was, in truth, a question of survival of the fittest.

Today, we raise our children no longer into a world where only the strong survive, but into what, we hope, is a world of law and order. Theoretically, all people are entitled to find their way without having to step on the weaker ones. Just as, collectively, we no longer sanction slavery today, we no longer consider children merely the extension and the property of their parents. We see them as human beings, entitled to their own chance at well-being and happiness.

In spite of this, reported child abuse cases have increased steadily over the past few years. Is it that people are more alert to the problem, or is child abuse truly increasing? The increase would be understandable. With so much of humanity standing packed like sardines in hot subways or fighting stop-and-go traffic on the freeways before coming home at night, it is really amazing that more violence is not committed. Every year, the gap between what is offered or advertized on TV and what people can actually afford becomes greater. And the more a parent is incapable of bringing home to his family those things he feels he should provide, the more angry he will become at those demanding little creatures who keep him caught in the rat race. If a woman is angry at the father of her child (whether he is there or has just deserted her), the child is right there under her hands and is the most convenient object on which to let out her anger.

Statistics indicate that child abuse is more common in families where the parents themselves had been abused as children. This latter generation, who are now abusing their own children were raised in the benign era of Dr. Spock and supposedly humanitarian child raising. Nevertheless, we have the following horrifying statistics.

TABLE 1   SUBSTANTIATED MALTREATMENT—PERCENT

(Compiled from *Highlights of Official Child Neglect and Abuse Reporting,* Annual Reports, 1976-1980, American Humane Association)

Type	1979	1980	1981	1982
Major Physical Injury	4	4	4	2
Minor Physical Injury	15	20	20	17
Physical Injury (Unspecified)	3	3	3	5
Sex Abuse	6	7	7	7
Deprivation of Necessities*	63	61	59	62
Emotional Maltreatment	15	13	12	10
Other	9	8	12	10
Number of cases (in thousands)	226	268	236	332

*failure to provide shelter, nourishment, health care, education, supervision, clothing and failure to thrive, as defined by the states.

TABLE 2 FATALITIES ASSOCIATED WITH CHILD MALTREATMENT

(American Humane Association, 1979-82 data)

Year	Total # Reported	# States Reporting	# With Maltreatment Type Known	Cases Associated With Neglect #	%
1979	350	25	261	142	54
1980	421	27	288	123	43
1981	585	25	381	212	56
1982	484	24	282	144	51

These are only the cases which were actually reported. In 1977, David Gelles estimated from interviewing persons who had witnessed some form of violence between parent and child that there were anywhere from 1,400,000 to 1,900,000 cases of such violence.

What had gone wrong?

One of the results of the fact that society is beginning to feel responsible for the well-being of children is that, with today's explosion of knowledge and the tendency of doctors, hospitals and universities to apply for government research grants, there has been a wealth of research in the area of abuse and an enormous amount of statistical information.

The information available through the National Center on Child Abuse and Neglect covers many areas: the incidence of abuse, the background of the parents, the possibility of prediction, and so on. The one area which has only recently come under scrutiny is the role of the child in the parent-child interaction which leads to abuse or neglect. Researchers have focused on several different ways in which the child may contribute to the tension or provoke the abuse. While in no way do we wish to imply there are not other factors involved, this book deals with these high-risk children, who in a high-risk situation will invite trouble.

There are statistics to show that as much as 70% of the abused children have shown some physical or developmental deviation! That these deviant children are even more readily abused if they are the children of poverty-stricken families does not alter this fact: They are in danger, and something must be done for them as soon as the condition is recognized. The question then becomes: What is the condition which must be recognized and changed? Much of our knowledge about proper child rearing initially came from studying mentally ill adults. Knowledge of nutrition has come from studying nutrition deficiency diseases. So it makes sense to look at that part of our population which has been abused.

Now, there are many abused and beaten children who have grown up and, to all outward appearances, are normal human beings. We know very little about them. The one group which has been studied from all angles and on whom we have all kinds of statistics is the prison population. Rightly or wrongly, the commercial sponsored by the Child Abuse Council claims: They have all been abused children! And this is what we find:

1. Jailed offenders have been abused children.

2. Seventy-five percent of prisoners are learning-disabled. (The average reading level in United States prisons is below the fifth-grade level.)

3. Eighty percent of prisoners studied have been found to be hypoglycemic. Hypoglycemia manifests itself in depression, mood swings, anxiety attacks, and incoherent thought.

4. In a study of the psychological background of juvenile delinquents, while there were numerous contributing factors involved, the only statistically significant fact which emerged was that the children had perception problems — visual, auditory, or intersensory. (Both perception and intersensory problems have been identified as two of the main causes of reading disability.)

The figures give us some characteristics, but not yet the causes for characteristics which drive parents to abuse their children. To find those, we have to look even further:

5. Forty percent of brain-damaged children are allergic.

6. Fifty percent of autistic children are allergic and hypoglycemic.

7. Almost all brain-damaged children have perception problems.

8. Almost all autistic children have sensory-perception problems.

9. Hypoglycemic children have perception problems.

Somewhere there is a statistician who can pull all of these facts together and make some sense, but for our purposes, we have here a modern version of the three blind men and the elephant. Each expert describes only what he knows and what he is looking for. The statistics are not contradictory; they are simply overlapping.

The general conclusion from all these studies is that, if we take a guess at evaluating prisoners, we will probably be right if we presume this: The abused children who have landed themselves in jail are allergic, hypoglycemic, and learning disabled. We can also presume with some accuracy, that these allergy, hypoglycemia and learning problems affected the child's behavior, thinking and actions. The result: the ultimate abuse — the denial of freedom — jail. What we have established is that we are looking not for one factor, but for many overlapping ones which need to be treated at the same time. With what we know today, we should be able to diagnose a child's problems before he gets in trouble with the law. But if we have failed at that, if we take a juvenile offender and treat him for hypoglycemia, we may have cured a few allergies in the bargain (They tend to become less or to disappear along with the hypoglycemia), but we have not cured his learning disability that way. Suppose we cure the perception problems which caused his learning disabilities; he would still have to catch up on years of missed learning, and even then, we have not begun to heal the emotional scars which have been caused by all his prior problems.

It would be so much more effective to fix these kids before they became a danger to themselves and to the rest of us. Unfortunately, until recently so little has been known about these problems and how to cure them that no one is really to blame for not doing more than has been done. Psychologists knew only about psychological problems, neurologists about neurology, teachers about teaching, and case workers about social laws.

To make matters worse, the problems of the offenders were often so minimal that they remained undetected. Could it be that many of these children were the bright kids who were able to fake their way through elementary school? Not until junior high school, when more reading was demanded than they could safely handle, did they fall apart. Had their problems been more obvious earlier, they might have gotten help.

Identification, then, is a primary problem. When it becomes a case of one individual child, all the statistics in the world are of little use; we still have to deal with the individual child. Sometimes, on the other hand, the reality of one single case of an abused child can make all the statistics suddenly fall into place and make sense.

Ruth Inglis, in "The Sins of the Fathers," describes the same connections in England. She describes not only the background from which many of these abused children come but also their characteristics. She talks about the low-birth-weight child and about how parents see the child they have singled out for abuse as evil and retarded. This is the same material which American researchers have found.

At one point, she quotes an abusive mother as having said, "When she looks at me with those queer gray eyes, she makes me think of how my mother looked when she was really nasty!"

Now, Ruth Inglis, being thoroughly familiar with Freudian psychology, sees that at this point the mother is having a reaction to her own childhood anger at her mother. There is nothing essentially wrong with that conclusion, but there is another piece of information in the statement which seems to throw light on an entirely different aspect of child abuse: "Those queer gray eyes..."!

Somehow, that sounded familiar! Myra Rothenberg had written a book, "Children with Emerald Eyes". The children with emerald-green eyes were the autistic and emotionally disturbed children with whom she had worked ... children with emerald eyes!

Those same autistic children were the ones Carl H. Delacato has been able to help, as he described in his book, "The Ultimate Stranger: The Autistic Child."

Dr. Lendon H. Smith has said about the ticklish, hypersensitive and school-problem children, "I see a lot of this in blond, blue-eyed children, in green-eyed redheads, in Indians, Jews, and Italians."

Ben Feingold, in "Why Your Child is Hyperactive," talks about the blond and blue-eyed ones as being more susceptible to allergies in food additives.

George von Hilsheimer, in "Allergies, Toxins and the Learning-Disabled Child," talks about the wispy-blond, blue-eyed children who are fairer than their parents.

I have seen a whole wall of photos of these children, almost all blond and blue-eyed, and many with the characteristic buck teeth of the brain-damaged child, in the waiting room of a developmental optometrist in Brea, California. Essentially, the optometrist was giving these children the same kind of vision training that the juvenile delinquents were being given at the Black Mountain School for delinquent boys, in Colorado. And this program in turn, was similar to the sensori-motor program given to the learning disabled prisoners in the reformatory in Green Bay, Wisconsin. Although the prisoners in this particular program had not been tested for anything other than learning- and motor-development problems, if the statistics are correct, they were also hypoglycemic, allergic, and abused children.

The cycle had come full turn: These cases made up some of the 70% of the abused children who, statistics indicate, have some developmental deviation — the children who invite abuse!

(It might seem ridiculous that there should be such overlapping of symptoms, but such connections are not arbitrary. Long after this book was first conceived, the late Dr. Norman Geschwind, who was one of the top researchers in neurology, discovered that lefthandedness is associated with a tendency toward immune disease, migraine and developmental learning disorders. This gives us further confirmation that we are on the right track, but does not show us how to counteract those tendencies. Geschwind has pinpointed the problems — our intent is to find ways to cure them!)

In the blue-eyed children, we can see the obviously genetic factors which predispose the children to these problems. The truth is, any child, given the wrong nutrition or a barren, nonstimulating environment, can be turned into a learning-disabled or otherwise deficient child.

Our society, for all its human intentions, for all its advanced techniques and supposedly advanced know-how, is very much responsible for creating such deficient children.

We live in a world where, for many, the birth process is shrouded in drugs and the mother is denied the first precious moments of holding her baby. Not until recently did we know how important the bonding of these first few minutes is in permitting maternal instincts to take hold and in creating a strong, warm bond between mother and child.

We live in a world in which "milk" and "love" are synonymous, and "The Good Stuff, Beautiful Milk" is pushed on all children, even though we know by now that 30% of white children and 70% of nonwhite children are allergic to milk. The shelves at the store are stocked with junk food, and the TV sets educate the kids that they cannot get along without those goodies.

We also live in a world where, in spite of "Sesame Street" and "The Electric Company," the children cannot learn, because in sitting in front of the two-dimensional screen, they have no chance to learn "up" and "down" and the concept of "three feet to the front" and all the things the brain needs to learn for the child to be able, eventually, to read, write and do arithmetic. If the children are taken out of the house, they are all too often driven everywhere by car.

Even in the supermarket, they may be driven in the shopping cart. To learn space perception we must walk and run and climb. Space perception is not learned unless the entire body is used.

To make matters worse, while in olden days there were many jobs requiring no great skill, so that even the "village idiot" could be tolerated with good humor, today, unless one is skilled in reading and writing one simply cannot survive in our society. Thus the pressure to force some children to do what they cannot do is on the parents, the teachers, and — worst of all — on the children.

In short, our advanced, benign society can be a destroyer of children.

Now, obviously, we do not wish to go back to the terrible old times. Since 1900, the infant death rate has gone down from 140 per 1,000 children to 1.1 per 1,000. In the process, however, we are keeping alive many, many children with damage of varying degree, from minimal to very severe brain damage.

We also have the medical knowledge to allow children to live through dangerous childhood diseases which only the strongest children would have survived in prior years. Again, many of those we have learned to save will have suffered usually minimal but nevertheless debilitating brain damage from the disease. It is most often these children who become the abused children, because they are expected to behave as they had before the illness, and no one can understand that something has happened to them.

We are only just emerging from a time in which it was a deadly taboo to tell a mother there was anything wrong with her child's brain. It is only recently we have learned about the extraordinary plasticity of the brain and that in many cases something can be done about brain damage.

Even today, the diagnosis of autism is considered so devastating that the knowledge gained from treating autistic children is rarely applied to those with similar, but less frightening problems.

We have only just — within the last 20 years or so — begun to explore the field of cerebral allergies.

To confuse things further, we are also emerging from a period of Freudian analysis which, while opening tremendous frontiers into the treatment of psychological problems, has blinded us to other factors which might cause emotional illness. Freud himself, toward the end of his life, was aware that there might be chemical or neurological factors involved in what he had been treating as an emotionally caused illness. Unfortunately, he left us with a legacy of thought which has been so influential, that if there is a problem with a child, many automatically blame it on the mother.

The time has come to look at the child himself and at his impact on the relationship with his parents. The time has also come to stop fracturing both diagnosis and treatment of a child and to put together all we know from various fields of knowledge. Only then can we keep our little ones from being destroyed, help the not-so-little ones to overcome their problems, and get the older ones on their way to living full, competent lives!

SECTION I

THE EARLY YEARS

Chapter 1

The Bonding Connection

Nature has a lovely way of insuring the survival of the species. The young of each species, whether they are bunny rabbits, baby polar bears, baby birds old enough to be out of the nest, even baby hippos, are appealing to the adult human being.

And every baby, every single human baby, becomes "the most beautiful baby in the whole world" to his parents.

Babies have a soft, strangely scented skin which simply invites touching and kissing, and, like the elephant mother who touches her newborn calf every 30 seconds, any mother is hard pressed not to nuzzle the soft folds of a baby's neck. Even children up to three and four years old have the kind of softness that one can barely resist.

After a baby has nursed, the muscles around the mouth, tired from sucking, relax into a smile; this smile elicits another smile from the mother, and the cycle of communication has started. At what point and in what situation does this protection built in by nature break down and the abusive cycle start?

Not three weeks prior to the writing of this book, a young mother threw her year-old baby off a freeway overpass in front of the oncoming traffic. She did this just hours before a member of the Division of Children's Services was to come and take the baby away from her. Was she protecting the baby from strangers who were

1

about to take him to a frigntening, uncertain future?

Was she really an abusive mother? Some animals will destroy their babies when there is danger to the nest. How many other mothers might have done the same thing rather than expose their children to the uncertainty of a system of child protection which is, at best impersonally benevolent; most often, truly uninformed? It is not that the people running the system don't care, but they are trained social workers, not doctors or psychologists. The need for child protection is so enormous, there are so many children and the services are so dreadfully understaffed. The mothers themselves are still often children, and when circumstances become overwhelming and the mother can't cope with the child, who will help the mother?

There are certainly abusive mothers and circumstances of extreme stress that lead to abuse, but these are not what this book is about. Again and again, we find there is only one child in a family who is abused, and when the mother is interviewed about the child, we find the baby made the mother feel rejected! The child made the mother feel inadequate and helpless — not the other way around!

Even a tiny infant can give the mother feedback that she is important and exciting and worthwhile. This feeling comes from the way a baby finds the nipple and settles down contentedly; from the eye contact, as those deep, dark baby eyes search her face; from the way a whole little body, all quivering legs and arms, gets excited when the mother approaches the crib! But what if that feedback does not happen? What if the child is sickly and colicky? What if the child will not nurse properly and is unresponsive to the mother's smile? It takes two to have a relationship, and soon the mother gives up, and her handling of the baby becomes routine and robotlike. It is a tragedy that strikes both mother and child.

Yet it seems as if, given the way we treat brand-new mothers today, all the cards seem stacked against the possibility of making mothering successful. Fortunately, there are now changes being made in more and more hospitals, but this is still the routine procedure in far too many hospitals:

You arrive in a state of great nervousness, wondering if, of all the millions and millions of women who have brought babies into the world before you, you alone are going to make a fool of yourself and behave in a cowardly fashion. There are people who have a generally easy time of it, but brother, it hurts! Maybe the doctor knows you're going to be all right, and maybe the nurses do, but that pain which is burning in your insides, does it mean there is anything wrong? Is the baby going to be all right? Is that thing in there going to tear your insides into pieces?

Then, finally, it is over. If the doctor is kind, he will let you awake from a drugged sleep to see what you have just produced. He is holding the baby upside down. The tiny head is covered with blood. Why didn't they warn you that would be the case? And you hear the birth cry and wonder if it is fair that the first thing they would do to your baby is make him cry! Then you see them out of the corner of your eye, wiping and cleaning the little creature, and see them bundle him into a fishtank (that, you find out later, is an isolette). Through the glass wall you see tiny arms and legs waving through the air, and then they roll away that tank and take your baby away!

Later, when you wake up a second time, there's a nurse with a face mask taking your blood pressure, and you drift off to sleep again, wondering restlessly if there is something wrong that they have to do that . . . and is the baby all right? They won't even let you see the baby for 12 hours! And finally, at the official time, the nurses come into the ward, each carrying a little bundle over her shoulder. The babies are carefully wrapped, like packages in a store, so carefully that you are almost afraid to open the folds, to touch the tiny body and to make sure that all the fingers and toes are there. They have fed your baby sugar water when he cried, and when they finally let you hold him — for a miserably short 20 minutes — he will not suckle. Rejected already, by your own child! And you feel that of all the things in your life which you can or cannot do, this — to nurse your own baby — this at least should be the one thing that you should know how to do!

If you happen to have a baby who is strong and has a healthy sucking reflex, there may be no problem. But it's very possible that, even if the baby was not given sugar water in the nursery, he might have just cried himself into exhaustion and is now too tired to suck. Almost all animals, from small ones like cats to big ones like horses or cows, after the placenta has been removed, lick their babies to stimulate them to nurse. Just a few minutes is not enough time to stimulate a baby to nurse. And here, at the hospital, when you have just become very, very slightly acquainted with that strange, small creature in your arms, here come the nurses again, all in green smocks and green caps, and each picks up a bundle. One of them disapprovingly surveys the mess you have made of the baby's blanket and carefully wraps the baby again with standard regulation folds, which seem designed to keep your body as far from your baby as

3

possible. And off goes the green brigade, leaving you to chat brightly and miserably with the other mothers.

And after the babies are gone — ostensibly so the babies do not get infected — they admit the fathers. You walk over to the "goldfish bowl" where all the little bundles with dark hair and red faces are lying, and you see that your bundle is crying, and no one is paying any attention! And there you stand — is it really the "baby blues?" — with tears running down your face, because your baby is crying and no one will let you near him.

Finally, if you are pronounced well and the baby healthy, they put you in a wheelchair — as if you were sick — and wheel you, baby in your lap, to the exit. There, they more or less dump you out of the wheelchair — and you're on your own!

So there you are, with a baby who has been thoroughly confused and frightened by not being with his mother. You don't understand what he wants and why he is crying, and you don't know if you're keeping him too warm, or too cool. If he cries, what on earth are you going to do with him? And if you think you're upset, you wonder how much more upset the baby must be!

Now, very slowly, and not in every place in the United States, the young women are beginning to revolt. They want to have the baby at home, and they're having the birth with midwives in attendance — and this not only because the cost of the doctors is too high. The midwife can give the mother far more personal support than she would get at the hospital, where the doctor might be supervising as many as five or more births in one weekend. (Fortunately, we hear less and less of nurses at hospitals tying a mother's legs together to keep the baby from being born before the doctor arrives. The number of babies who suffered brain damage because of this practice is tragic.) While there is slowly beginning to be some doctor support for home births, a recent British study has shown that 20% of them do run into some trouble. In some cases, the birth cry was delayed for over a minute; in other cases there was a delay of from one to three minutes. Out of 150 home births monitored, in five cases an ambulance had to be called. The first few minutes of a baby's birth are so vital to the child's neurological development, that a 20% risk of something going wrong is way too high.

Some hospitals now provide birthing rooms which, though sterile, look like living rooms. Here the baby can be born with a midwife in attendance — if this is preferred — but close to medical help if needed, and the mother can relax. This seems by far the most desirable of all options. If all is well and both mother and child are safe, they can go home right afterwards.

What does all this have to do with child abuse? Taking such precautions is not a case of being over-protective. What happens during the moments of birth and then during the next few hours has a lasting impact on the child's later neurological development. Mishaps at that time may cause what we generally call "minimal" brain damage, but which makes the child just a little bit different from the others. This kind of child gets abused more often than the one who has a major handicap. Allowances will be made for a child with a visible problem. The subtle problems are the ones which will get the child into trouble.

Allowing mothers to "bond" — to hold the baby right after birth — is becoming more and more the practice, but it is not universal yet. At a hospital, or at home, mothers must insist, over everybody's objection, if necessary: We want to hold our babies right after they are born! Raising a child is difficult under any circumstances. We need that extra bit of love between us and the child to cope with the inevitable conflicts without resorting to violence.

We have known for a long time that right after a duckling hatches from an egg, it can be made to follow any object that makes a clucking, rhythmic noise, and it will follow that object from then on as if it were his mother! Konrad Lorenz has done extensive research showing that birds raised by people from the start will accept those people and imitate them. The geese he had raised did not learn to fly unless he ran ahead of them, flapping his arms. Only in imitating him did they learn to use their wings.

A different study explored the impact of the first contact on animal mothers. If a baby goat and its mother are allowed to be together the first few days and are then separated, the mother will resume nursing the kid when it is returned to her later. If, however, the baby is removed during the first few minutes after the birth, the mother will reject it when it is brought back to her and will butt it and kick it away. Interestingly enough, if the kid of another mother is introduced to the goat within the first 10 minutes after birth, she will nurse both her own and that other kid and continue to care for both as if they were her own. (Farmers have found they can make a ewe accept her own or another's lamb even long after birth, if they stimulate the ewe's womb!)

Finally, someone had the brilliant idea that, after all, we humans are also a species of animal, and maybe we too have a period during which the maternal attachment is formed. So investigators tried to find out what would happen if they did what in many "primitive" societies is taken for granted: They allowed the newborn to stay with the mother right after birth. As soon as the mother was able, they permitted her to hold the naked baby next to her skin on her stomach. Later, after the baby had been cleaned, the mother was again allowed to hold the baby, to touch him and examine him, to stroke him, talk to him, and allow him to nurse.

Right after birth has taken place, infants are wide awake for a period of about three hours. They are alert and amazingly competent. They can see, and they are particularly interested in faces, especially eyes. They can make sounds which follow the rhythmic pattern of whatever language is being spoken to them and they can reach for an extended finger with amazing accuracy and cling to it with great strength.

The mothers, on the other hand, are suddenly overwhelmed with a great feeling of ecstasy. It's a feeling which is so strong that it makes them immediately forget all the pain of the birth. The combination of feeling that ecstasy and the delight of seeing and touching that alert little creature, forges the kind of bond which will last a lifetime. In the early '70s some studies were made that proved that mothers who were allowed to "bond" with their babies developed a far more intimate relationship with their children. Even a year later, they smiled more with them and the babies laughed more. Mothers treated in the manner of unfortunately still too many hospitals today, showed far less intimacy and contentment.

There is far more involved in this question of separation after birth than emotional satisfaction. If there is a potentially abusing mother, this early bonding can well make the difference between potential and actual abuse. Without these moments, not only does the mother feel less close to the baby, but the baby is less emotionally attached to the mother and is more likely to make the mother feel rejected.

That is not as ridiculous as it sounds. A friend of mine recently had a caesarean. The doctors wanted to whisk away the baby and send him off to the nursery, but the father said: "No way, I am going to bond with this baby!" and he held and talked to the newborn. When the mother came out of the anesthetic and was finally allowed home, for the first three days the baby would only pay attention to the father — in spite of the fact that the mother was nursing him! Bonding with fathers affects both father and child. From what information we have today about incest, men who bond with their children, or at least spend a good deal of time with them when they are little, are far less likely to abuse them sexually.

With a mother who is able to love, separation at birth can be overcome. Even so, I have talked to women who had several children. They loved all of their children, but they admitted they felt a special closeness with the ones they were allowed to hold at birth.

In comparing children who were allowed these first few moments of contact and those who were not, it was found that in those who were not bonded, there were more cases of hyperbilirubenemia (a condition, similar to jaundice, that can cause brain damage), more mild respiratory distress, more sleep apnea (those frightening spells during which the baby does not breathe), and more cases of poor sucking. That's pretty scary, especially since some of these symptoms are found in infants who later die of crib death.

And who do you think gets blamed for these conditions? Psychologists say, "Poor mothering! Emotional problems!" In some ways they are right, but it is our culture with its customs which is causing the problems, not the already harassed mother who has to live with a child who has been affected by this collective ignorance.

At least there is a lesson to be learned from these studies. If you have a baby who seems to have trouble breathing and who refuses to nurse properly, it might be an indication that there is need for stimulation that the infant missed in the beginning. (Appendix II gives suggestions for providing stimulation.)

Unfortunately, mothers are not always warned that their babies are at risk. This may be because the area of high risk is so nebulous and, sometimes, simply because the doctors do not realize what is at stake.

In crib deaths, for instance, even though we know the parents were not at fault, there is still always the terrible suspicion that there might have been faulty mothering involved. Not only do relatives, friends and neighbors feel that way, but the thought that something might have been left undone that would have kept the baby alive, will haunt the parents for the rest of their lives.

Dr. Augusto Paris, a pediatric neurologist in Avezzano, Italy, does not make any distinction between high-risk and normal infants. He shows all mothers how to stimulate their babies, and both he and the mothers are delighted with the results. In Italy, swaddling the infants and keeping them immobile was a common practice. Since these mothers have abandoned this practice and are giving their babies more physical contact and freedom to move, Dr. Paris says he no longer sees as many cases of children with dislocated hips as he used to see. In the United States a similar situation was found among the Navahos, who kept their infants immobile on cradle boards; hip problems among Navahos were unusually high.

We know today that deformed children are more likely to get abused. If we can cut down on the incidence of hip dislocation, we have saved many children from experiencing the physical and emotional agonies of going through life as a cripple.

What a large reward for something as simple as giving a little extra stimulation and allowing an infant freedom of movement! Babies are not born with fully developed hip sockets. These are worn in to fit, so to speak, as the baby crawls and later walks. That crawling and walking depends on the development of the brain. For the brain to fulfill its preprogrammed function, the baby must be allowed to receive input through the senses from the outside world.

The adult brain weighs roughly three pounds. At birth the brain weighs roughly one pound and by the end of the first year that weight has increased to almost two pounds — almost one-third of its total growth. What is programmed into the brain during this first explosive growth period determines how the child can develop during the next 18 years. The comparison between the brain and a tree is not quite accurate, but the same way you cannot climb to the top of a tree unless there is first a trunk and lower, larger branches, there are areas in the brain which must first receive basic information before the information can be further processed in other, more complex areas. Unless information from all the senses about touch, gravity, light, sound, movement and so on, are allowed to register in the brain, the brain will not be able to direct the child's body to move correctly. The hip sockets will not be worn in properly and the child might become a cripple.

If normal, relaxed stimulation is permitted during the first year, the brain is given a chance to fulfill its preprogrammed human potential.

We have learned to save many children. A hormone has been discovered which will prevent cretinism. Thyroid deficiencies, which would cause retardation can be remedied by only a minimum of medication. PKU, which causes retardation can be diagnosed by a simple urine test, and retardation can be prevented by eliminating milk from the child's diet. Other such miracles are performed every day. It seems just about the only remedy which has to be found is one which eliminates child abuse — still one of the greatest dangers to our children today.

We have learned, from interviewing thousands of women, that the way a mother talks about her infant can give us clues that she might be a potentially abusive mother. We also know fairly well which children are high-risk infants. If a low-risk infant is born to a high-risk mother, with immediate emotional support and maybe a little psychotherapy, mother and child may yet get along. The bonding process, allowing such a mother to hold the child soon after birth, may make a tremendous difference.

If the mother is a caring mother but the child is high-risk and promises to be a difficult child to raise, there can still be an abuse problem. Showing the mother how to stimulate the child and otherwise cope with the problems that are likely to arise, can break the rejection cycle.

But if a high-risk mother and a high-risk infant are thrown together by fate, we can almost predict child abuse. We must then use all the knowledge we have been able to gather over the last few years to try to prevent this tragedy.

Chapter 2

The Parent/ Infant/Deficit/ Toxicity Syndrome

Some mothers come home from the hospital with their newborn, and after a few weeks proudly announce that the baby sleeps through the night. Some mothers come home from the hospital and a year later the infant still wakes up every two and a half hours.

Some infants come home from the hospital, suck early, are easily comforted if they do cry, and generally think living is a pretty neat sort of experience.

Others come home, are fussy and will not nurse well, have colic if they do eat, and generally act as if they already knew from birth on that this is a pretty dreadful world into which they were so hastily catapulted.

Scientists at this point have pretty well established that there are difficult children and easy children. As a matter of fact, a recent study of infant abuse among monkeys and the evolution of child abuse said that while there are many outside factors which lead to monkey infant killing, some monkeys tend to get more abused than others. Like humans, some monkeys are simply harder to raise than others.

Some thirty years back, to measure the different types of temperament which human beings seem to possess, they were, for the sake of convenience, divided into three major categories. Supposedly depending on which part of the embryo was developed most strongly, they were called mesomorph, endomorph and ectomorph.

The endomorph loved to eat and was the easiest to get along with. The mesomorph liked to exercise and was the one who was active and healthy, but beware the difficult ectomorph! The ectomorph was fussy and needed to be fed often; the ectomorph slept little and was delicate and sensitive.

There was one major advantage to being able to put your child into one of these categories: It was easier to tolerate the child's idiosyncracies. It was also easier to sit back and do nothing about changing the behavior of a difficult child. You simply gave the child a label — that is, if you had heard of the label. If you hadn't, and the child was screaming his head off for the tenth time during the night and you had to be up and go to work the next morning, you'd find yourself with your fingers around the baby's neck and wondering which was the greater force — the drive to strangle him, or the protective instinct.

The statistical graphs show a high rate of abuse-caused deaths during the first few months. Then there is a lower rate of such incidents until the second and third year when there are again many, many fatalities. It's not that parents really want to hurt their children, it's just that some kids can be unbearably difficult, and many parents do not realize how extremely fragile these little creatures really are!

It is most often the low-weight or premature children who get murdered. Those are the ones most likely to be born to very young mothers, who themselves are still children and have not fully developed their civilized self-restraint. There seems to be an atavistic desire: The desire to destroy the smallest of the litter. "Atavistic" is that beautiful-sounding word which means: "Showing a reversion to the instinct of our remote ancestors." Over millions of years of evolution, this infant murder became the way of insuring the survival of the fittest and, at the same time, a way of strengthening the species.

The weakest of the litter, the runt, the pup who needs the mother's milk even more than the others, is not only pushed away by the other pups, but is totally ignored or even killed by the mother. It may seem harsh to state that human behavior still has this kind of rejection of a child, but if the bonding instinct is still part of our make-up, why not this? Besides, statistics prove that weakly infants

11

are abused more frequently than the strong.

Now: If you take the runt away from the litter, pamper it and feed it, it just might survive. In today's society we try to do this by having a social agency — often called Children's Services — to remove a failure-to-thrive infant from his mother. While this is sometimes necessary, by removing the child we create a great many tragedies, simply because we still know so little about infants. I know of one case in which a baby was removed from the mother. Six months later, the now one-year-old was returned to her with the information that the baby was brain-damaged. No information was given the mother on how to treat the child.

Another case, this one involving twins, was luckier. One twin, considered more fragile, had to stay at the hospital for a longer time. When he was finally allowed to come home, the baby did not thrive. This time, however, no one could blame it on the mother, because the other twin did just fine. Finally the baby was taken to a hospital in the nearest large town, where all kinds of tests were performed. The information was fed into a computer and compared with similar symptoms of other cases all over the country. It was eventually discovered that, for some reason (possibly the special formula which the baby had been given) there was a lack of copper in the child's nutrition. The baby's diet was changed and the child improved visibly.

When we snatch babies away from their mothers, we usually do not go to such lengths to find out why the child is not thriving. I dread to think what some agency might have done, had there not been a healthy twin!

We do know that, in many cases, a little assistance to the mother might prevent child abuse. Part of the problem is that, just as unceremoniously as the mother is escorted out of the hospital in a wheelchair and then just left on her own, the doctor who delivered the baby washes his hands of the whole affair. Usually, there is a financial contract which pays the doctor for prenatal care and, maybe, for a single postnatal checkup. The gynecologist does not consider himself a pediatrician, and if the mother asks for help, he — often quite rudely — tells her so.

Especially in welfare cases, this break is unforgivable. Not so long ago, the newspapers carried the story of a case in which a very young mother left her newborn infant alone in the apartment with a huge German shepherd. The dog had not been fed while she was in the hospital, and there was no food in the house. While she went out to buy some, the German shepherd ate the baby! Didn't anyone know — or care about — into what kind of situation the girl had been discharged? When an agency undertakes to help a young mother, shouldn't it include the responsibility of seeing that the baby is safe?

Gynecologists are usually aware of the situation in which the expectant mother finds herself. They should pass this information on to the pediatrician. Today we know from statistics what, not so long ago, had been considered merely an old wives' tale: Mothers need to be protected from stress during their pregnancies. Dr. Lendon Smith says most of what he describes as "goosy, ticklish and hyperactive kids" come from mothers who had a stressful pregnancy.

There used to be two common fallacies about the mother and the fetus. It was believed that, even if the mother was malnourished, the fetus would draw whatever nourishment it needed from the mother's depleted stores. It was also believed that toxic substances would not cross the placenta and that the fetus would automatically be protected from whatever poisonous substances the mother was taking in.

We know today that malnutrition of the mother can severely affect the infant's intelligence. The mother's alcohol consumption can cause the severe mental retardation called Fetal Alcohol Syndrome, and smoking — even the father's smoking — can adversely affect the birth weight of the infant.

There are many other factors, factors that Dr. Ray C. Wunderlich, Jr. calls the Parent/Infant/Deficit/Toxicity Syndrome: "Deficiencies of nutrients and toxic conditions in parents and/or children interact to produce wrong living. Parents and/or kids are nervous, irritable, pathologically tired, and often hyperaggressive with a 'short fuse'. The result? Misunderstandings which spawn precipitous actions — with the conspicuous absence of measured problem solving." This makes it so vital that the pediatrician consult with the gynecologist. Unfortunately, even if the gynecologist has warned the pediatrician that there were problems (physical or emotional) during the pregnancy, the pediatrician will usually treat only the baby. At that early stage — and sometimes, of course, all through life — mother and baby share the same problems. We may have a mother who is exhausted and probably hypoglycemic either because of the stress during the pregnancy, or even from before the pregnancy. (See Chapter 4.) In those moments when her blood sugar is low, she is not entirely rational. Now she also has a baby who is fussy and demanding, and if her own self-control is low at a time when the baby refuses to be comforted, anything can happen.

It is for those cases that one wishes for a pediatrician like Ray C. Wunderlich, Jr. — No, Dr. Wunderlich is not a made-up name, although his name in German is the equivalent of "someone at whom one should marvel." After Dr. Wunderlich had already decided to become a consultant for this book, I was going through some clippings and articles which I had accumulated over the years. Here and there I had marked off a paragraph or a small article, and I found, to my amazement that much of this material was by Dr. Ray C. Wunderlich, Jr. Originally I had not paid much attention as to who had written these articles, especially since they all seemed to be on different subjects: Emergency crying, allergic symptoms, vision problems. Who would have thought that all these would come from the same man?

Then one day, in a book called "Vision and Learning Disabilities", put out by the American Optometric Society, I came across the diagram reprinted here, and it seemed to be what I had been looking for all these years! It is the diagram of the neuro-allergic syndrome, but I am always tempted to call it "Dr. Wunderlich's magic spiral," and in a sense, this spiral is a diagram of the contents of this book.

Dr. Wunderlich, who has been very active in the education of teachers and parents of learning disabled children, is one of those rare professionals who believes in a team approach. There is much research available, but there are very few pediatricians who will take the research in all fields and apply it to help the children. Dr. Wunderlich has written two books, which have dared to make a statement that, especially at the time they were published, most pediatricians did not dare voice for fear of chasing away their clients: The child has a brain. These books are *"Kids, Brains and Learning,"* (1970), and *"Allergy, Brains and Children Coping,"* (1973).

The child has a brain! And Wunderlich dares to suggest that the mother has a responsibility to influence what is happening in that brain! Heredity is one of the factors affecting the brain, but also significant are allergies (which might be inherited), nutrition and the stimulation the parent gives the child. While his intent is to help the children, Wunderlich never for a moment forgets that the health of the mother is an integral part of the child's health.

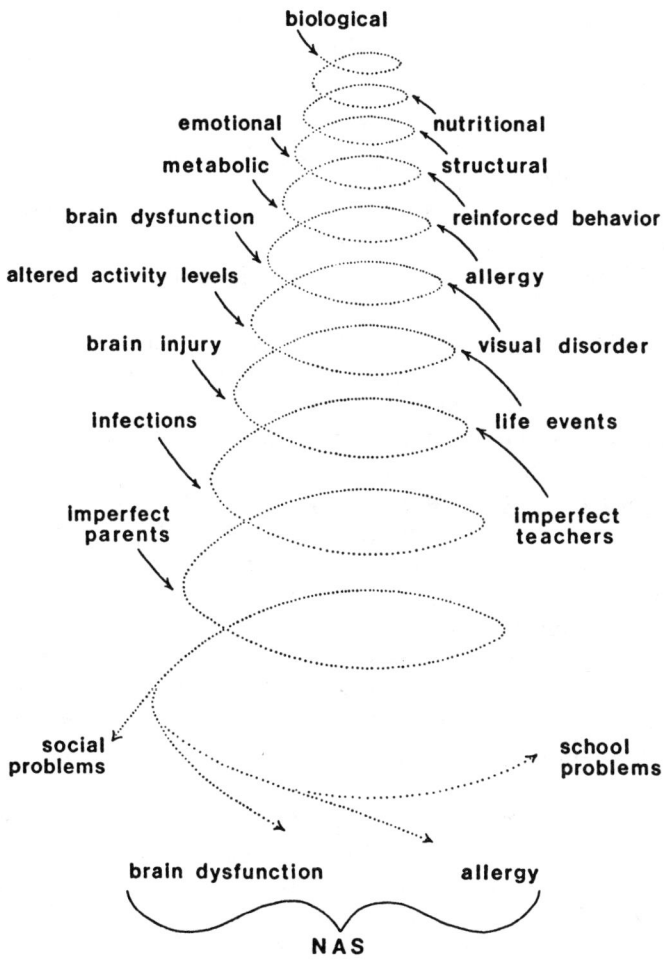

biological

emotional · nutritional

metabolic · structural

brain dysfunction · reinforced behavior

altered activity levels · allergy

brain injury · visual disorder

infections · life events

imperfect parents · imperfect teachers

social problems · school problems

brain dysfunction · allergy

NAS

BIO-SOCIAL DECLINE

Various factors, biologic or cultural, may be responsible for
a child's entrance into the spiral of developmental decay.

15

Parents usually bring their children to the doctor if there is something obviously wrong. Especially the inexperienced mother may send off a volley of phone calls to the pediatrician, who gets annoyed and makes her feel she is an overprotective mother. After a while she gives up and stops asking what she thinks the doctor might consider foolish questions. The line between overprotection and neglect is a very thin one — one which few pediatricians have learned to find.

On the other hand, there are many symptoms for which the mother will not take the child to the doctor. It is not considered a sickness if the child is cranky and irritable. It is not considered a sickness if the child tries to hit out at the parent or at other children.

If the child is lethargic and a little slow, she may say: "Well, he's an endomorph!" If the child does not seem to learn very well, she thinks, "Well, he's not very bright." (In the old days, she would have said things like, "Well, he takes after Uncle Charlie!")

A mother usually does not think the child needs to be taken to the doctor if he eats enormous amounts of food and does not gain weight. She's proud of his appetite.

Things are a little more abuse-provoking if the child does not eat! One of the classic examples of nutrition deficit in children is iron-deficiency anemia. The iron-deficient child doesn't want to eat. Try to make him eat — Smash! — the ungrateful brat knocks the spoon out of your hand and, next thing you know, the bowl of cereal is all over the kitchen floor. If the mother is already at her wits' end over other problems, she spanks his little bottom and throws him into his crib. There's screaming and yelling, and eventually either the child or the mother gives up trying.

If the mother is a little more aware, she may take the kid to the doctor, and she closes her eyes tight as the lab technician takes some blood from the child's finger. The blood test, however, comes back and reads "normal." Hematocrit, hemoblobin, and red blood cells are all within the "normal" range. So the mother takes the kid back home, and he continues to be testy, snappish and high-strung. Then, one day when the mother is tired and the child still prefers dirt and clamps his teeth tight against a spoonful of string beans, mother has finally had enough and the kid ends up with a bowl of mashed string beans on his head!

Now if the mother is lucky enough to have a Dr. Wunderlich in her town, after listening to her complaints about the child, even if the blood count is normal and shows no signs of anemia, he will be aware that the child may have a very significant lack of iron. (This would be manifested only as a decrease in iron stores.) Not only will he not think the mother is overprotective, he will probably also suggest she might take an iron supplement herself. Mothers are generally so delighted at having this marvelous little infant of their own that they don't realize how totally exhausted they are. And so now, after taking iron for a few days, she will suddenly realize how much stronger she feels, and the baby, having also received some iron, will stop being so fussy and may even start to enjoy his lunch. Mealtimes are no longer a battle and peace is restored.

Other mineral deficits contribute to picky eating. To a child who has a deficiency in zinc, everything has an awful taste or no taste at all. Zinc deficiency can lead to toxic cadmium excess, digestion problems, urinary tract and growth problems. If it leads to urinary tract problems, this means the child will have problems with toilet training, because it may be painful for him to go to the bathroom! Toileting problems are very frustrating to a mother, and can easily lead to a blow-up.

Zinc deficiency is not just a rare occurrence. Zinc deficiency has become so widespread today that the American Chemical Society held a special meeting on the problem. One of the researchers suggested that out of the 16 million people in the United States who have taste and smell problems, about 4 million have these because of zinc malabsorption. And spinach — after millions of children have been forced against their will to eat that stuff — can cause overexcretion of zinc, because it has too much oxalic acid. Another culprit is the modern way of baking bread. If the flour were not refined, then zinc would be present to balance the toxic metal cadmium. Also, if the dough were fermented longer before baking, the phytic acid would be broken down to liberate the zinc for absorption.

Minerals, unlike most vitamins, can easily be given in too large doses and can become toxic. It is, therefore, important to have some authority to provide guidance, and nutritionally oriented physicians are hard to find. Dr. Wunderlich's book *"Nourishing Your Child"* is a great help to parents, but should be required reading for all social agencies dealing with children.

In the past few years, doctors have reported much success in giving magnesium and calcium to children. Calcium deficiency makes a child edgy and jumpy. Lack of magnesium, potassium, and selenium may make the muscles of a child weak. Weak children do not get sympathy; on the contrary, there is something slightly irritating about a child who is flabby.

Here's another nutritional problem which can get a mother-child relationship off to a rocky start. Especially during the first six months, the mother gets very little sleep. When the little one drops off to sleep, there's some respite, and she can get a little rest. In the normal process of a child's development, if there is a strange noise within the baby's hearing, the baby will wake up. Once he has waked up, and convinced himself all is well, the next time that noise is repeated he will sleep right through it. There is nothing more amazing than to see infants sleeping blissfully in the noisiest of all places — the New York subway, for example — but they can do it. If the baby lacks magnesium or B vitamins, he may not be able to suppress the noise. Even the slightest noise can wake him up, and there goes mother's chance to nap and her patience for the rest of the afternoon.

Dr. Wunderlich has found that hypersensitivity to light is a sign there is a need for riboflavin (vitamin B2) or vitamin A. Hypersensitivity to touch — something which can simply mean ticklishness or, in severe cases, be quite painful to the child — usually lessens when calcium, magnesium and selenium are prescribed in the right amounts. Leg pains — "growing pains" which were almost taken for granted in earlier generations — will go away with extra amounts of calcium, magnesium, selenium and vitamin E.

If the child craves sweets and is always climbing up onto some high shelf to get into the cookie jar — the more sugar the child gets, the worse the craving gets — then we have broken cookie jars and spanked bottoms. Wunderlich has found that chromium and manganese deficiency usually accompany this craving for sweets. Sometimes, too, the sweet-addict is driven to sweets because of the presence of a chronic yeast-fungus infection (candida albicans).

Nutrient deficiencies are the underlying causes for most infection. If these deficiencies are not recognized and the needs met, the child is likely to run into further trouble, because not only do these deficits make the child uncomfortable and cranky, but they lead to something far more dangerous. Nutrient minerals have a protective function. They protect the child from various toxic metals which are all over the environment today. The child who lacks a full quota of nutrient minerals is more likely to be affected by today's pollution. For instance, the child who lacks selenium may develop mercury poisoning (selenium is antagonistic to mercury). Zinc deficiency increases the effects of cadmium, which we get from cola drinks, cigarette smoke, and air pollution caused by the wearing of tires stabilized with cadmium.

Calcium and vitamin C counteract lead. Lead poisoning was formerly thought to be a "poor children's disease" caused by lead paint from old buildings, but is often caused simply by automobile exhaust in the air.

Lead poisoning is probably one of the more common toxic conditions, and here we can really see this downward spiral which keeps creating more and more difficulties for the child. At Harvard Medical School, researchers collected the baby teeth of 60 youngsters. These teeth were analyzed for their lead content. Those children who had been exposed to lead — as the analysis of the teeth proved — were then rated along with the other youngsters by their teachers. Not only was there a difference of 10 points in I.Q. between the exposed and the nonexposed children, but the teachers consistently rated the children with little or no lead in their teeth as being better behaved and happier in school.

It is possible to reduce the lead in a child's system by giving massive doses of vitamin C or other chelating agents. However, pulling the lead out of a child's body has to be handled by an expert. If the lead is drawn out of the bones, it may end up in the digestive tract, and from there not only get absorbed again, but may actually end up in the bloodstream, where it can do more damage than it would in the bones.

Another side effect of hidden mineral deficits is that the child may have an enormous appetite: He eats and eats in an attempt to gain the nutrients he needs.

In one case an eight year old boy simply was not recuperating from an illness. Luckily, the child lived on a farm, and one day he saw a beautiful red pepper and started eating it. Over the next few weeks, he continued to eat a great many peppers and, apparently, they contained exactly what his body needed, because almost from that moment on, the child started regaining his strength. (Incidentally, red peppers are a fine natural source of vitamin C.)

Most children are not that lucky. The foods coming from the supermarket have been processed out of most of their vitamins and minerals. In former times, even the poorest of children got more vitamins and minerals out of their crust of bread than today's child gets out of the prettiest bowl of "enriched" sugar flakes. And so the child eats and eats in an attempt to get the foodstuffs he needs. He gets fat, and the other kids make fun of him. And there is little anyone can do. If a child is scrawny and pale, and obviously neglected, one can turn to Children's Services to look into the matter. But if a child is so fat he can barely run across the room without getting out of breath, and still the parents send him to school with huge sandwiches and creampuffs for dessert, no judge has the slightest authority to step in. Unfortunately, eating habits are passed on from generation to generation, and chances are that the mother is equally as fat as the child. (As a matter of fact, although this is not a book about the abusive parent, excessively fat women are more likely to abuse their children than normal-weight women.)

Children with nutritional deficits have intestinal tracts which are easy prey to parasites. If parasites set up residence in the child's intestines, they further weaken the child. Such a child is overwhelmed by every little problem a stronger child would cheerfully take in stride.

Healthy infants coo and gurgle and are their mother's joy and delight. As they get older, they are so enthusiastic about the many wonderful things they discover in the course of the day that they make their parents suddenly see the world with different eyes. And so they give their parents a new lease on life and more strength to cope. But the lethargic and whiny child only adds to the difficulties and the burdens of the parents, and he becomes one more irritation among the many others which life brings. This little irritating creature, however, is small and weak, and it is so easy to let out one's anger on a little one who can't strike back!

Sometimes, a child who is normally quite amiable and happy suddenly turns into a little monster. He won't do what he's told, puts up a fight at everything and anything he's asked to do, and is generally totally unreasonable. Look out! He's coming down with something. Carl Delacato says even though autistic children with whom he works have long given up some abnormal behavior, two weeks before they come down with a virus infection, they may revert to that autistic behavior!

Children (probably even adults), suddenly become cranky when they are about to get sick. Then, during the sickness, they turn quiet and very well behaved. Wait until they are getting better: The first sign of recovery is they are being mean and ornery again. It's not that they have been spoiled during their sickness; the systems in their brains are just not "go" at that period.

The child with a fever, with a runny nose, even one with a sore throat can be identified quite easily as suffering from an infection.

But any one of many low-grade infections can cause a child to be grouchy and uncooperative. Unfortunately, again, mothers don't take their children to the doctor at such times. He'd probably think she was nuts! Mothers have been made out to be the villains if the children are not well-behaved. Four generations of post-Freudians have now blamed everything on their mothers. As it is, even if a doctor were called, most of them would not know how to help. As Dr. Lendon H. Smith says: "Medical schools don't teach classes in 'crummy kids'."

A difficult child may have a low-grade infection in the bladder, in the vulva, on the skin of the lower legs, in the nostrils, or in the middle ear. Even the cuticles can harbor insidious infections. Usually, says Dr. Wunderlich, at the heart of these infections are nutrient deficiencies or even allergies. Antibiotics may be needed, but the real cause must be uncovered.

The child who has been normally cheerful and suddenly becomes difficult may be more at risk than the one who is perpetually difficult, because the mother does not know how to cope with the sudden resistance she is getting. She thinks, "Boy, my mother-in-law must be right, I really did spoil him. And now look what I've done, I better crack down on him!"

She hasn't yet learned the little tricks that make it possible to live with a contrary child — tricks like distracting him with something else while you're quickly doing what he doesn't want you to do or, knowing he will invariably do the opposite of what you ask him, telling him to sit down when you really want him to get up.

Children who are generally whiny or who just seem to be slow and lethargic, children who are slow to learn and never seem to get excited by any activity, children whose eyes are lack-luster, and those who are always complaining — these children are usually sick. It is not the kind of sickness which is apparent, like a sniffle or a cough. It's a subtle, low-grade illness, usually chronic, for which the mother hesitates to call the doctor. If she has a healthy child, she may be able to compare the two and suspect there is something wrong. But if it's an only child, she has no way of judging what is normal behavior. Even doctors have a hard time finding the problem, because it is what they call subclinical — the symptoms are not strong enough that the child would show clear indications of a specific disease.

If the child has a high fever and is obviously ill enough to be kept in bed, he gets a lot of loving and extra sympathy from the parent. But if he's just a little below par, he is simply told, "Cut it out!", "Quit being such a fusspot.", or "Behave yourself!" (as if children know what "behave yourself" means). Finally, some parents blow up and knock the child across the room.

Curiously, the first symptom of an illness or a toxic state is that the child's vision is affected. Even as adults, just before we come down with a flu or some other sickness, we seem to get dizzy and our eyes don't seem to coordinate. After an illness is over and the fever long gone, the eyes may still hurt, and the numbers in the telephone book seem to flip around and will not stand still for us to read.

Hearing goes, too. There is a soft buzzing sound, not really a noise, but something similar to how one would hear under water, which makes it hard to pay attention. The nurses who work in those departments of hospitals where abused children are brought for admittance say how devastating it is to see how many of the abused children had hearing problems at the time of admission. The children were ordered to do something, and they simply did not hear what they were told to do. They had no way of changing their behavior to please their parents; they either did not hear or did not understand what they were supposed to do. (So many of these children do not get enough magnesium and water-soluble vitamins, and this influences their hearing). Many, many children simply do not live fully, because they suffer from chronic middle ear disease (usually serous otitis media — a collection of fluid in the middle ears).

Of course, some perfectly normal children get abused for no fault of their own. Social factors are involved in the abuse! In Oregon, which is dependent almost entirely on the lumber industry, there are some towns inhabited mainly by the employees of the lumber mills. During the recent economic depression, two terrifying statistics emerged. When the lumber mills closed and laid off the workers, the consumption of alcohol went up 25% and the incidence of reported child abuse went up 50%.

But social factors are certainly not the only ones. Some interesting facts have become known since we started keeping track of abused children in this country. One is that a great many of them had been brought to the hospital, often more than once, during the six months just before their admission for the child-abuse injury. They were brought in by their parents for conditions which would normally be treated at home, such as a sniffle or a scraped knee.

This unusual fact has been interpreted as a sign that the mother was really asking for help in not being able to cope with the child.

What we need is a new kind of office interview. We need a whole new breed of doctors — doctors who are aware, as are all the consultants to this book, that there are many factors involved if a mother asks for help. If there is trouble between a parent and a child, the kind of problems which cause it may be a clue to what is wrong, not merely a sign that there is a potentially abusive mother. The underlying cause must be removed. Perhaps those long questionnaires which patients are asked to fill out when they first come into the office should include a whole new set of questions. Answers to those questions — later fed into a computer — could alert a doctor not only to physical symptoms of the child, but to emotional and developmental problems as well. They should include the health and the emotional state of the mother. The doctor, who has little enough time to spend with his patients, can at least have a warning that a problem exists, and if the problem is outside his expertise, can call on a colleague who specializes in that particular field.

Chapter 3

The Allergy Connection

Get rid of that little snot-nose!" What a perfectly abusive concept, and how often do we hear this expression! It evokes all kinds of pictures of a sniveling, whining, dirty little creature. When I was still a child myself, people thought these children with streaked faces must have had a terribly neglectful mother. After all, perfect little girls and boys did not have to sniffle up the nose. I supposed they had maids and mothers who blew their nose for them into nice, clean hankies.

Even today, when these whining little ones hang on the pantlegs or the skirts of their mothers, sniffling and wiping a dirty hand under their nose, they get little sympathy from anyone. Usually they are between the ages of two and four before they are old enough to know how to use a Kleenex by themselves. We've all come to connect discharge from the nose with colds and flu germs. We automatically reject messy little faces as something dangerously dirty, even if the mucus is simply nice, germ-free stuff which is caused by teething or perhaps by allergy.

Of course, the allergy also makes the little one uncomfortable and cranky, which makes Mother irritable and Daddy even more so, and a perfectly awful time is had by all.

There is always the hidden emotional impact: A child who has just been crying also will sniffle, because his nose is running from the tears. And somehow, when a child cries, we tend to feel he is crying to annoy us. There's always the chance he is not really allergic, he just may need a good cry. If so, why doesn't he just come out and say what's bothering him? Either way, the child makes the parent feel inadequate and guilty, and since no one likes to feel guilty, the allergic child is often in bad trouble.

There is one advantage in having an allergy that shows in a runny nose: Sooner or later, some doctor may do something about it. It is far more devastating if a child has an allergy causing symptoms not so readily visible as those which affect the nose. In such a case, the child is in double jeopardy, because the allergy is all too often not being recognized.

The field of allergy, as it is beginning to be understood today, is only about 25 years old. As a matter of fact, clinical allergy has often been treated as the stepchild of medicine. Psychology, education, dietetics, neurology, all still fit neatly into their own pigeonholes. The wholistic concepts which include allergy, however, are far too slow catching on, and counselors and teachers are not permitted to mention such heresies, lest they lose their jobs!

Nevertheless, today any child therapy program worth its salt will take the influence of allergies and allergy like conditions into consideration. We have only just begun to be aware of cerebral allergies which will change the mood and the performance of a child.

The Full Circle School in Bolinas, California, deals with violent, disturbed and criminal children. On admission, their children were given a thorough, detailed physical and neurological examination. All of them had severe eye or perceptual problems. Even though this kind of learning problem is the rule, rather than the exception, in disturbed children, Z. Michael Lerner, the founder of the school and his staff were surprised by the appalling results. The percentage of learning problems was enormous. The school also hired Dr. Clyde Hawley to test the children for allergies.

Again the results were shocking. The children were put on an elimination diet. Foods suspected of causing problems were taken from their diet. Then, after two weeks, these foods were again introduced and the change in the behavior of the child was observed. As the specific foods were reintroduced, some of the children went into a state of stupor, some erupted into angry outbursts, some became violent. One child's throat constricted dangerously. It is frightening to think what might have become of those children had they been sent to an institution rather than to a school in which the administration was exceptionally aware. The findings of this school were very similar to those of another school for "incorrigibles" in Florida. George Von Hilsheimer used many different methods to help his charges, including nutritional therapy and games which stimulated their sensori-motor development. The aim was to return the sparkle to the dull and discouraged eyes of the youngsters. Von Hilsheimer, too, reported similar findings of allergies that changed the way the kids behaved.

The field of cerebral allergy is still essentially in virgin territory, and we still don't quite understand why allergies go hand in hand with brain damage and perception problems. Why, when we cure hypoglycemia, for instance, do many allergies disappear? Dr. Broda O. Barnes has found that in certain cases, simply the prescription of small amounts of thyroid medication has alleviated hypoglycemia and all the problems which are symptoms of that disease. It is important that we recognize the so-called classical allergies of immune origin as well as the allergy-like states which as yet have no clear origin in the immune system. Until we gain more insight, we can at least eliminate the offending foods from the diet. Statistics indicate that when emotionally disturbed children are treated for allergies, 60% are greatly improved, 20% improve some, and the rest are not helped by this kind of treatment at all. If such a high percentage of children are helped by eliminating some food, it is certainly worth the effort to try and find the culprit. It is very important, however, that if a certain food is taken away, some other way is found to provide a balanced diet.

Sometimes it is easy to spot an allergy, especially if the child becomes difficult only at certain times. When the behavior is consistent, the allergic link is harder to find.

A young woman I know lost a child in an accident. With a perhaps unfair wish to make up for the lost one, she decided to adopt a child through the Holt Agency, an agency specializing in adoptions of foreign children. The infant who was given to them turned out to be a 6-month-old Korean boy, who came to them round and rosy and with obviously good prior care. The parents felt an almost mystical sense of awe when they found out the child had been born on the same day their own had been killed. With gentle fingers, the new little boy explored the strange round, blue eyes of his new mother, and he still got deeply excited when someone with dark eyes entered the room. Nevertheless, slowly, bit by bit, he got used to his strange-looking parents, got used to sleeping in a bed instead of on a floor, and slowly started to enjoy the attentions of his new blue-eyed sisters. Then suddenly, after about three months, all was chaos. The little Korean fellow no longer wanted to have anything to do with anyone in the family. He screamed and cried and rolled on the floor. In despair the adoptive mother found a baby sitter and escaped from the home. "He's had it with us! He's fed up with our strange culture!" she moaned. Heartbroken that the child did not want her, she complained bitterly about it to her friends.

Finally, one of her friends had an idea. "Hey, wait a minute, that child is an Asian! ... Perhaps he does not tolerate our milk!" The mother looked puzzled for a minute and then suddenly said, "My God, yes, we took him off his formula about two weeks ago, just when all this terrible screaming started!" After a consultation with the pediatrician the child was taken off milk and, overnight, just as suddenly as the tantrums had appeared, they stopped again.

This particular problem had an easy solution. The onset of the problem had been sudden, the behavior violent, so a solution had to be found immediately. In this case, the mother was caring and loving, and the child was not beaten.

Things are not always that simple. Recently the newspaper reported that a comatose infant was brought to the hospital by a young couple, and both father and mother were immediately arrested for endangering the life of their child. When they could not stop the infant from crying, they had fed him an opium ball to calm him and had nearly killed the 6-month-old. The paper never once mentioned why the child had been crying so hard.

In emergency cases like these, generally, some sort of help will be found sooner or later — if the child survives the abuse. But far, far more dangerous are those cases in which the allergy is very mild and is not spotted. These are allergies which seem to come on slowly, and the comparatively mild symptoms can be easily tolerated. If the allergic child fails to digest his food properly, then the symptoms of poor nutrition will not show up for a long time. The mother believes the child is getting a balanced diet, but he does not absorb what he gets. In such a case, the child's fatigue and poor behavior seem to have no reason whatsoever. These types of children seem always a little on the sluggish side — not really sick, but not quite alert and enthusiastic about life. And the cause for that kind of problem is so hard to detect!

The child may be a chronic mouth-breather. The nose is clogged, so he has to sleep with his mouth open to get air. The result of this mouth- breathing is generally a dry mouth in the morning. A dry tongue can be very painful and that does not make for a happy child.

Some allergies can cause fluid in the middle ears, which cuts down tremendously on what the child can hear. Thanks to antibiotics, ear inflammation is no longer the problem it once was, but an antibiotic will not clear up the fluid accumulated in the ear because of an allergy. Now there is a new problem: If a child is given antibiotics too often, a certain yeast fungus — candida albicans — exists in overabundance.

Some children suffer from recurrent middle ear fluid because of the presence of this organism. The treatment for candida albicans is anti-yeast medication, not antibiotics.

The symptoms of excess middle ear fluid are not so starkly evident as those of an ear infection. As a result, they are often not treated. The symptoms may well be simply diminished hearing or ringing in the ears; also, lack of balance, since the whole balancing mechanism is channeled through the ears. The more subtle the symptoms, the more irritable — and irritating — the child, who does not really know what is the matter with him. Even if he did, he not only does not have enough speech to tell others what he feels, but he does not realize this discomfort is not normal or that someone might be able to help him feel better.

There is a great danger that once the doctor has detected the pressure in the ears and even has cured it, you expect great changes in the child. Here you have spent all this energy and money to make sure the child is healthy, and the kid is still stupid! Of course he is stupid. He probably has heard very little during the six months before the visit to the doctor. There has been no input to his brain from the vestibular system which coordinates his adjustment to movement, and in a small child an interruption of normal neurological development, even of just a few months, has serious consequences. Give the child extra chances for listening, tumbling and rolling to make up for the input he missed during the time his ears were stuffed, and he'll catch up. (See Chapter 7.)

It is best to presume that no child is "ornery" on purpose. A mother may swear up and down she is feeding her child properly, that the child is not getting candy or coke or the other junk which can cause hypoglycemia, yet, simply because of allergy, there can be enormous fluctuations in blood sugar. When the blood sugar starts to fall, the child will, without being conscious of it, try to raise the sugar level. A good fight can raise the adrenalin, and also the blood sugar.

A good scary TV show can do the same thing. I have often wondered if this is the reason there are so many TV-addicted children. Do they need the scare to raise their blood sugar? The Quolla society, in Southern Peru and Bolivia, has a crime rate worse than that in our overcrowded cities. The reason seems to be their appalling diet, which leads to a craving for sugar. They love to fight, perhaps because a good fight raises their blood sugar and makes them feel better!

These blood-sugar fluctuations can also be caused by chemicals, by foods, or by fumes the children inhale from waxes on the floor, insulation in the walls, or gases from spray cans.

Far too often these symptoms remain masked because, as Lendon H. Smith states, children become addicted to the food to which they are allergic. The first food to suspect is the one which the child just absolutely must have every day. I know a child who loved Campbell's chicken noodle soup. He wanted it with his school lunch every day. And every day he came home from school banging doors, stamping angrily, or sat pouting in his room. Come vacation time, when a different lunch was served, there seemed none of this behavior. But with the onset of school, the child, who had seemed perfectly contented during the summer, turned into a little monster again. Was it the tension at school? Somehow it occurred to the mother that the child did not have the noodle soup during the summer, and that the child's behavior started when he carried the noodle soup in his thermos to school every day. She made soup from scratch for the child, and lo and behold, who was that strange child who appeared cheerful and relaxed at her door every afternoon? Surely the tensions at school had not changed! The monosodium glutamate in the chicken soup seemed to be the culprit. From then on, every food label at the grocery store was scanned for ingredients.

There are only about three soups in the entire supermarket which do not contain monosodium glutamate. Almost every other kind of processed food contains it. But the family was careful, and while there is no record of the child having turned into an angel overnight, at least 90% of the stamping and door slamming was eliminated.

Almost any food can cause problems. Any and all of the grains, for instance, can give the child an allergic reaction. I know of an infant girl who had constant diarrhea from the time she was six months old, until finally some specialist diagnosed that she had sprue, or celiac disease. The child could not tolerate any kind of gluten. Gluten is in wheat flour, oatmeal, rye and barley. To have to clean up the mess of an infant with constant diarrhea is a test of anyone's patience. A child like this, born to a parent who tends to be abusive, would have easily triggered a catastrophe. It is to the everlasting glory of motherhood that when I saw her, this child was a delightful, happy baby, resplendent in a neat pink dress, and with carefully combed blond curls. (Remember: Blond and blue-eyed children are more likely to be allergic!)

Allergies can be responsible for gradual and cumulative damage. There is no count of how many children have been diagnosed as retarded but are simply in a constant fog as a reaction to a cerebral allergy.

About 50 years ago, no one talked about allergies. The most we heard, was that little brother broke out in a rash whenever he ate strawberries, and that Uncle Joe swelled up like a balloon and nearly choked to death the last time he ate shellfish. But even when the word allergy became accepted — first in medical circles and then in popular usage — it was still believed the allergic substances could not cross the blood-brain barrier. We believed the brain was nurtured entirely by blood sugar, and other substances would not affect its function.

Then, during World War II, something happened that changed the entire concept of the influence of nutrition. In the mental hospitals of Greece, as everywhere in Greece, wheat was hard to come by, and there was a shortage of wheat bread. The inmates had to live on whatever else was available. Suddenly, to all the psychiatrists' surprise, half of their schizophrenic patients got well, packed up their belongings and went home. It seems like a strange thing to have happened, but the connection between allergy to gluten and schizophrenia in a large number of patients has since been scientifically established.

It is not only wheat which can cause an alteration of behavior. Some years back, a psychologist to whom I went for therapy suggested that, to make myself a little more aggressive, I should eat rye cereal for breakfast. I had childhood memories of a rye cereal with a picture of a centaur on its container — a handsome mythological beast, half horse and half man. So, delighted by the prospect of turning into something strong and brave, I faithfully ate my rye cereal. The result was this: I became so irritable that at work it took all my self-control not to throw the telephone through

30

the office window down some 50 stories onto some innocent passerby!

It was a great comfort to me, that I was not the only person who reacted like that to the rye cereal: Another patient to whom the therapist had recommended eating rye was jailed for punching someone in the nose.

I had almost forgotten the incident when, twenty years later, I suddenly found I was unbearably irritable. That is, I wasn't the one who was irritable — it was just that everyone around me was completely irrational, demanding from me ridiculously stupid things and driving me up the wall! Again, with the kind of memory which makes a dog not eat the same thing twice that made him sick the first time, I started putting two and two together. We had just discovered an absolutely fabulous rye bread, and I was eating about two loaves of it a week! I cut out the rye bread, and it was amazing how the world suddenly became quite reasonable and how problems which had seemed horrendous became simple annoyances.

When a child is in the grip of a cerebral allergy, you can stand on your head to try to please the child. All the cajoling and all the threatening will fall on deaf ears. To him you are simply one more irritating object in his way.

Cerebral allergies can cause edema (swelling) of the brain and give rise to the symptoms of brain damage. Dr. Ray Wunderlich, Jr. states that sometimes just eliminating the allergy can make learning problems disappear. (At other times though, he states — and Delacato also has found this to be true — a sensori-motor approach to learning problems seems to alleviate the allergies!)

To a child in an allergic fog, all the best methods of teaching will do no good. These reactions can vary tremendously from food to food and from child to child. Allergic fatigue can vary from a slight listlessness to a tiredness which seems to settle like lead in the child's arms and legs, so that he can barely stand up. He becomes "spaced out" at times and can hardly think straight. These are conditions which are particularly hard to detect in infants, because they sleep a great deal, anyway.

Infants, on the whole, seem to be very good at spitting out food they do not want. Unfortunately, in our Puritan society it has become a cultural matter to make the child eat everything on his plate. Soon the limbic system, the part of the brain which normally tells the body a certain food made the child sick the first time, gives up and stops telling the child the food is bad for him.

31

How, then, can we tell what food to give a child? Somehow the old tricks of feeding children, handed down from generation to generation, seem to have been lost. When introducing a new food to the baby, don't feed that kind of food more than once every four or five days. That way, if the baby is allergic, the body may still handle the insult.

Also, if there is an adverse reaction to one of the foods, it is easier to detect just which food is the culprit! Wheat, milk and eggs are the first suspects. Twenty-five percent of white children, and 75 % of nonwhites cannot tolerate milk. (The allergy to milk of the adopted Korean child is not an isolated case, but rather the rule among children who come from the East into our culture.)

Big tonsils? Suspect milk! Some children can tolerate raw milk better than homogenized. Homogenized milk with its added vitamin D has just about eradicated rickets in the United States, but there have been other, unfortunate results. In Finland, the rate of death from heart attack went sky high after homogenized milk was introduced. Our own young men killed in Vietnam, who had presumably been raised on homogenized milk, were found to have the clogged arteries usually found only in much older men. The fat in homogenized milk is saturated and can cause all kinds of problems, so don't feel obliged to continue giving it. Alternative sources of calcium are found in green leafy vegetables, broccoli, almonds, tofu, sesame seeds, sardines and other foods.

Eggs are another source of allergies, which is too bad, because they are high in iron and sulfur and have lots of high-quality protein. Wheat is another suspect which can be eliminated to see how it might be affecting the child. Many children are hypersensitive to wheat, a grain closely allied to rye. Many react adversely to wheat but may still be able to tolerate oats, barley, millet, flax and brown rice.

Dr. Lendon H. Smith suggests that not introducing wheat before the infant is at least one year old, can prevent a later wheat allergy. In general, Dr. Smith says, suspect the food which the child "must" have every day — that's the one to check out first for allergy problems. Eliminate those foods which the child seems to crave, and then introduce them again. Any allergy symptoms will show up almost immediately. However, look also for reactions which occur within a day or two. It is quite a lot of work, because the food must be controlled carefully, but it is better than having to scold your kid all the time!

Be sure to check for the onset of symptoms. If they come after a move into a different house, the child might be upset by the move. However, if the symptoms don't clear up, he might be allergic to the chemicals in the panelling of the house or sensitive to the gas escaping from a gas heater. (On the other hand, if during the drive to the new house both you and your husband are sniffling all the way there — you may have left all your friends behind, and it's not the pollen in the air which makes you sniffle — you both probably need a good cry!)

Irascible kids, with their tired, short-tempered parents, when carefully evaluated, are usually found to have allergies or allergy-like conditions. Social agencies must be aware of this possibility, and show parents how this can affect them and the children. No matter what other factors are involved, alleviating the allergies can play an enormous part in preventing a situation which could so easily lead to family violence!

Chapter 4

The Blood Sugar Connection

There is a very subtle form of child abuse going on today, and it is one no judge will condemn and no Children's Services will step in to change.

There was a sample of it at a restaurant of a local shopping center the other day. A young, attractive, and well-dressed mother had a little three-year-old girl sitting at one of the tables. Beside her was a year-old baby in a stroller. With a big smile, she put an enormous donut in front of the little girl, uncapped a bottle of cola, and then, with obvious love, she poured half of the cola into the one-year-old's bottle.

It was then ten o'clock in the morning!

This took place in Oregon, and I don't know about the law in other states, but Oregon has laws which require that child abuse be reported. Basically, however, even in Oregon people are taught to mind their own business. If the young mother had beaten her child, someone might have stepped in and stopped her. In a case like this, however, even if someone had been aware enough of what was happening, who was going to do anything? Nobody was going to go over and yank the donut out of the little girl's hand or knock over the baby's bottle! No one was going to go up to this smiling young lady and say: "Hey, do you know what you're doing to these kids? Do you know that you just gave those kids 200 calories of pure, unadulterated nothing in that donut? That the coke has 300 milligrams of caffein and 200 calories of pure sugar? That a three-year-old uses 1,200 calories a day, and that this junk — one-fourth of her daily intake — has no vitamins, no minerals, no fiber — nothing?" Or who'd have guts enough to say, "If you give these kids that stuff at 10 A.M., by noon, unless you manage to get some decent food into them, the girl will be a miserable, cranky little brat, and the baby will be yelling his head off! And if you keep this up, by the time the kids are five years old, they'll be asthmatic, allergic, and hyperactive!"

We are far too sophisticated or too well brought up — too cowardly perhaps — to interfere in a case like this. Perhaps, with a little bit of luck, the young woman might eventually come across Lendon Smith's incredibly comprehensive book, "Feed Your Kids Right." Perhaps someone might buy it for her as a present!

Dr. Lendon H. Smith, probably more than anyone, has tried to make mothers aware of the importance of nutrition, and he admits that for him, too, this is a comparatively new awareness. He is well known for those charming three-minute health-advice vignettes which are shown on local TV when the news is slow. He is even an occasional guest on the Johnny Carson show, because he is also a witty and delightful man. In 1979, we invited Lendon Smith to do a videotape program for the Eugene Public Library, as part of a series made under the auspices of the Department of Health and Welfare, to give information to parents which will help keep them from abusing their children.

Lendon Smith lives in Portland, Oregon and not in Eugene, but he agreed to do an hour show for a fee much smaller than what he would get for 10 minutes on the Johnny Carson show. Only on the night of the taping it was dark and stormy, and Portland lay under a blanket of six inches of slushy, awful snow, and we were afraid he would not make it.

As he drove down the hill from his house, one of his snow chains broke. So he slushed back up the hill through the snow and the wind, to borrow another snow chain. Back down the hill he went and drove through rain and snow that long, nasty, two-hour drive to Eugene, and a bit further to Lane Community College, where we were to videotape the show.

There he was, snow or no snow, bright-eyed and bushy-tailed, with a big grin on his face, a tall, lanky man, looking somewhat like a Don Quixote about to tilt at the windmills of ignorance!

Lendon Smith, in spite of his views on sugar and other delicious things, is quite aware that "a spoonful of sugar makes the medicine go down," and so his lectures are full of humor, quite ribald and totally devoid of respect for all the sacred cows, like apple pie and motherhood.

For the audience we collected members of a "parenting class" consisting entirely of parents of hyperactive children. As the program went on, they roared with laughter of recognition as Dr. Smith described their children. (This and other tapes from this series are available through the Eugene Public Library, 100 West 13th Street, Eugene, OR 97401).

This chapter, then, is essentially the content of what Dr. Lendon H. Smith explained to us that dark and stormy night at Lane Community College.

And here is a "portrait" as drawn by Portland "artist" Dr. Lendon Smith, as he explained the impact of nutrition on the brain on that dark and stormy night at Lane Community College:

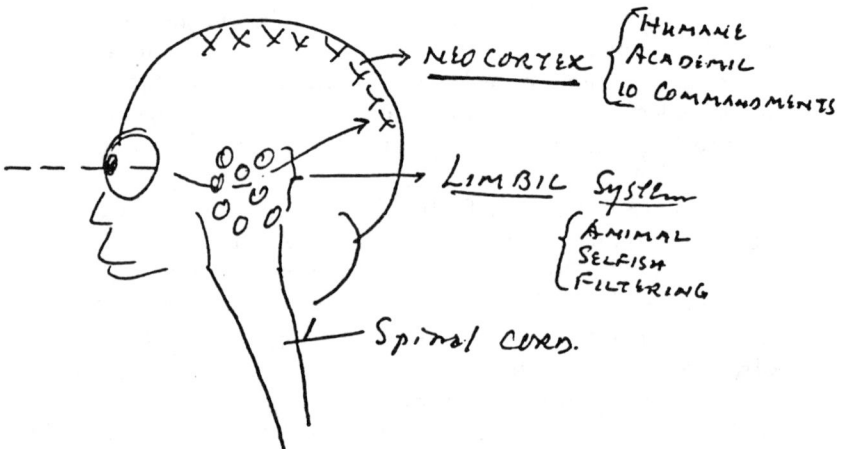

The messages from the nerve endings are sent along the spinal cord up to the brain where they are consciously perceived in the cortex. The messages which come through the eye are perceived by the visual cortex. The message of pain, received when a person steps on a tack, has to travel up the spinal cord, through the midbrain, and then to the cortex, where it tells the body, "Pick up your stupid foot!"

There is another system, located just under the midbrain, which is known as the limbic system. The limbic system is composed of many parts. Basically, it is some of the thalamus, some of the hypothalamus and some of the spinal cord. It is our animal brain. In it is a center for breathing, a center for eating, and a center for temperature control. It also has a sex center, which is very close to the eating center. All these are our animal functions in that area. You can think of this as our gorilla or dinosaur brain. It keeps the entire individual informed as to what is happening and how to react to what is happening. (If you get cold, you shiver; this helps the body keep warm.) From this center our temperature is controlled at about 98.6 degrees Fahrenheit.

But the limbic system also serves another purpose. It is actually a sort of screening device, a kind of colander, or switchboard, or whatever you will, and all the incoming messages have to go through this before they are conciously perceived.

At this center is decided what information the person needs to be aware of for survival. If some messages were not ignored, one would notice everything. (For example, when you're driving in heavy traffic, you must keep your mind on the traffic; if you are driving on an open, clear freeway, you can take time to admire some of the beautiful scenery.)

In vision, for instance, you could not pay attention to every message coming through your retina and still pay attention to one specific thing. The same holds true with sound. Normally you don't notice most of the sounds in your house — the dishwasher running, the humming of the furnace. This is why the furnace sounds so loud at night: There is nothing else to which you need to pay attention. The limbic system acts as a sort of screening device.

We think that many children, and many adults too, don't have a very good filtering device. This may account for the fact that they are particularly sensitive. Some are so sensitive that they notice every change in temperature. To them the water is too hot, or it's too cold. They don't like the feeling of an egg sliding down their throat. There are all different kinds of sensitivity. And when the limbic system permits all the different messages into the cortex, the person feels threatened. The cortex is sort of "on fire" all the time for people whose screening device won't work properly.

Dr. Smith found in his practice that the people whose limbic system allows too many messages to go through are the ticklish ones.

Ticklish people are overly sensitive people. And while he admits that this does not sound like a very scientific diagnosis, he has found in his many years as pediatrician that children who are having trouble in school, who are waking up every night, who feel every wrinkle in their sheet, the children for whom the cereal is too hot or too cold — these children are also the ticklish ones.

And they are also the ones who, more than the others, are affected almost immediately by faulty nutrition!

When he gets these children into his office for an examination, they won't let him look into their ears. They gag on the tongue depressor. If Dr. Smith tries to put a stethoscope on the chest of such a little fellow, he giggles and says, "It's too cold!" When he finally gets to put that little stethoscope disk on the child's chest, and moves it around, the kid might say, "What's the matter, can't you find my heart?" And when he tells him to lie down and tries to put his hand on the child's stomach to feel for the liver, he can just about count to four before the kid doubles up and screams with laughter. There are many children like that.

Lendon Smith says that if he has a six-year-old who is like that on the examination table, he will casually turn to the mother and ask, "Trouble in school?" Invariably she will nod: Trouble in school! He says that for the 4,000 children he has examined for school problems, there were at most 2 who were not ticklish.

Ticklishness, then, is a giveaway for hypersensitive people. Not every child who is ticklish will have trouble in school, but out of the ranks of the ticklish ones, there are more who are likely to have trouble.

Dr. Smith explains it this way. The screening out of distracting sensations occurs in the limbic system. This screening-out process is controlled by a chemical factor called norepinephrine. It's almost as if there were a little chemical factory in the nervous cells of the brain which manufacture norepinephrine. Other cells have different chemicals, such as dopamine and histamine, alphabutyric acid, and serotonin. These are also chemicals which do the work of the brain, chemicals that the nerves need to fire — in other words, to send messages to the different parts of the brain.

Difficulties in sending messages can also be caused by enzyme problems related to genetic effects; that is, these defects are passed on in the family. An injury to the brain, either at birth or through a blow to the head, can also keep messages from going through.

There are two enzymes that influence the production of chemicals that in turn influence what the limbic system does. It is now thought that there is a neurobiochemical that causes ticklishness. Now, we are not talking about the fact that the ticklish child, when touched lightly, just about has hysterics; that by itself is not a catastrophe. The child who is ticklish, however, is also the type of child who is likely to have colic and is more likely to have trouble falling asleep at night. You can't just tell him to go to sleep and expect him to turn around and sleep. He's not that kind of a person. If his relatives come over for a holiday like Christmas or Thanksgiving, he's all worked up and can't sleep for several days. He may even fall apart completely with the excitement and throw up. He makes a mess of everything. At first he gets all excited, and then he also gets disappointed. This kind of child always gets disappointed, there's really no pleasing him.

He's the child who, when you take him for a walk down the block, touches every picket on the fence and then goes back half a block to touch a picket he missed. In a big building, he has to touch every button on the elevator. In the supermarket, the checker can diagnose this child immediately. These kids come into the supermarket and think, "Wow! Look at all these treasures!" And they'll have to touch everything. Other people keep their hands off things.

Another thing which can be said about these children is that they are unable to disregard anything. Whether this puts them under a special amount of stress which other children do not feel, and whether this stress causes hypoglycemia or makes them more susceptible to hypoglycemia, is not clear. It is very important, however, to watch the diets of these kids especially carefully.

Their terrible hypersensitivity makes it almost impossible for them to function except on a one-to-one basis. In a crowd or in the schoolroom, this child's life becomes a nightmare. In school he looks around, and there's a kid who has the hiccups, and he has to go over and talk to him about that. Someone drops a pencil, and he has to go and look. A car passes, and he runs to the window to see what make of car it is. The teacher thinks he hasn't been disciplined enough at home and says "Shut up, sit down!" So, here's this six-year-old who's always cheerful and excited about all the wonderful things he will get to do in school, and pretty soon, he's been yelled at so often that all the fun is gone out of his life.

There are so many things getting into his nervous system that he cannot concentrate or think straight. He won't put anything down on paper, because he is constantly interrupted by something which is capturing his attention. The teacher says: "I know he can do that, but he won't try!"

So he gets a bad self-image. Those are the kids who by the sixth or seventh or eighth grade are sitting there with their arms folded — and their jackets on. They don't like to take their jackets off, because when it comes time to get your coat out of the locker, there's always a line. They don't want to wait because when the bell rings, they're ready to split. They're "low man on the totem pole" in the class social order. These kids band together for comfort and become a sort of subculture. If they can't compete in class, they can compete in being tough, and come eighth or ninth grade they're running away or pulling a knife. They're depressed and they consider suicide, or they dream up ugly things that we don't consider very civilized. We do know these kinds of things depend on the part of the brain which controls their behavior: The limbic system.

If you are what we call a nice human being, you live in the cortex part of the brain — the part of the brain where the Ten Commandments are practiced (or whatever number of the Ten Commandments are practiced in our society, says Dr. Lendon H. Smith). The animal part of the brain is the part which says: "I'm better than you are!" "I'm King of the Mountain!" "Get out of my sandbox!" That's the animal part of the brain talking. So if you are a Jekyll-and-Hyde person, you are Mr. Hyde when you are functioning mainly in the limbic system, and Dr. Jekyll, the civilized gentleman, when up in the cortex.

Now, all people have these kinds of fluctuations, but in these types of children you can really notice when they are functioning in the cortex or in the midbrain! There seems to be no reason for the changes in behavior. Some days you may call them to come in for dinner, and they'll yell at you and throw a tantrum as if you'd suggested hanging them by their thumbs. The thing to do is to give them a small glass of orange juice half an hour before dinner; then, when you ask them, well, maybe they'll deign to show up.

The thing which Lendon Smith found is that ticklishness means hypersensitivity, and in these same children, the Jekyll-and-Hyde behavior is related to a special sensitivity to food.

The Jekyll-and-Hyde behavior grows out of an abnormal fluctuation of blood sugar, which is caused by the "pseudodisease" called hypoglycemia. It is not recognized by most people in the medical profession because, for some reason, it does not happen to everybody. Actually, hypoglycemia has almost become a household word. Magazines have come out with articles about it, and books have been written since the early fifties.

That snowy night in the TV studio at Lane Community College, Dr. Lendon H. Smith drew us this nice, neat picture of a blood-sugar curve with white chalk on a green blackboard:

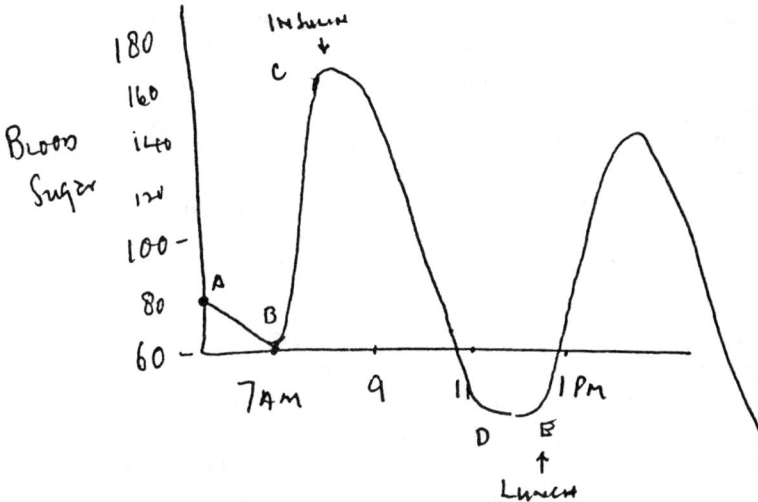

This is Charlie's blood sugar curve according to Lendon Smith's art work:

Here at point "A" is our Charlie, whose blood sugar has slowly fallen during the night, so his blood sugar is now maybe 80 gm. percent sugar. (We all have to have blood sugar in our bloodvessels to make the brain work.) At point B, he's having a typical American breakfast, which is a glass of Tang and a bowl of Sugarpops, which already has so much sugar in it that there is a bunch of that gritty stuff in the bottom of the bowl. He has a piece of white toast with jam on it and, because it's a cold morning, some hot chocolate with marshmallows in it. It's mainly carbohydrates he's eating, and at that, it's more than most American kids are getting.

So Charlie eats this junk at point B, and within half an hour (and this has been tested), the blood sugar shoots up to 160 milligrams of sugar at point C. He's almost diabetic at this point, because diabetes starts when you're over 160 milligrams. The body does not like this. There is a safeguard which keeps the body from going into a diabetic coma, and this safeguard is the insulin system.

41

The pancreas squirts out insulin, and in about three hours, the insulin has knocked the blood sugar back to normal.

In a normal child, this process takes three hours. But Charlie is one of the hypersensitive children. His pancreas squirts out too much insulin and drives the blood sugar down too far, down to point D, and there it stays until lunchtime, point E. At lunchtime he's eating a bowl of instant noodles and chocolate pudding, so later in the afternoon, after an initial rise at point F, the blood sugar comes down again to point G! The insulin system does not like these sudden changes and, in a child like Charlie, brings the blood sugar down far too low.

The problem is that with children or adults with a blood sugar curve like this, when the blood sugar is way down there, the brain does not work. What we do know about the brain, says Lendon Smith, is that the cortex is a very busy organ. One-fourth of our blood goes right to the brain, one-fourth to the liver, one-fourth to the kidneys, and one-fourth elsewhere. This shows how important an organ the brain is. This small gray matter which doesn't look like much is busy, busy, busy all the time.

A child's brain has two or three times the energy needs that an adult's has. But there is no room for storage in the brain. If there were to be room for storage, like there is in the liver or in the muscles, there would have to be such a big head that it would be impossible to carry it around. So mother nature fixed it that people would have a big blood supply. The brain would be served by the blood which brings it all the nutrients: Sugar, oxygen, amino acids, certain vitamins, and all the other things a brain needs to function. This works provided people eat right. But if Charlie's blood supply is not bringing all the brain needs, and all the time the brain is being bombarded by outside stimuli, our Charlie is having a hard time coping.

Let's presume some young teacher meets her new class for the first time and wants to get the class to write the alphabet. She wants to see how much they already learned from "Sesame Street", so she says, "Get out your crayons and do your alphabet."

Our Charlie pulls out his crayons and gets through the first letters just fine — A,B,C,D — and now he can't remember if the prongs on the E go backward or forward. When you're six it's rough. You can't cheat, because someone else might have it wrong also! So Charlie just sits there, he can't figure it out. No matter how hard he tries, he can't remember, so he throws his paper in the air, drops his crayons on the floor, gets down next to his crayons, and has a big temper tantrum. The teacher is worried; she prods him a little with her foot. "Are you all right, Charlie?"— but Charlie just carries on. So she does a little behavior modification and pays no attention to him. After a while Charlie calms down and just sits there for a couple of hours, and finally they send him home.

Now, the next day, the teacher asks Charlie, "Can you do the alphabet?" He says, "Sure!" and he writes: A,B,C,D,E,F,G... the whole alphabet!

There is an obvious, big difference between Monday and Tuesday — a sort of Jekyll-and-Hyde performance. He couldn't function on Monday, and on Tuesday he could. We could say it was obstinacy or stubbornness, his mother gave him a bad time, or his father kicked him. You can find any sort of reason for his noncompliance on Monday and his compliance on Tuesday. What was the difference? Had he stayed up late the night before and was out of sorts? Chances are it had something to do with his breakfast, because on Tuesday, when he could function, someone had managed to get something lasting into him, like a bowl of soup, or even a piece of whole-wheat bread with a lump of peanut butter. On Tuesday, his blood sugar stayed high all morning; the complex carbohydrates and the fat from the peanut butter were absorbed slowly. The blood-sugar curve rose slowly and just a little bit, and so the insulin system was not called in to knock his blood sugar way down. The little memory-storage circuits which say, "The E goes to the right and not to the left!" were way up in the cortex, and the messages just did not get way up there. On Monday, "the lights were out" up there. On Tuesday, when he had eaten properly, his energy sources were functioning all the way, and it was possible for Charlie to know: "Ah, of course, the E goes that way!"

Lendon Smith, in his joking way, but nevertheless very seriously, suggests that the teacher line up the class every morning and ask each child, "What did you have for breakfast this morning?" If someone says, "I can't remember!" chances are his blood sugar is already way down.

If Charlie answers, "Well, I had 'Sugar Bear' flakes like Tony the Tiger, had Wonderbread, which helps the body grow 13 ways, Tang, like the astronauts do..." and so on, she knows he's still all right. He can still remember. But in 20 minutes his blood sugar will be down and he'll be out of it. She might as well send him back home.

Then, of course, says Lendon Smith, there's the dentist's little girl whose mother runs a health-food store. She's had a glass of fresh-

43

squeezed orange juice, a soft-cooked fertilized egg, a slice of whole-wheat bread her mother bakes fresh daily, spread with peanut butter, and, of course, all her vitamins and minerals and lecithin.

It might make sense to deputize her to watch the class, while the teacher goes to the teachers' lounge for coffee and a donut.

A survey has been made of children's breakfasts, and the results have been appalling. In Sweden and Denmark, the government provides fish at break time for children to keep up their blood sugar. Even long before hypoglycemia was recognized, the Swiss, who are famous for their boarding schools, would not dream of letting their students go through the day without supplying them with a handful of nuts or a slice of cheese at midmorning and then again in the afternoon!

The concept of hypoglycemia in children is comparatively new. It was only in 1981 that Columbia Medical school finally introduced a course in nutrition for its medical students!

Even Lendon Smith admits that his knowledge of what food does to the body comes from his disenchantment with what drug therapy was doing to children who had been labeled "hyperactive" or "problem" children. This awareness does not keep him from constantly stressing the fact that there may be many other factors involved. There are times when emotional problems can well be helped by a psychiatrist. Stress certainly builds up, especially if the child is particularly sensitive. But there has been enough work done by this time to know that if a child is having problems, it might be because of the way he is eating.

If a child comes home from school, kicks open the door, and lets loose with a stream of abuse and generally acts like Attila the Hun, it's difficult not to get mad at him and act like Attila the Hun yourself. But it displaces the anger a little bit if, instead of getting mad at the child, you get mad at something which happened to him. Instead of smacking him and sending him to his room and grounding him for the next six months, it makes more sense to say to him, "What on earth did you eat for lunch!?!"

A prudent parent would stand there and shove a big spoon of peanut butter down his throat, then get out of the way and wait for things to calm down. In 20 minutes the kid will have joined humanity again: "Hey, need any help, Mom?" If you want him to do something for you, like take the garbage out, and he does it for you, pat him on the head and say, "Thanks for helping me! You're a great garbage-taker-outer." You even give him a reward, so you'd think that the next time he'd be glad to take out the garbage for you. But if then, when you ask him again, he throws it on the floor and yells, "I don't want to! Let someone else take out the garbage!" don't throw something at him, feed him! Feed him, and wait a while. His blood sugar may have just been a little low at that point.

Things, of course, are not always as simple as that. If they were, there would have been no need to write this book, and Dr. Lendon H. Smith would not have agreed to be part of the book. We must be aware, for instance, that stress in life can lower the blood sugar just as fast as food can. It has even been suggested that the excitement which kids experience watching television causes enough stress to start the spiral of hypoglycemia. They may well become addicted to the excitement, purely because this excitement starts the adrenalin, which then raises the blood sugar and makes the child feel better.

The important thing is to be able to identify the "goosy" baby as soon as possible. These children can't understand all the sensations which come on to them far stronger than to other children, and they conceive the world as a very dangerous place. Lendon Smith likens it to having a space bubble, the same sort of situation as being in a crowded elevator. You can't wait to get out of it. You get an anxiety attack. When the child's cortex gets this overload, it sends messages to the adrenal gland and the pituitary. Now, the glands have no perceptions of danger on their own. They can't tell if it's a real emergency or not. All they can tell is that they got a signal to squirt out their chemicals. It's the same as if there were a tiger out there somewhere, and the body had to get ready for a fight. So each time, when they get the signal, the adrenals squirt out adrenalin and cortisol. Pretty soon the adrenals get exhausted. As the adrenals get exhausted, allergies start to show up along with psychosomatic illnesses, headaches and migraines, colitis, ulcers, and high blood pressure. Hay fever is one of the symptoms. This is the basis for psychosomatic medicine.

There are lots of people who live with these problems. Somehow they survive and are even very successful. Thomas Edison was like that, Winston Churchill and Attila the Hun, restless people who had to keep doing things to discharge the tension which builds up in them. The question is how to raise such a person to be a useful person and to have a good self-image? When you have such a child, he seems to do nothing for which you can reward him. Does a mother say, "I love you for the way you run from the living room to the dining room, the way you throw the food around and jump up from the dining room table! I love the way you stay up till midnight waiting for the test patterns to come on!"?

Dr. Broda O. Barnes has had success treating hypoglycemia by giving thyroid medication. He states that hypoglycemia is essentially a thyroid-deficiency disease, not a disease in its own right. By giving thyroid, he eliminates the same problems which Dr. Smith lists as being the results of hypoglycemia: The anxiety attacks, the bed-wetting, the nightmares, the sudden behavior problems.

To see if thyroid therapy might be indicated, Dr. Barnes suggests taking the child's temperature under the armpit first thing in the morning for one week. If it reads consistently below 97.8 degrees, it might be a good idea to find a doctor who is willing to give this kind of therapy a try. What these findings indicate is that the child's entire metabolism is off. If thyroid therapy is given, it must be handled very carefully and with continual monitoring by the doctor, at least in the beginning. Even then, all the good can be undone by continuing with poor nutrition.

We would not feed our animals the way we feed children in this country. Ask any farmer, any owner of a racing stable. The animal's feed is carefully monitored for protein content, and vitamin supplements are given.

Of course, the farmer does not have to contend with doting relatives who insist on giving your child all kinds of awful food. And don't forget: As little as 15 years ago, if you took your child to a doctor, the doctor would give him a lollypop as a reward for taking his shots. Dentists were a little ahead of the game. It's been 20 years since they gave away lollypops.

Under any circumstances then, nutrition is a very important influence, no matter what other steps are being taken. Sugar and white flour are the first things which should be avoided.

The danger is that hypoglycemic children are not fat. Lendon Smith says that out of 4,000 hypoglycemic kids he has seen, maybe two were fat. The mother thinks, well, he's burning it all up, so he must need it — and continues to feed the junk food. What she does not realize is that when the body metabolizes these empty nutrients, since they have no vitamins of their own, the body's store of vitamins is used up. The body needs these lost vitamins to function well. They use up the B vitamins, which are necessary to help the brain make norepinephrine. This is the chemical which keeps the limbic system of the brain functioning smoothly, and it is this system which regulates all the automatic functions of the body. Mess up these automatic controls, and a host of allergies and diseases will follow. The psychiatrist will call them psychosomatic, but there is a very real chemical reason for the problems.

White sugar and white flour are the main culprits. It will take about three weeks for the child to cease craving these, but once you take the child off sweets and institute a hypoglycemia regimen (feed nuts or cheese between meals and, especially, some protein before bedtime), the change will be evident in three days! Children even as young as four or five years old should be told what you are doing; and they readily feel the difference and usually cooperate quite willingly.

In any case, donuts and cola at ten o'clock in the morning are definitely not the thing to give to children. A small bag of peanuts is cheaper and will last the child a lot longer. The nutritional approach is so easy to follow that if you give yourself a three-week limit to sticking to it, you will see if it works or not. Sometimes it takes only three days before you can see the results. But it is the long-range effect which will be more and more evident when the child not only ceases to have mood swings but many of the allergies will slowly disappear. (For further information on hypoglycemia, see Part VI of the Appendix.)

SECTION I

$\langle\!\langle\times\!\times\rangle\!\rangle$

THE EARLY SCHOOL YEARS

$\langle\!\langle\times\!\times\rangle\!\rangle$

Chapter 5

The Sensory Connection

Jimmy is a first-grader, a perfect little gentleman. Yet, at least once a month, you see him sitting in the principal's office. Regular as clockwork, while he is an absolute angel in class for three weeks out of the month, the fourth week, the teacher cannot control him at all. That's the week the teacher menstruates.

Johnny is considered hopelessly hyperactive. He knocks his feet against the chair, taps on his desk with his pencil, clicks his tongue, slams books. He is considered hyperactive; yet, when you really observe him, he does all these things without ever moving out of his chair!

Mary is an intelligent, attentive girl — as long as it is summertime and the sun shines through the window. Come winter and it is dark outside and the teacher turns on the lights, Mary can no longer sit still or pay attention and is always disturbing the class.

Andy is pale and white. He has dark circles under his eyes, sits in a corner most of the time, and completely shuts out all the activity going on around him in the classroom. The teacher is very concerned that Andy might be a neglected child.

QUESTION: Which of these children is an abused child?
QUESTION: Which of these children may end up being an abused child?

Your average classroom has five high-risk children. Their problems can range anywhere from learning disabilities to emotional problems at home. Perhaps they are simply overplaced: The child was developmentally too young when he entered school.

The teacher, somehow, has to teach an entire classroom of normally rambunctious kids, yet also work with these five problem children. And among those five kids, more likely than not, there is also a Jimmy, a Johnny, a Mary and an Andy.

For the dyslexic, she may order special tutoring; for the overplaced, she may reassign the child to a lower grade. But what about Jimmy, Johnny, Mary and Andy? If she calls in the school psychologist there will be much probing and testing. The parents will be upset. The mothers will blame the father's influence, and the fathers will blame the mother's. The children will be getting all kinds of extra attention and, as a result, will continue the behavior the teacher is trying to eliminate.

Contrary to what the teacher might have suspected, none of these children behaves that way because of abuse! But any one of them may well get himself abused, because no one can understand what is wrong with him!

It is actually the Jimmys, the Johnnys, the Marys, the Andys and the many variations of such children, who have been the motivation for writing this book. They are in grave danger of being abused, because they are the children who fall between the cracks. They are not ill, they do not have a mysterious sickness, yet they behave in strange ways which are doubly annoying because we can find no reason for their behavior.

The clues to helping these children come from an unexpected source. In 1974, Carl H. Delacato published the findings of his work with autistic children and opened a door to a whole new way of seeing problem behavior in children. His book "The Ultimate Stranger: The Autistic child" is a landmark in child psychology. Yet, hand this book to a teacher or a student teacher, both of whom are overloaded with other required reading, and they will turn it down, saying, "Oh, we never see any autistic children in school. I can't take time for that." Suggest it to a psychologist, and he will say, "Oh, these children are so rare, I have no need for that!" And you don't dare hand the book to a mother, or she will be horrified that you are implying her child is autistic!

And so Jimmy, Johnny, Mary and Andy are not likely to get any help. Neither their school psychologists, their parents, nor their teachers know what to do with them.

These children are definitely not autistic. Autism implies that they do not react to people; that they have repetitive, apparently meaningless movements; and until just recently, that the chances of their ever getting better would be close to nil.

These children, however, do have some of the same symptoms of the autistic child. No way near to the extent that the autistic children have them, but to a far greater extent than we all do, and because we all have a little bit of this "brain disease", as Carl Delacato puts it, they are really not that difficult to understand. They are the "hypersensitive" children, or the "hyposensitive" children, or the children "with white noise". ("White noise" children have ringing in their ears, the same ringing we hear on a really quiet stretch in the snow-covered forest, when the snow has deadened all the noise. Or they have a strange taste in their mouth, or see flashes in front of their eyes. We are less likely to find these in the schools.)

Most of us can find a way to identify with hypersensitive kids. For instance, if we put on a wool sweater in the morning, it may feel perfectly soft and comfortable. As the day goes on and we get more tired, suddenly the sweater seems awfully bothersome and itchy, and we can't wait to take it off. The annoying quality of the sweater, or whatever is bothering us — a collar too high around the neck, a pair of pants that don't fit, shoes that are a little bit too tight — this annoyance is often so subtle that we are not quite sure just what is making us irritable. Again, we do not actually zero in on the sensation until we get very tired and our nerves are "raw."

In the same way, we may be able to tolerate all kinds of noise, just simply ignoring it, and then, suddenly, every sound becomes a painful intrusion on our sensitive ears.

The senses of the "hypersensitive" children are always as "raw" and as sensitive as ours are only when we are tired. When such a hypersensitive child comes to school and his sweater bothers him, he is so uncomfortable that he has a hard time paying attention.

Jimmy, who is a good boy three weeks out of the month, is hypersensitive to smell. He can smell things none of the other children smell. When the teacher's body odor changes because she is menstruating, he finds this smell so obnoxious that he will pull any kind of maneuver to get away from the odor. That week he becomes a problem and is sent to the principal!

Mary, who is well-behaved unless the fluorescent lights are on, is one of the many children who are affected by such lights. It is not entirely certain whether these lights affect the children visually or whether the very fine whine that these lights give off — and that most of us cannot hear — bothers them.

And then there is Andy. You see a lot of Andys, with dark circles under their eyes and very, very pale faces. The only time Andy looks a little bit rosy, is when he himself is making quiet sounds, singing, or tapping his fingers. Andy is so sensitive to sound that the only noise he can tolerate is the sound he makes himself. (This is not surprising, as experiments have shown that the brain processes the sounds a person makes himself quite differently from the way sounds made by someone else. When you run the vacuum cleaner, the noise does not bother you at all; if someone else runs it in another room, the racket may drive you up the wall.)

As long as Andy makes his own noises or is in quiet surroundings, he is comfortable and relaxed. School hallways and classrooms usually echo the clatter of shoes, slammed desks, scraped chairs and the constant chatter of the students. No industrialist would expect his employees to work under such conditions and still be able to function. Bombarded by all this noise, Andy's sympathetic nervous system shuts down all the sound sensations in Andy. This switch to the sympathetic nervous system is what is also causing the child's pallor — a kind of ashen quality, which you can recognize even in black children.

It is this ashen quality which makes the child look as if he were in shock — that is the giveaway. Our bodies are controlled by two different nervous systems: The central nervous system, which controls the functions that we do consciously; and the autonomic nervous system, which, unless we are trained in biofeedback, is not under our control.

The autonomic nervous system consists of two networks of nerves: the parasympathetic and the sympathetic. As either set of nerves is stimulated it counterbalances the influence of the other, so that between the two systems our body functions are kept running smoothly. Our blood pressure, heartbeat and perspiration are under the control of these two systems. If the parasympathetic nerves are stimulated, there is a generally calming effect. The sympathetic nervous system readies the body for fight or flight. If neither fight nor flight is possible, the body can go into a state of suspended animation — actually a form of flight, like the playing dead of an animal in danger. Andy's body has learned that to his hypersensitive ears noise is painful. When he is faced with a noise level that is threatening, his body automatically puts him into a withdrawal stage (very similar to shell shock) which protects him from the overload of noise to his brain.

This state of shock is what is causing the pallor. When Andy has that ashen look, he does not hear. He cannot hear, because his hearing system is shut off. It can make a bright child look very stupid. It can, unjustly so, make him look stubborn.

Quite often a mother does not realize her child can be that gray color, because she sees him only at home. There he is comfortable and relaxed. Should a teacher go to the child's house to try to find out what is wrong with his home environment that gives him that abused look, she may be startled to find he is quite a different child there. It will be hard to convince the parent that the child needs help. But — blow a shrill whistle and, within seconds, the child will turn pale, and if he is then asked a question, he will not hear it properly and may ask to have it repeated. It's not that he is not paying attention, his sound system has shut down.

What about Johnny, who keeps making all those tapping noises and is considered hyperactive, even though he never moves from his chair? He's the one who is probably "hypo" in hearing. Not enough sound reaches his brain, so he desperately tries to stimulate his hearing by putting in more noises. I say "probably" because he might also be using these tapping sounds to help locate himself in space, because his eyes and his proprioceptors do not help him find where he is. He uses the noises the same way a blind man taps his cane.

Dr. Larry Burr, one of the desperately few developmental optometrists in this country, says that with some of his young patients he can tell, even before they enter his office, whether they are wearing the new glasses he prescribed for them. If such a child makes a lot of noise, it's 10 to 1 the eyeglasses are in the child's pocket and not on his nose. Somehow, these children use the sound of their voices as an echo locator. The moment they put on their glasses and can see, they know where they are and become very quiet.

Each child is different, and it takes a good deal of detective work to find out what is wrong so the child can be helped. This detective work is made easier by the techniques which Carl H. Delacato lays out in "The Ultimate Stranger." The book reads like a detective novel; indeed, it's so entertaining it is hard to appreciate just how much research it took to achieve this breakthrough in the understanding and treatment of autistic children.

Even though the children we are seeking to help are not autistic, the same principles of testing them for sensory distortions apply. To understand the reasons for these tests and for the treatment, we must have a look at the work which led to Delacato's discoveries.

Carl H. Delacato had been working with brain-injured and learning-disabled children for over 15 years. After a long period during which he had a constant struggle to justify his procedures to a skeptical world, in 1974 the National Association for Retarded Children, which had been challenging his theories, finally did a study of the theories and procedures based on the work which he and Glenn Doman had been pioneering at the Institute for the Achievement of Human Potential, in Philadelphia. Their official statement at the end of this research declared they had found these methods to be a legitimate approach in the remediation of certain handicapping conditions.

Delacato now took on a new challenge: Finding clues to the puzzle of children with strange, unexplainable behavior. The more he saw of behavior-problem children, the more he felt that they were like the brain-injured children with whom he had been working all along. To make sure he was dealing with autistic and not with brain-injured children, he chose to work specifically with those who had been labeled autistic by other experts before they had come to see him.

The label "autistic" is a diagnosis which strikes terror into the heart of any parent. Autism, or childhood schizophrenia, is still considered the childhood mental disease which has the least chance of ever being cured. The generally accepted symptoms of autism are:
— lack of interaction with other people
— repetitive, non-goal-directed (purposeless) behavior
— insistence on sameness in the environment
— lack of use of language, but with occasional signs of normal, even superior, intelligence

In short, these children live in a world of their own. they make movements or noises for apparently no reason. they don't speak to us but, nevertheless, do not seem stupid.

The children who were sent to Delacato for help were indeed strange and sometimes even terrifying. They rocked back and forth, they hit their ears and their eyes. Some went into hysterics if someone made a loud noise; they vomited if someone blew smoke in their direction.

One child had to wear a helmet, because if the helmet were removed, she would bang her head on the nearest table corner or other sharp surface and smile beatifically at whoever would then wipe the blood from her forehead!

Then there was Annie. Annie had to wear gloves all the time, because given a moment alone, she would bite her hand until the fingers bled.

Delacato watched these children and listened to them and collected data. While he was collecting information on them, and studying their case histories, he also went to institutions for the mentally retarded where these children were being warehoused. He saw the same kind of behavior repeated in endless variations: The same withdrawal, the same repetitive motions which seemed to make no sense, the same strange cries for which there seemed no reason. These types of behavior were labeled "autisms" by the psychologists.

Delacato also went to the schools for the deaf and hearing-impaired. There, too, he saw some of the same strange, repetitive behavior. The children rocked back and forth and hit themselves on their ears. They made strange noises, though their teachers knew they could not hear them. Their teachers called these behaviors "deafisms" — signs that the children were deaf.

In the schools for the blind, there was a similar situation; only here the children hit their eyes with the flat of their hands. They too rocked back and forth. It was as if — not being able to see where they were — they used the change in gravity to tell them when it was necessary to move the body so as not to fall over. Their teachers called these motions "blindisms".

While Delacato was doing his research, an unexpected thing happened. The brother of little Annie, the child who bit her hand, had slammed the car door on that hand. Now the hand was black-and-blue — and Annie stopped biting it. The hand hurt, and Annie was not biting it any more.

Delacato continued to collect his observations of the behavior of the autistic children and noticed that the behavior fell into specific patterns. The blindisms — or what would have been considered blindisms if the child had been diagnosed as blind — were efforts aimed at getting input into the eyes. If, for instance, the children hit their eyes, they were trying to see flashes which the pressure might cause, or if they waved their hands before their eyes, they were trying to see something.

The deafisms were efforts to get information into the ears. The behavior of the autistic children also related to smells (were aimed at the nose), or taste (aimed at the mouth), and in other cases there were attempts to get more information into the proprioceptive (touch) system.

What had been loosely labeled an "autism" — a sign that the child was withdrawn, all those strange, repetitive behaviors — were not really autisms but, specifically deafisms, blindisms, tastisms, tactilisms, and smellisms. Not only that, but there seemed to be a specific reason for each kind of behavior. If the sensory channel at which the behavior was aimed did not allow enough information to get into the brain, then the children hungrily created the sensory stimulation they seemed to need. If too much information entered the channel, the children made efforts to escape — from the light, from sound, from smell, or from whatever else threatens to overwhelm them. At times there seemed to be a sound or a sensation coming from within: A bad taste in the mouth, a ringing in the ears, flashes of light seen inside the eyes, or there is an uncomfortable sensation in the proprioceptive system, the channel through which we perceive the small but important sensations from our muscles.

The concept that autistic children have sensory problems was not really a new one. Other researchers of autism had gathered information and described unusual sensitivities and perceptual distortions resulting from a barrier which did not let information enter the child's brain.

There was one major difference between the approach of the others and that of Carl Delacato. Delacato had been working with brain-injured children for 20 years, and he had seen blind children — some blind children — learn to see. He had seen deaf children — some deaf children — learn to hear, paralyzed children learn to walk, and mute children learn to talk. Carl Delacato never accepted for one moment that a condition caused by brain injury could not be remedied, at least to some degree. And these autistic children he studied were not even completely deaf or completely blind and, generally speaking, were not even very badly brain-injured.

Annie, who had stopped biting her hand while it was black-and-blue from the accident with the car door, returned for another visit. Her hand was now healed, and she had started biting it again.

And so Carl Delacato treated Annie's hand as he would have the hand of a brain-injured child who had lost control over an arm. He started to send as many different stimuli as possible from the hand into Annie's brain. He had Annie's parents dip the hand alternately into hot and cold water. They were to pinch and poke that hand, rub it with rough towels and massage it. They gave her arm and hand deep, almost painful massage, and eventually the channels from her hand to her brain told Annie there was a hand attached to her body. She no longer had to bite it to feel that it was there. If she bit it, "It would hurt!", as she now proudly said.

A whole new way of treating autistic children had been discovered, a whole new way of looking at these children. They were not schizophrenic or emotionally disturbed; they were brain-injured. They were brain-injured in ways that affect, not the out-going channels, but the channels which bring information into the brain, and they were reacting to this distorted input. For us to get a general concept of how these behavior problems originate, we might imagine this:

We have just come from the dentist's office. We have just had a shot of novocaine and our cheek and tongue are still completely numb. In an effort to change that dead, numb feeling, we find ourselves rubbing the numb cheek and poking at it.

We may meet a close friend, who sees us poking and slapping our face, and his reaction might be: "Hey, what's the matter with your face?" But a stranger coming by, who didn't know that we don't normally go around slapping our own face, might think, "Gee, look at that weird character hitting himself!"

Now that the puzzle pieces were beginning to fall into place, Delacato began to decode the behavior. If the behavior was in front of the child's eyes, it related to vision; near the ears, it related to hearing; in front of the nose or mouth, it might relate to smell or taste; and so on.

If the child fled from the stimulus, it meant that he was too sensitive; if he was seeking it, there was not enough coming in; and if he seemed to be listening or paying attention to some inner noise or sensation, it was a question of white noise or static in the particular channel involved.

The treatment was then carefully tailored to each child's needs and was essentially divided into three parts.

To begin with, once the parents understood that the behavior had a purpose, they could tolerate the child's behavior more readily and were less likely to abuse or to institutionalize him. Once they could see the reason for the child's actions, these actions seemed no longer frightening nor quite so unacceptable.

To begin, Delacato taught the parents to make the child more comfortable, to shield him from the sensations which were making him withdraw from people. Once the parents and the child could live with each other, the child was given treatment that would make the affected channels as close to normal as possible.

Delacato worked with autistic children with very severe sensory problems. Perfectly normal children, however, can have some slighter sensory problems which also can affect their behavior. In such cases, their behavior is far more likely to cause them to be abused and belittled, because to all intents and purposes, these children are normal and no allowances are made for them. It is, therefore, of vital importance that anyone dealing with children be at least aware of Delacato's techniques.

Somewhat the same methods Delacato uses in first evaluating and then treating behavior problems will hold true in the classroom. A teacher might say, "That's all well and good, but what am I supposed to do about it? I have to teach 25 kids, I can't just sit there and observe the ones with problems, much less do anything about fixing those kids!"

Well, to begin with, even a little bit of awareness will go a long way. The truly autistic child will probably not show up in the classroom, even with the new policy of mainstreaming. But suppose a teacher notices that a child seems to be "hypo" in vision — he does not see too terrribly well. The child may work better with a black flow pen than with a pencil! A hypervisual child, who is interested in every little thing that moves, might function better in the front row, where he is not distracted by every move his friends make. Since the teacher is now aware that the behavior of the child is not aimed at challenging her, but caused by a specific problem, such treatment of the child no longer has a punitive quality to it. The child will sense this. Also, because his behavior will no longer cause an angry reaction from the teacher, it will no longer bring extra attention. Such emotional reinforcement would eventually have to be carefully eliminated by painstaking behavior modification.

There are easier ways to cope with children who have slight sensory deviations than to use behavior modification. Let's suppose the teacher has observed that Mike has a "tactility" problem. Some tactility problems have a way of happening in spurts. That is, the child seems to be going along fine, then suddenly seems to be unable to sit still. It is as if he were uncomfortable in his skin. He must move and squirm and wiggle his body or touch something.

Understanding this, the teacher will know just what to do. When she sees this sort of thing happening, she may call him over to her desk and gently say, "I see you are having a hard time sitting still. I have a note to deliver to Mr. Jones (who just happens to be in the classroom furthest from her own and is in on the act). Do you mind running over to deliver it? That will give you a chance to stretch your legs and help me at the same time." Then she can apply a little behavior modification, telling him how wonderful he was that day not to have bothered the other students.

Eventually, when Mike gets that sudden spurt of restlessness again, instead of getting himself into trouble with the kids sitting next to him, Mike will come to the teacher and suggest to her, "I have a hard time sitting still. Can you send me somewhere? I have to stretch my legs!" Mike will have acquired a certain amount of biofeedback and learned to deal with his problem without thinking himself a bad boy.

Another point: With this new awareness, parent-teacher conferences will take on a different quality. The teacher will no longer look askance at the mother of little Andy, the boy with the pale face and dark circles under his eyes, and wonder if his parents are taking proper care of him. Chances are the mother is equally concerned about those dark shiners. The teacher does not have to say to her, "I wish Andy would pay more attention in class!" If she did, Mother might take Andy outside later and yell at him to pay more attention, and Andy would turn even more pale and tune her out completely.

The teacher might instead try this: "Some children are terribly sensitive to noise, and I have a feeling Andy is one of them. School must be a real strain for him!" (By now, Mother already loves the teacher.) "Of course, it's just a feeling I have. Can you tell me a little bit about how he reacts to noises outside the school?" And chances are that Mother will have a whole history of how Andy used to scream when the vacuum cleaner was running, how he hates barking dogs, and can hear an airplane before anyone else knows it is there. Once the teacher's hypothesis has been confirmed, a good rapport will have been established, and she can then suggest that maybe Andy might be more comfortable coming to school with a little cotton in his ears.

The interview with the mother of a hypotactile little fellow, who seems always to be starting a wrestling match during recess, can be even more fruitful. This kind of child gets so few sensations from his own body that he has to get them from the roughest kind of play. He usually ends up being the school bully and invariably ends up sitting in the principal's office. Poor Mother is constantly being called to school to be told what kind of monster he is. He may be taken home and spanked, which is a complete waste of time. First, he does not feel very much, being hypotactile; and second, he might only be learning what he is already doing in school — that beating up on someone smaller is an all-right thing to do. (These kinds of children are a football coach's dream.) It is far more productive to explain to the parents that some children need a lot of deep touching and that daily sessions of rough-and-tumble, deep massage, and bear hugs will give the child the sensory input he needs. After a few weeks of such a routine, his behavior in school should improve measurably!

Awareness and knowledge are the key. This does not mean having a know-it-all attitude. At best, we are guessing what the problem might be. Of course, the first question which comes to mind is, Why doesn't the child tell us what's wrong? The reason is that he has no idea that the world can be any other way than the way he experiences it. There are ways, though, of making children aware, of making them able to express how they see and hear their world. It is possible to teach reading and writing with games that explore the senses and the children's feelings. This will give the children necessary biofeedback so they can ask for help when they feel overwhelmed by their sensations.

The second question which comes up is, What about all this behavior-modification stuff they have taught us to use? There is nothing wrong with a little behavior modification, especially if the youngster has learned that his attempts to deal with his sensory problems have also given him some extra attention, good or bad. Ignoring the bad and encouraging the good may cut down on some of the behavior — if the school is no worse for wear in the meantime — but while it may cut down on the frequency of the behavior, it has not solved the child's problem. And it is important to remember that to a hypotactile child a big bear hug is a reward; to a hypertactile child a big smile is sufficient — indeed, a hug would be punishment!

To find out which child is "hypo" and which is "hyper", the best rule of thumb is that the "hyper" one draws away from you. It's not that he dislikes you; he just hates to be touched. (How hard it is to like someone who seems to reject you!)

Sensory problems are not always easy to evaluate. The child with

59

the vision problem, who has been mainstreamed into the classroom, probably has very fine hearing — not because of an injury to the brain, but as a compensating factor. The child who has to touch every little thing may have a vision problem rather than a tactility problem. He must touch things, because if he doesn't, he cannot see what they are! The trick is to find out what needs to be done.

Teachers have been using volunteers, usually mothers, to sit in the classroom and take notes on everything a certain problem child does. Unfortunately, the report turns out to be a long list of accusations.

"Michael sat there kicking his legs against a chair. Then he pulled a hair out of his head and studied it. Then he broke a pencil, tore a piece of paper. He put one leg under him and squirmed around, etc., etc." Read a list like that to Michael's mother and her reaction most likely will be: "Well, this stupid teacher probably bored the poor kid to death. What else does she expect him to do?"

The intent of the observation is not to blame "the poor kid." Michael obviously sees very well up close, or he would not study his hair so minutely. But there may be some trouble with his hearing, because he is constantly making some kind of noise. He bangs the chair, tears the paper, breaks a pencil. If his hearing is affected, it may also affect his sense of balance, since vision, balance and hearing connect in the vestibular canals of the ears. This might be causing the constant squirming — his need to orient himself in space through the feedback from his muscles rather than from the information he receives through his eyes. Now if Michael is also having problems with his phonetic reading although his sight vocabulary is good, the parent-teacher conference may be used to establish whether Michael might have a hearing problem.

One such child, though his hearing tested as normal, nevertheless had auditory-perception problems. At age four he had had an infection, and for six months after that, the parents thought he might have turned deaf. Infections in early childhood often cause minimal brain dysfunctions which go undetected. In this case, there had been at least a suspicion of something going wrong. The infection had obviously caused problems which affected his hearing and his sense of balance — the vestibular system had been affected. In those days, children were still treated with erithromycin, since it was not known at the time that the drug was ototoxic, that is, it could cause hearing damage.

With this particular child, a sensori-motor program with great emphasis on tumbling and rolling (vestibular stimulation) was started, and within a few weeks he was a much calmer little boy, more attentive in school, and his reading improved by leaps and bounds.

There is a final question which is being asked over and over again: Why weren't any of these problems taken care of before the child went to school? These problems are very subtle and can easily escape detection. At home, prior to going to school, the child can find a way to cope or to escape into some corner if there is a sensation which is bothering him. The problem children we see in the classroom are not heavily damaged, and as long as they were at home, the parents usually tolerated a certain amount of eccentric behavior. If the behavior had been very strange, they would have either abused the child or received help from a doctor or agency.

What we see in school is a situation similar to seeing an animal in a cage. For children who see, hear, feel, or experience smell in a different way from the rest of us and can't escape from what is bothering them, the adjustment to this situation becomes more difficult.

So what is the answer? We don't have all the answers yet on how to detect and treat these children. Many of them do survive in the school system, but life is very hard for them. Some ways to make things easier can be found in Part IV of the Appendix to this book.

Chapter 6

The
Time
Connection

"Everybody swears that their child is a genius!" my grandmother used to say. "So then, where do all those stupid adults come from?"

Many preschoolers are brilliant. A two-year-old can name all the butterflies in the butterfly book after being told their names during just a few sessions on Mom's lap. He can tell the names of all the presidents from their pictures if someone shows him the pictures a few times. He may even know a Cadillac from a Chevrolet, a Mazda from a Toyota. Did Dad teach him that? He just seems to have picked it up. By three or four, given a modern mother, a child knows that chickens lay eggs, but that the facts of life are different for animals like dogs and cats. At four, he knows all the four-letter words which circulate among the older boys in the neighborhood, and at five, even before he enters kindergarten, he is fascinated by all those scary dinosaurs and knows their Latin names.

And then something terrible happens: He enters school. The more brilliant a child is, the more devastating the event may be, because the more brilliant he is, the more likely his parents are to push him into school too soon!

Louise Bates Ames of the Gesell Institute has been pleading for years to make sure the child is ready for the grade assigned to him — that the time of starting school should depend on his behavioral age rather than his chronological age.

But on October 4, 1957, when Sputnik went into orbit around the world, the government came down on our educational establishment and blamed it for not educating Johnny as well as Ivan was educated in his country. The pressure was on. Not only did the schools want to bring the children in earlier, but all the proud parents wanted their own child to be "the youngest but brightest" in the classroom.

Even if a child knows how to read before coming to school, it does not mean that he is ready for formal education!

The signs are not always immediately obvious. They don't necessarily show up in school, especially if the child is very bright. At school he fakes it. It is dreadfully important for a five- or six-year-old to be the best at everything. Ask a class of five-year-olds who is the fastest runner, and they will all put up their hands! And there is no sense calling each reading group the blue group and the green group and the lavender group: These kids know when they are in the bottom group! So they'll fake it and memorize the whole first reader from start to finish. By the time they get to the second reader, they are having a harder time. By the third one, they start to complain of headaches!

The first signs usually show up at home. Johnny is irritable and cranky. He throws things at the slightest provocation and won't do what he's told. It's as if having to behave himself in school is all he can handle, and when he gets home, he's had it. But Mother doesn't know that. She thinks her soft, gentle five-year-old of last year has learned all the bad tricks from the other kids in school. If she understands, she'll put up with at least some of it; if she doesn't, she'll punish him.

Now Johnny is twice in trouble: At school he feels stupid, and at home, his loving mother has suddenly turned into a tyrant!

Sometimes it's the other way around. If the only way Johnny gets love at home is by being good and by being smart, he may cut up in school. Rather than admit he can't do the work, he'll misbehave. At least he'll draw some attention away from his failure!

Mother excuses his lapses: "Well, he's really too bright for the class, so he's bored!" But it's not that he's bored, he can't do the work. And so, before long, he becomes one of the regulars outside the principal's office! There are long parent-teacher conferences, but Mother refuses to keep her child back another year (it seems like a terrible disgrace). Now the pressure is on the child to perform at home — and at school — and life becomes a continuous series of failures.

Why do we insist on putting our children into school before they are ready? The laws set an arbitrary birthday date at which children are to enter school. This means that some of them are barely six when they enter school, others may be almost seven. And these children are pitted against each other in competition! At age 20, a year more or less does not make much of a difference. At age six, great changes occur in just a few months! It is a very subtle form of child abuse to place a child into a classroom before he is ready — ready not only to do the work, but to make the adjustments which are necessary to be part of a class.

Most children, for instance, have developed a preferred side by the time they are six years old. If the child has not, he should be tested to see which eye is the dominant one. The child who is totally right-sided or totally left-sided has an easier time learning to read and write than one who constantly has to decide whether to pay attention to the messages coming from the right side of his body, or those coming from the left. Today, teachers rarely try to force a left-handed child to be right-handed. But if there is no hand preference, it is better to go with the side of the dominant eye. If it is not established which eye is dominant, someone might try to teach a left-eyed child to be right-handed and thus cause all kinds of unnecessary problems.

The elementary school at UCLA, the "Harvard" of elementary schools, to which parents apply for their child's admission practically by the baby's first birthday, never even tries to teach the boys to read before they are seven years old. The parents are horrified at first. What is being done to their little geniuses? It is only at the junior high level that these children really take off and do exceptionally well. That little waiting period has a reason and pays off.

There is a horrendous gap between what the government wants and what is possible to do. The law-makers cannot be expected to know any better, but it makes no sense to put more pressure on the teachers when they are not able to teach the children simply because the children are not ready to be taught.

When, in 1980, the University of Oregon sponsored a convention on brain research related to the learning process, it drew some 600 teachers for a week-long conference. The neurologists who had been studying the growth and the organization of the brain confirmed what the teachers had known for a long time: There is such a thing as school readiness.

The confirmation of this fact should make the administrators have another look at those children who are not succeeding.

The human brain weighs approximately 350 grams (about 12 oz.) at birth and by brain maturity around age 18, will have increased to about 1,450 grams (3 lbs., 3 oz.) in males around age 18, and to about 1,300 grams (2 lbs., 8 oz.) in females. (Since females weigh less than males, their brain has less area to control, so this does not mean that men are "brainier.") It was discovered that this weight gain does not occur at a nice even pace; it increases in spurts during various ages of the growing child. Another finding, even more important, but one which came as no surprise to the teachers, was that not only do these spurts of brain growth happen at certain specific ages, but the times at which they happen in boys are later than the ones at which they happen in girls.

These brain spurts are still under study and teachers will become even more aware of how they can utilize this knowledge in the classroom. The findings are a neurological confirmation of the studies of Piaget, who said that the way a child thinks, changes at rather predetermined stages. Chances are, that during the periods of growth the child may be at odds with himself, trying to find out how to cope with the new awareness each brain growth allows him to experience. Teachers still are not sure if the child should be challenged more or challenged less during these growth spurts.

The brain has all the nerve cells it will ever have by the end of the child's second year. The growth in weight and volume of the brain, therefore, seems to occur in the number and in the lengths of the dendrites and axons of the neurons. Electrical messages are sent along these dendrites and axons, which in connecting with cells in other areas of the brain, make up the communication network that runs the body.

Since the number of cells no longer increases after age two, the brain's growth indicates that the dendrites increase in number and possibly reach out further toward different cells, making new connections with different parts of the brain.

The change in brain size, therefore, is not related to changes in brain function, but in changes IN THE WAY the brain functions.

Educators have been aware of these changes for thousands of years. Ancient Greece and Rome had a primary school which the child entered at age 6, a "grammaticus" at about age 10 or 11, and a school of rhetoric at age 15. The ancient Jews had a similar arrangement. Bible stories were started at age 5; at age ten the Mishna (a set of oral instructions on the conduct of life) was taught. Even at 13, at the Bar Mitzvah, the students still were given mostly memorization work. Not until age 15 were they exposed to more intellectual discussions.

By 63 A.D., educators had found, apparently through experience, that age 5 was too young to start school, and the child should wait until age 6 or 7.

The new neurological findings will give the teachers simply an extra confirmation that some changes are needed in our educational procedures and that the child's development cannot suddenly be changed just because it is politically expedient to do so.

The brain spurts occur during the time spans from 3 to 10 months; between ages 2 and 4; between 6 and 8; 10 and 12; and 14 to 16. Professor Herman Epstein of Brandeis University states that these spurts actually account for a brain increase of only 5 to 10 per cent weight increase and that in each individual the increased growth period lasts only just a few months.

The brain continues to grow all through the childhood years, but not nearly as rapidly as during these months. While the start of these spurts varies with each child, even children with very high I.Q.s do not experience these stages before the minimal age at which they happen in other children. This holds true for the entire world population.

What is even more important — all through the period of schooling — is that the brain spurts in boys happen during the higher limits of the growth-spurt years. This presented no problem in earlier times, because girls rarely received an education and then they were not taught alongside the boys. Today, however, the boys are being judged by the same standard as the girls, even though they have not arrived at the same stage of maturity.

Teachers have known for years that boys are far slower in maturing than girls, and they generally make allowances. It is far more difficult for a mother, and especially for a father, to be so understanding. If, as happens frequently, the first child is a girl and does well in school, the younger boy is constantly being compared with his sister, who did so much better when she was his age. It is devastating to the boy not to be able to do the work, and the tests which children are given during those first few years, unfortunately, do not have two separate grading systems for boys and for girls. The boys won't like the girls in their class any better if the girls always get the better grades, and it certainly will not help a boy love his sister if she is always held up to him as a shining example! It is very comforting to a worried — and usually angry — parent if the teacher can explain that the brain growth of boys occurs at a later age than that of girls.

Even if parents understand the situation and try not to compare, the child is aware of the difference and may even magnify it in his own mind. And so by all means, until the schools start to act on what is already known about the ways boys and girls grow, keep your son home from school a little longer. Doting relatives who insist that you are over-protecting the child can always be told about the brain spurts. Spread the knowledge to your friends and neighbors; it might keep some other child from becoming a learning casualty if his parents understand that his problems might simply be time connected.

In a few schools, even before they were corroborated by neurologists, the findings of the educators were being put to use. Shining examples of such success stories are the elementary schools on Coronado, the small island just off the San Diego coast.

Here there are no stupid children, no unmotivated children, and no lazy children, although some might well have been mislabeled as such, had they gone to another school. At first grade, 90% read above the 50th percentile. At third grade, 86% read above the 50th percentile, and even at 5th grade, 82% read above the 50th percentile. This is a sign of superb schooling, even if you have a pretty high level of intelligence and affluence in the neighborhood!

Not so long ago, when the school's rating in comparison with all the other California schools dropped from the 99th to the 93rd percentile, the school board was so disturbed that they called a special meeting! The sudden drop, it was explained, was caused by the presence of several oriental children who had only just arrived and did not speak fluent English as yet.

The board members were so overly concerned because they expect nothing but miracles from the school, which, under the guidance of Ann Breslauer, has made educational history with the so-called Coronado Experiment. (This experiment proved that a sensori-motor approach can be successfully implemented in the public schools to improve the children's performance skills.)

The Coronado School District's staff is trained to look at the whole child and then find ways to give the appropriate help where help is needed. Many school problems simply never arise because the children are tested to see if they are ready for first grade work. The school follows the guidelines established by the Gesell Institute after years of research. A great deal of emphasis is placed on the age at which the child is admitted. Boys are counseled to wait until they are at least six and a half before they enter first grade, and the school accepts a child's teething pattern as the outward indicator that he is ready to learn to read without too much strain.

One study by Gesell found that of those children who were ahead in their teething schedule, 60% were in the top academically, 36% were doing well, and only 4% were doing badly. In those behind in teething, only 6% were in the top group, 40% were questionable, and 54% needed to repeat a grade.

As in all matters relating to children, the variable is high. Nevertheless, given this evidence, it is advisable to give a child another chance at first grade if he is not doing well and if his baby teeth have shown no signs of wanting to come out. While he may be perfectly normal in his development, this development is just a little bit slower than that of his schoolmates.

Usually the first teeth lost are the two lower middle front teeth. The new ones come in around five and a half to six years of age. At six come the six-year molars. Next the child loses his upper middle teeth, and the new ones come in when he is around six and a half years old. The Gesell Institute has found that there is a close correlation between the child's behavior and his physical maturity as it can be recognized by the level of teething.

We know about the difference in brain spurts between boys and girls, and we know about the generally slower development in boys. But what about the difference in tooth loss? Here, too, while there are variables, boys' teeth tend to be lost later than girls' teeth. In short, while there are other physical signs of school readiness, nature has provided us with a convenient, readily observable sign: The loss of the first set of teeth.

If a child is already beyond first grade and is not doing well, the child may be perfectly normal but simply overplaced. The Gesell Institute provides us with some statistically proven clues for which to look:
— inability to finish the work and sit still
— trouble with motor tasks, especially writing
— trouble with handling stress
— not wanting to go to school; frequent illness or claims of being sick

— temper tantrums at home or at school.

On Coronado, Ann Breslauer, as the school district's remedial education specialist, found that 63% of the children in the remedial reading class had too early an admittance to school and were simply overplaced. These children, essentially normal in their development, simply were not ready for what they were being taught. When she reassigned them to a lower grade, they did just fine.

Let's give an example of how this kind of maturity lag may be causing problems. Suppose the child's visual function is not developed enough to differentiate letters and to see the word dog as "d-o-g" and as a unit. If he is bright, he will find a trick way of remembering the word. He may take the word as a whole and say it looks like a dog, with the "d" being the dog's head and the lower length of the "g" reminding him of the dog's tail. He may find many such pictures to help him remember words and will give everyone the impression that he knows how to read. The sad thing is that he cannot use these pictograms for more advanced reading. They do not help him use letters to read other words. He has developed what is known as a "splinter skill." Such a crutch works fine for a while — until he gets into a higher grade and is then accused of malingering because he seemed to know his work in the first grade!

Rarely, at that point, does anyone explain to the child that he is having problems because he simply was not ready in the beginning, and now has to start to learn to read all over again because now, at last, he is ready to find a better way to do things.

The dentist, the optometrist, the teacher, the mother — all must pool their observations. Larry Burr, examining a second-year schoolchild referred to him for what seemed to be vision problems, may find that the child's teeth have not come out yet. In that case, the child's vision is normal and Burr simply has a very slowly developing child in front of him. On the other hand, if the child's teething schedule is normal, but the visual performance is not up to the expected level, he knows that visual training will help the child catch up in that area.

We do not know why one child develops more slowly than another. We do know that boys develop more slowly than girls. We also know that there are more boys who are slightly brain-damaged or hyperactive than there are girls. One of the theories is that, since the boys' brains develop more slowly, the boys remain longer in the very early brain stages during which the brain is most vulnerable to damage by every virus and by every ever so slight accident.

Because the signs of an overplaced child are so similar to the clues given by a child with neurological problems, we must be very careful in checking all the different aspects of the child's growth. The secret in the success of the Coronado schools is not only in making sure each child is placed correctly according to his maturity, but also in watching for other problems and giving the children any help they might need.

Chapter 7

The Neurological Connection

On November 22, 1979, the Associated Press sent out the following story which was carried in large and small newspapers all over the world.

DYSLEXIA TRACED TO ANATOMY OF BRAIN
BOSTON (AP) — Researchers have found evidence that dyslexia, the learning disorder that affects the reading or writing of an estimated 10 to 15 million Americans, may be caused by abnormalities in the brain, it was reported this week.

Neurologists examined the brain of a 20-year-old dyslexic man killed in an automobile accident and found "striking" abnormalities only in the section of his brain considered responsible for language function, the Boston Globe reported.

"Dyslexia has been thought to be a psychological problem, but is really a neurological abnormality," said Dr. Anthony Galaburda, who conducted the research with Dr. Thomas Kemper at Beth Israel Hospital in Boston.

"Our study shows for the first time there are actual differences in the anatomy of the brain of a dyslexic person."

Dyslexia most often manifests itself in reversed reading of words and letters, but it may also affect writing. It frequently affects children with above average intelligence.

Roger Brown, Massachusetts associate commissioner for special education, said he and other learning disability specialists have long suspected that dyslexia resulted from a brain abnormality, but the Beth Israel research is the first evidence.

Dr. Norman Geschwind, head of Beth Israel's neurological laboratory, said the discovery could lead to successful treatment of the disorder, even though there may be other causes of dyslexia, too.

"Whenever we have made a finding of distinct organic problems, it has led to a remedy," Geschwind said. "Obviously this is only one case, but the changes found in the brain in this particular case are nothing borderline. They are striking and clear-cut."

What a devastating piece of information for those 10 to 15 million Americans who have been labeled dyslexic! How convenient for those teachers who somehow have not been able to teach a child to read! And, indeed, it would be a devastating piece of information if it were not for one fact: There is no truth to the belief that nothing can be done about the function of the brain! Carl H. Delacato, among others, has been achieving such changes — without surgery — successfully for over 25 years.

At a time when controversies were raging in educational circles over whether it was better to teach by the look-see method or by phonics, Delacato published *The Treatment and Prevention of Reading Problems.* In it, he suggests that if Johnny cannot read, it is not a question of the teaching methods which had been used. Rather, the organization of the child's brain causes the problem. In 1962, he followed up with *A New Start for the Child with Reading Problems*, in which he outlines procedures which parents can follow to change that organization and make sure the child's brain has all the information the child needs to read well. Yet today, in most schools, children with learning problems are still being treated as if nothing could be done to help them.

In far too many schools, the children with reading problems are still simply pushed through from grade to grade, to flounder more and more as they get into the higher grades, where reading is absolutely necessary for them to be able to do the work. These kids experience one failure after another until, finally, they drop out.

Their failure is not only in school; it is all-pervasive. The teacher accuses the child of being able to do better "if only he would," and the parents are pushed into service to help the child with his homework — homework that is simply more of what the child cannot do in school! Tempers become raw, the parent becomes impatient. What started out as a learning problem can easily become a power struggle, and the life of the child becomes a nightmare.

There is an advantage. The children are no longer called "lazy" and "stupid" or "unmotivated," which are devastating and abusive terms. They are given a new name: they are now the "learning disabled," the "hyperactive," and, somewhat more frighteningly, the "Minimal Brain-Damaged," or "MBD" children.

These terms are a cop-out. They are supposed to give the mother an explanation, but they do not give her the slightest help. The diagnosis may even give her a strange feeling of self-importance: It gives her something to talk about, sort of like showing off her appendix scar.

But these terms mean almost nothing. It is as if you called in a doctor to look at a sick child and the doctor came and said, "Johnny has a fever!" and sent you a bill for $40.00.

The new diagnosis may keep the parents from abusing Johnny in regard to his schoolwork, which is good for Johnny's self-image, but it may also keep them from doing anything about the fact that Johnny is not functioning.

Reading failure is usually the first symptom which shows that the child is having a problem. It is indeed a symptom — not the cause — of the child's problem.

If the two sides of Johnny's brain do not function together, his eyes do not function together. In a normal child, the words THE CAT are seen by each eye. The brain superimposes the two pictures and the child sees

THE CAT and **THE CAT**

simply as one picture:

THE CAT

If, however, the two eyes — for whatever reason — do not fuse the two images into one, the child may see:

THE TCAT CAT

73

The teacher says, "Come on, Johnny, look at it. What does it say?" And Johnny looks again, and this time it says:

THE CATHE CAT

Johnny thinks the teacher is pretty unreasonable to expect him to try to make sense out of this mess.

Perhaps there ought to be a law that states that no teacher under 40 should be allowed to teach children to read: Until a teacher's eyes start to give her trouble, it may never occur to her that there might be something wrong with the child's vision.

These are the 1980s. I often talk to young education students who are doing their practicum in teaching remedial reading. Nobody, but nobody, has taught these young people anything about vision.

Actually, this is not surprising, considering there are only about 300 developmental vision specialists in the entire United States. It is only within the last 10 years or so that the eye has been recognized as being something more than a camera. It is a highly sophisticated computer which works through the brain in coordination with the entire body.

So here is poor Johnny, and Johnny can't read, and the teacher does not know why. So the teacher tells his mother to work with him at home. And the same thing happens to Johnny at home. Here is Mother's bright little boy, and suddenly the dumb kid can't even read CAT! I have known otherwise calm and rational mothers of perfectly bright children to slap them during these reading sessions, which had become a daily torture for both of them.

If the child's two eyes do not function together, chances are the same brain dysfunction also affects the child's hearing. If this is so, Johnny does not have stereo hearing. To know what effect this has, simply hold one ear closed the next time you are in a crowded room.

Normally, if someone in the room makes a nasty remark, you can tell immediately where the remark came from. The brain knows that if the sound reaches the right ear in one hundredth of a second and the left ear in three hundredths of a second, the voice came from a point closer to the right ear. If you are unable to judge this minute difference because you have closed off one ear, you can no longer tell where the speaker's voice came from. All the voices have become one general hubbub, in which you cannot distinguish the location of an individual remark.

If Johnny's brain does not connect the input from the two ears in such a way that he has stereo hearing, he cannot tell that it was the teacher who just said, "Sit down, everybody!" He will know that she said it only when all his friends have suddenly disappeared from his side and are already seated. He is then the last one to slink into his seat and, even if the poor child never did anything else wrong, he is labeled uncooperative and a troublemaker.

It is not simply a question of seeing and hearing. The child functions as a whole; efficient reading depends on many skills. If the child's inability to read is the result of incomplete neurological organization, there will be other side effects. If his eyes do not function well together, it could mean he is easily fatigued. It might be difficult for him to do certain sports. Not only that: most likely his entire coordination is off and his movements are awkward.

Kids pick up on this, and the awkward children are the first to get singled out for attack by the others. The way children pick on the different, clumsy ones is like the way sharks attack only the fish that are obviously in trouble. Parents, too, especially fathers, are uncomfortable and irritable around children who seem to be not quite up to their idea of a "perfect" son or daughter. Some abusive parents in England have described their offspring as "eminently bashable."

The message that the uncoordinated body sends out is so strong that it carries into adult life. Fascinated as to why some people in the cities get mugged several times while others go unscathed through dangerous neighborhoods, Betty Grayson, a professor of behavioral science at New York City College, conducted a study. Why do some people seem surrounded by an aura of "muggability"? Some of her students were policemen and had told her that often they would follow someone who looked like a victim, and sure enough, quite frequently, that person would be assaulted. The officers could not explain what criteria they used to spot their victim; they chalked it up to experience.

Betty Grayson decided to find out just what kind of nonverbal communication was going on to make these people victims. With a hidden camera, she videotaped 60 pedestrians, each for only seven seconds. (She presumed it would take about that long to size up a stranger.) She grouped these tapes by age range and then showed them to a selected audience of prisoners who were all in jail for mugging someone. They were asked to pick out the potentially easy victims. More than half of them agreed that 20 of these 60 people would have made easy targets. They had rated these 20 people as

1, 2, or 3 on a scale of 1 to 10 (1 being the most easily victimized, 10 the least).

Although women above 45 were nearly twice as likely to be judged easy victims, an equal number of men and women in the 35-or-under group were picked. Betty Grayson then had the tapes of the "most assaultable" ones analyzed by a trained dance analyst. Five movement characteristics were common to all victims. First was the way they lifted their feet: Instead of walking from heel to toe, they picked up the whole foot and put it down flat, like a Spanish dancer might. They all used exaggerated strides, either too long or too short. And they moved laterally: Instead of swinging the right arm at the same time that they moved the left leg forward, they moved the arm and the leg on the same side. Then there was the way the top of the body moved in conjunction with the lower part of the body: It was as if their torsos moved at cross-purposes. They also walked so that it seemed as if their arm and leg movements came from the outside of the body instead of from within.

We know that the movement of people's bodies is controlled by the brain. Even though these people may be considered "normal," there is obviously something not quite right in the way the signals from the brain coordinate their bodies. Had they showed signs of smooth coordination, this would have signaled to the attacker that the intended victim would have fast, sure reflexes which would allow him to defend himself quickly and to give as good as he was getting.

Many of the children who have learning problems have this lack of coordination. They have the same faulty neurological organization. With a child like that, the parent can't win. If he refuses to pressure the child into doing more of what he cannot do at school, he is accused of not caring; and if he does, he just might make matters worse. It is not a matter of the parent not caring — it is a question of not knowing how to fix the problem.

The teacher, too, has a problem. She is accused by the parents of not teaching the child properly. What about the other children, whom she manages to teach just fine? Unless she has a superb back-up system, such as the one Ann Breslauer developed in her famous *"Coronado Experiment,"* all the teacher's efforts at helping these children may fail.

In the Coronado School, the children who are found to be uncoordinated and also to have a learning problem are given a sensori-motor program. This gives them a chance to coordinate their bodies and their senses by experiencing once more some of the movement stages which a child normally goes through. It gives them a chance to catch up on periods of development they might have missed. To give a child this extra chance is not just a matter of helping him learn to read, but one of making him more comfortable in the world.

Oh, yes, you can teach a brain-damaged child to read, but it does not take care of the other problems created by this damage, wherever in the brain it might have occurred. You can do it by tracing letters with your finger on the child's back, or by having him touch letters which have been cut out on sandpaper. There are many ways. But they are merely teaching an isolated skill, a splinter skill, which is used as a crutch. It does not help coordinate the other senses and the movements of the child.

I have worked with an adult who had graduated from a school well known for its successes in working around children's disabilities. A graduate from a stiff master's program at the University of Oregon, a perfectly bright young man, but he walked like an idiot, talked like an idiot, and moved like an idiot. Within about six months of his (I must admit) somewhat half-hearted effort of putting himself on a program which would coordinate his whole body, he started to walk like a man, talked more fluently, and generally began broadcasting to the world that he was a capable human being.

If you work only on the skill that the child lacks and not on the reason why he never acquired the skill, you will have to continue working around the disability.

A sensori-motor program for a reading-problem child takes approximately one-half to three-quarters of an hour of fairly strenuous exercise a day. That is quite a lot to ask of a child who has already experienced a share of failure and is beginning to doubt himself. Right from the start, at whatever level of understanding the child has, the person who teaches him the exercises explains to him, honestly, what the problem is.

"You are not stupid!" I heard one such programmer tell one child. "You have a perfectly good brain. It's just like in a car, you have a good machine, only some of the wires are connected wrong. With these exercises you are going to connect them the right way." Far too often, the child has already come to terms with the idea that he can't learn, so he quits trying. He often volunteers the information that he is stupid.

"You don't have that excuse," says the programmer. "You have a perfectly fine brain. It just needs a little tune-up!" And the first good test score the child brings home certainly deserves a shiny quarter!

When you solve the basic problem — if the problem is poor neurological organization — then the child will be able to function on his own. I have personally seen this happen over and over again during the last 10 years. Once the intersensory connections have been established in the child's brain, the child suddenly takes off and develops rapidly in all areas. He makes social contact, functions in school, and becomes a relaxed, often superior athlete. (This last ability is terribly important, because so much of the child's self-esteem depends on his athletic skills.)

Teachers who are not aware that a child went through such a program will comment, "He has it all together now!" It is a comment I have heard over and over again. And that is exactly what has happened: We have put it all together for the child.

Sensori-motor exercises are given routinely to all children at Coronado to make sure they have all the skills it takes to learn to read. The children are observed carefully, and if a child seems to need further help, he is given a special sensori-integrative program which emphasizes visual skills as well as auditory ones. The end result is the tremendously high success rate of the children and, later, a higher-than-usual rate of college entrance.

The orginal concept of using a total-body sensorimotor program was developed by Carl H. Delacato some twenty years ago. What we call "putting it all together" is what he calls neurological organization.

At that time, Delacato was working as part of a team of specialists who were exploring ways to help brain-injured children. The team consisted of brain surgeon Dr. Temple Fay, physiotherapist Glenn J. Doman, and Carl H. Delacato, educator. In those days, although it had been established that a certain child could not move because his brain had been injured, most therapies were aimed at the arms and legs that were not functioning. Since the injury was in the brain and not in the arms and legs, the therapies were doomed to failure. Not only did those children not improve but, surprisingly enough, the team found that those children who, for one reason or another, had been permitted to stay home and were there left on the floor to fend for themselves as best they could, had improved more than the ones who had been put into braces and who had spent hours and hours in physiotherapy.

78

Intrigued by the question of why this should be so, the team surrounded themselves with normal infants and children of all ages, to see just how they developed from stage to stage.

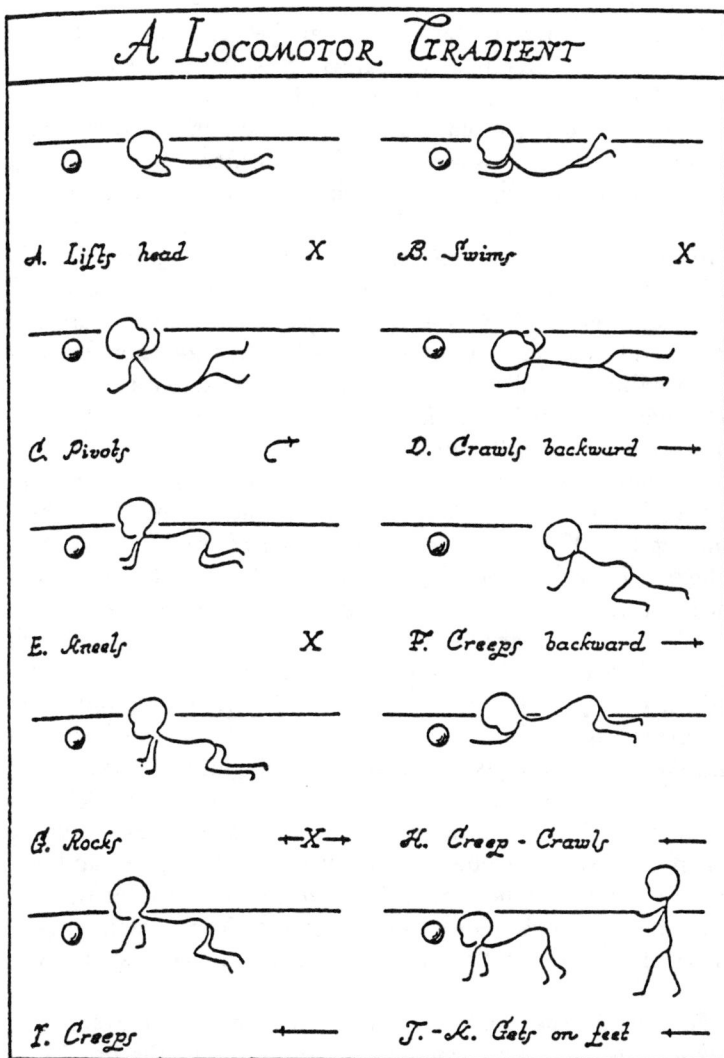

A LOCOMOTOR GRADIENT

A. Lifts head   X   B. Swims   X

C. Pivots   ↻   D. Crawls backward ⟶

E. Kneels   X   F. Creeps backward ⟶

G. Rocks   ←X→   H. Creep - Crawls   ⟵

I. Creeps   ⟵   J.-K. Gets on feet   ⟵

From "The Child from Five to Ten"
Arnold Gesell, Frances L. Ilg and Louise Bates Ames,
rev. ed., N.Y., Harper & Row, ©1977.

They observed how during each of these stages, through touch, through sight, through hearing, through movement sensations, even through taste and smell, input went into the brain which gave it the information it needed to permit the child to function successfully in the next stage.

At that time, too, it was found that the brain develops as it is used. What is a perfectly good brain at the start can be made quite useless if it is not stimulated, and a normal brain can be made superior by providing it with varied and, often, intense stimulation.

The team knew it was impossible to influence what messages came out of the brain; they could, however, influence what went into the brain. They theorized that they might be able to give a brain-injured child the information which normally would be received by the body at each stage of development. So, if a child could walk, but not well, they gave the child a chance to creep on hands and knees. That way, they gave the child another chance to feed into the brain all the information he needed to move on to the next stage — to walk well. If the child could not creep, they gave him a chance to crawl on his belly, until the brain received enough information to move on to creeping, and then from there to walking. If the child could not move at all, they had adults move the child's arms and legs. Eventually, as the limbs were moved over the sheets of the bed, or wherever this "patterning" took place, the information sent from the muscles and from the skin sensations, would, it was hoped, teach the brain to control the limbs without outside help.

The theory, translated into techniques and put into practice, worked. It was hard to predict how far each child would improve, but many did. Children who could not move, learned to walk; children who could not speak, learned to talk; and even some brain-blind children learned to see.

The brain is not a static thing. Neurologists have experimented with monkeys. They opened the little animal's skull, and with electrical probes, found which brain cells, when stimulated, would make the monkey's hand move forward. They then carefully destroyed those few cells and closed up the monkey's skull with a silver plate.

For a while, the monkey could not move that hand. Before long, however, the monkey learned anew how to make the hand move forward. At this point, the scientists removed the silver plate and exposed the brain. Again they tested to find which brain cells made the hand move. To their amazement, they found that the cells which now moved the hand forward were nowhere near the place that the original injury to the brain had been made!

It is not possible to restore the function of dead nerve cells. If, however, the brain of the child had been normal before the injury to the brain — even if the injury had occurred at birth, and sometimes even before then — there were usually enough normal, healthy cells to take over the missing functions.

At the time Delacato first became involved with the treatment of brain-injured children, he was still headmaster of a private school. There, much to his dismay, he had found that no matter what methods of teaching used, no matter how much time, love and attention had been lavished on certain students, they continued to be extremely poor readers. And the more Delacato worked with brain-damaged children, the more he felt that, somehow, his students who could not learn to read had some of the same symptoms.

Reading was obviously a brain function. The team had been able to restore the functions of brain-injured children, and if proof could be found that reading disability was linked to poor brain function, that would not only explain the reading failure but would lead to a neurological approach to remedy it.

So, just as the research team had surrounded themselves with normal children to study development, they now studied those children who could not learn to read. These findings emerged from careful observation of 200 of these dyslexic children:

— They lacked coordination. Running, walking, even creeping and crawling were awkward and lacked grace and smoothness.

— They had a hard time deciding which side to use: For writing, for throwing, for seeing, for drawing, for hammering, for kicking a ball, or for stepping on a stool. This lack of dominance existed way beyond the six-year-old level by which most children have developed a favored side.

— There were three times as many left handers as there were among good readers.

— They seemed to love music more than their brothers or sisters.

— Their handwriting had no consistent slant; their letters all seemed to have different angles and directions.

— Even though their eyes tested normal, all seemed to have great difficulty in seeing efficiently. Many practically held their nose to the paper when reading or writing.

— A large number reversed letters, mixing up the directions of an individual letter, such as "d" or "b," the way a much younger child might. They read "saw" for "was" or got numbers backward.

— Most were poor spellers who, even if they had been drilled thoroughly for a test, a day or so later, they forgot what they had learned. — Many seemed to do better in arithmetic than in reading and far better in verbal discussion than in writing.

— Every one of them had better language understanding through the ears than through the eyes.

Delacato then tested 200 normal readers and found that they had no similar problems. The problems that had been isolated in the poor readers all indicated that the child's nervous system was not well organized. And now the question was not only why it was not well organized, but how to improve this organization — how to put it all together for the child! The work with brain-injured children had shown that the brain does not develop normally if a stage of development is missed. Most of the learning-disabled children had no history of an injury to the brain, and they rarely had an abnormal EEG. It seemed as if the child might have missed a certain stage in the normal development.

The eyes, for instance, learn to work together during the time a child creeps on hands and knees. Every time there is the input of touch to the forward hand, the eyes will, through some reflex, focus on that hand. This helps both eyes focus on one point at the same time. The two images are superimposed in the brain, and the child sees one image and not two. Creeping is also of vital importance in helping a child judge distance, an ability very necessary in writing.

At the creeping stage, just as the brain learns to judge space from the information received from both eyes, it also learns to evaluate the information received through the ears. When the child creeps, as each hand hits the floor, the head moves gently from side to side as the eyes follow that hand. This provides stimulation to the vestibular system in the ears, and much of the information leading to the speech center is coordinated through that system. The vestibular system coordinates the visual perception with the ability of judging where sound comes from and it helps the brain to make the postural adjustments to allow the child to move freely.

Delacato, from what he had learned through testing functions of the brain-injured, theorized that it was not only this particular stage, the creeping stage, which had been lacking in many of the reading-problem children, but might also have been caused by lack of crawling. To find more support for what, at the moment, was still theory, he and Glenn Doman traveled all over the globe to search out primitive tribes who, for one reason or another, did not permit their children to move around on the floor. This taboo may have existed to keep the children off the jungle floor where they might encounter dangerous snakes or insects. Or it might have been, as in Eskimo tribes, that the weather was too cold to permit the children to be on the floor.

If Delacato's theories were correct, then none of these cultures would have a written language! It was a serious challenge to the theory, but wherever the team knew of the existence of such conditions, they investigated and found Delacato was right. If, as part of the cultural heritage, the children were not permitted to crawl and to creep on the floor, that society did not have a written language of its own.

Curiously enough, our own society today has similar conditions. We keep our babies in playpens, for the sake of convenience or for reasons of sanitation. What is even worse, we push the sale of "walkers." We prop up the baby in a cloth sling hung from an aluminum frame placed on four legs with casters. The infant can get around quite easily and keep himself amused, but he will not have learned the normal crawling and creeping patterns which would put important information into the child's brain and which are so vital for coordinating all the functions of his body.

In normal development, after the child has learned to crawl, to creep, and to walk, he develops a favored side, or what the educator calls "dominance". In short, if he picks up a hammer, he knows immediately that he will pick it up with his right hand. Not only that, but he will use the entire side — the right foot, the right eye, and the right ear — for most of his activities, using the other side mainly for balance and to help him judge space in all of his activities.

In all but 11 percent of infants, the left side of the brain — the side which controls the input coming from the right side — is the one which is stimulated the most when someone speaks to the infant. The other side "lights up" more when music is played. This is an inherited tendency. There are, however, some outside factors which can later influence the development of each side. It can happen if a baby is held mostly in one position when being fed a bottle, rather than being shifted from the right breast to the left breast. There could also have been a slight injury to one side of the brain, or even to both sides. There might possibly be an injury in the corpus callosum, the bridge between the two sides of the brain. These minor injuries can happen during a viral infection, from a blow on the head, or during childbirth.

Delacato also found that, though the child's medical history might provide clues, unless there was a major injury, it was not always possible to know exactly what had influenced the development of the brain. What the child could or could not do, how the child moved or how coordinated he was, was sufficient to tell him at what stage the injury had happened, and which stage the child needed to repeat to make the necessary connections in the brain.

At that time, it was already known that left-handed children who had been forced to become right-handed often stuttered. Since today we no longer feel it is necessary for all children to be right-handed, we hardly ever see children who stutter. Delacato recognized the link between verbal stuttering and reading stuttering. The final developmental stage of making one side of the body dominant was important to allow a child to read easier.

To understand this concept fully, one need only to imagine what it would be like to try to nail something without knowing automatically whether to pick up the hammer with the right or the left hand. It would be a very confusing and time-consuming situation.

For a long time though, teachers continued to fight the idea that dominance had anything to do with reading. If you tried to talk to teachers about it, they would ask you, haughtily, "Have you read the Robbins reports?" Melvin P. Robbins did two studies, both beautifully designed, with experimental, non-specific and control groups. They were carefully written up with all the statistical factors taken into consideration, and they neatly reported the results with several statistical tables: Delacato's methods did not work — or at least were not statistically significant. The reports were so impressive that evidently no one realized that the procedures he tested were not those used by Carl H. Delacato!

Neither Robbins, nor the majority of people who read the studies understood Delacato's basic premise: The total neurological development, not handedness alone, determines the ability to read. And so Robbins completely left out the crawling part of the program. (Several other studies later made the same error.) For the brain to function in stereo, each side must first have the same information. (While some people who have not developed dominance manage to read, they may have other problems, such as being tone deaf, or stuttering, or sometimes just being more mathematically inclined than verbally. They function at great cost to themselves.) Both of Robbins' studies, even if they had actually been testing Delacato's methods, lasted for only three months — far too short a period to have shown any positive results in reading improvement. One of the symptoms of the truly disabled reader is that, while you can make quite some progress during tutoring, the improvement disappears after a short while and the student falls back again.

While the first study used reading-retarded students taken from the first six grades, the second study used only second-graders, who did not necessarily have reading problems. This time Robbins included five minutes of homolateral patterning, but still no crawling. Using students who do not necessarily need this kind of neurological recapitulation along with those who do, is similar to splinting ten people's legs when only five have broken bones and then being surprised when the improvement is not statistically significant. One had to be very familiar with Delacato's theories to recogize these errors.

The first study was published in the *Journal of the American Medical Association*, and thereafter many doctors refused to investigate Delacato's theories further. The second article appeared in the *Reading Research Quarterly*, and a whole group of teachers closed their minds to the possibility of trying this approach. It was mostly education teachers who tended to read this professional material and they in turn taught their students. Now most teachers go around saying wisely, "Have you read the Robbins reports?" No one seems to go around saying, "Have you read the Vivian reports?"

Sister M. Vivian Skluzacek, S.S.N.D., did a five-year study, which started in October, 1964 and did not end until May, 1969. The first year, children in the experimental class were given the developmental program designed to take them through the level of pons, midbrain, cortex, and cortical hemispheric dominance — following the design of Delacato. There was a time span of seven months involved. Not only did the final results at the end of the school year show up in greater than normal reading improvement, but Sister Vivian reported other individual changes as they occurred from month to month. Hyperactive children calmed down; speech problem children — whose speech was recorded every ten weeks — showed clear improvement; short attention spans became longer; and one child's older brother who did the exercises just for fun stopped wetting his

Five-Year Reading Report*

No.	IQ	Sex	Chron. Age	Reading Readiness	Experimental Group				
					Gr. 1	Gr. 2	Gr. 3	Gr. 4	Gr. 5
1.	126	F	6-0	Average	3.5	4.5	5.1	—	—
2.	123	F	6-1	V. High	4.1	5.4	6.0	7.6	8.8
3.	123	F	6-1	H. Aver.	4.3	6.0	6.0+	7.9	9.2
4.	123	M	6-1	Average	2.7	3.5	4.5	4.9	4.5
5.	122	M	6-2	High	3.9	4.8	5.8	7.6	8.8
6.	117	F	5-11	Low	3.3	4.4	5.0	5.7	6.9
7.	117	F	5-11	Low	3.0	4.0	4.4	—	—
8.	120	M	6-1	High	3.8	4.6	6.0+	7.9	8.7
9.	121	M	6-0	High	2.9	3.5	4.0	5.1	5.9
10.	117	F	6-3	Low	4.3	5.2	5.8	6.9	8.1
11.	117	F	6-2	High	3.0	4.3	5.0	6.2	7.8
12.	117	F	6-6	H. Aver.	3.9	4.8	5.7	6.6	7.9
13.	116	F	6-5	High	4.0	5.8	6.0+	7.9	8.6
14.	117	F	6-2	High	4.5	5.8	6.0+	8.1	9.3
15.	115	M	6-2	High	2.9	3.9	5.3	5.4	5.7
16.	113	F	6-2	Average	3.4	4.4	5.2	5.7	6.9
17.	117	F	6-3	High	3.7	5.1	5.8	6.7	7.8
18.	114	M	6-4	Low	3.7	4.6	5.6	6.7	8.8
19.	113	F	6-4	High	4.0	—	—	—	—
20.	113	F	6-6	Average	3.0	3.4	4.0	5.1	5.7
21.	110	M	6-6	Low Aver.	3.3	4.6	5.0	6.2	7.1
22.	111	F	6-0	Low Aver.	4.5	5.0	6.0+	7.6	8.7
23.	110	F	6-2	H. Aver.	3.0	4.4	5.0	5.8	6.9
24.	110	M	6-11	Average	4.0	4.9	5.7	6.5	7.6
25.	110	F	6-9	Average	3.9	4.4	5.3	5.7	6.4
26.	109	M	6-3	V. High	3.8	4.6	6.0+	6.9	7.8
27.	108	F	6-7	Low	2.7	4.2	4.9	5.2	5.8
28.	108	F	6-7	V. High	4.5	5.8	6.0	7.6	9.2
29.	108	F	6-5	Low Aver.	3.5	4.6	5.4	6.1	6.8
30.	108	M	6-2	Low Aver.	3.0	4.3	5.3	5.0	5.9
31.	106	F	6-6	H. Aver.	3.5	4.4	4.9	5.8	—
32.	106	M	6-8	Low	3.8	4.6	5.3	5.2	6.1
33.	103	M	6-2	Low	2.9	3.5	5.1	6.3	6.6
34.	103	M	6-1	Low Aver.	3.1	3.8	4.7	5.2	5.4
35.	106	M	6-4	Low	3.5	—	—	—	—
36.	104	F	6-6	H. Aver.	3.3	4.6	5.6	7.1	8.6
37.	103	F	6-6	Low Aver.	2.9	4.1	—	—	—
38.	101	M	6-4	V. Low	2.7	3.8	4.3	4.3	—
39.	101	M	6-11	V. High	2.8	4.0	5.1	5.4	6.1
40.	103	M	6-10	Average	3.1	4.4	4.8	5.0	5.8
41.	100	M	6-4	Low Aver.	2.7	3.6	—	—	—
42.	100	F	6-10	Low	3.4	4.3	5.0	5.6	6.4
43.	102	M	6-8	Low Aver.	3.1	3.7	4.8	5.1	5.9
44.	78	M	6-10	V. Low	2.7	3.3	—	—	—

*Grades 1 & 2:   *Developmental Reading Tests* (Bond-Clymer-Hoyt)
    Grade 3:   *Developmental Reading Tests* (Bond-Balow-Hoyt)
Grades 4 & 5:   *DRT* (Bond-Balow-Hoyt and Bond-Clymer-Hoyt)

Five-Year Reading Report*

No.	IQ	Sex	Chron. Age	Reading Readiness	Control Group Gr. 1	Gr. 2	Gr. 3	Gr. 4	Gr. 5
1.	125	F	6-1	H. Aver.	2.5	3.4	4.5	5.8	6.0
2.	124	F	6-0	High	3.7	3.5	4.2	5.7	5.9
3.	123	F	6-2	V. High	4.3	4.8	5.6	—	—
4.	122	M	6-3	Average	2.3	3.5	—	—	—
5.	120	M	6-1	V. High	2.5	3.3	3.7	5.7	6.3
6.	119	F	5-11	Average	1.9	—	—	—	—
7.	119	F	5-11	Average	2.8	3.7	4.2	5.2	6.1
8.	118	M	6-1	High	2.4	3.3	4.1	5.6	6.4
9.	117	M	6-3	V. High	2.4	3.7	4.1	5.8	6.2
10.	116	F	6-3	Low Aver.	2.5	3.2	3.8	4.2	5.6
11.	116	F	6-4	V. High	2.6	3.8	4.2	5.6	6.7
12.	115	F	6-7	High	3.6	4.0	4.1	5.1	6.4
13.	115	F	6-7	High	2.2	3.8	4.0	5.1	5.9
14.	114	F	6-9	V. High	2.6	4.4	5.1	5.2	6.6
15.	115	M	6-3	High	2.4	3.5	3.8	4.7	5.6
16.	114	F	5-11	Average	1.6	2.6	3.2	4.1	5.0
17.	115	F	6-6	V. High	2.4	3.8	4.2	4.8	5.5
18.	113	M	6-6	Low Aver.	2.2	4.2	4.6	5.4	5.7
19.	112	F	6-5	V. High	1.9	3.8	4.1	5.2	5.7
20.	112	F	6-8	H. Aver.	2.6	3.9	4.2	5.3	5.8
21.	111	M	6-3	Low Aver.	2.7	3.8	4.3	4.0	5.4
22.	111	F	6-3	Average	3.8	4.0	5.1	5.8	6.2
23.	110	F	6-0	High	2.5	2.6	3.4	4.1	5.0
24.	110	M	6-11	Average	3.6	4.1	4.2	4.2	5.7
25.	110	F	6-8	Average	2.7	3.8	4.2	4.5	5.7
26.	110	M	6-0	V. High	2.9	3.8	4.1	4.8	5.6
27.	108	F	6-6	High	2.2	3.7	4.2	4.4	5.9
28.	108	F	6-5	V. High	3.4	3.7	4.4	5.3	6.0
29.	107	F	6-7	H. Aver.	3.2	4.0	4.5	—	5.7
30.	105	M	6-5	Average	1.9	1.3	2.1	1.4	2.0
31.	105	F	6-7	High	2.0	2.9	3.6	3.9	—
32.	104	M	6-8	Low	1.4	1.9	2.4	3.5	4.5
33.	103	M	5-11	V. Low	2.5	3.4	4.0	4.4	4.9
34.	103	M	6-9	Low Aver.	2.7	3.8	4.3	4.1	4.6
35.	103	M	6-10	Low	2.7	3.6	3.4	4.1	5.5
36.	102	F	6-11	High	2.3	3.1	4.1	4.5	5.2
37.	101	F	6-9	V. Low	1.8	—	—	—	—
38.	102	M	5-10	V. Low	1.9	2.5	3.8	4.0	5.1
39.	100	M	6-3	H. Aver.	1.9	2.9	3.6	3.5	4.4
40.	99	M	6-10	Average	—	3.2	2.9	3.8	4.2
41.	98	M	6-6	Low	2.3	3.1	3.2	3.8	4.2
42.	94	F	6-11	V. Low	—	1.7	2.2	2.1	—
43.	93	M	6-1	Low Aver.	1.5	1.8	2.3	3.1	3.0
44.	88	M	6-8	V. Low	1.6	2.1	2.6	3.1	2.8

*Grades 1 & 2:   *Developmental Reading Tests* (Bond-Clymer-Hoyt)
  Grade 3:   *Developmental Reading Tests* (Bond-Balow-Hoyt)
Grades 4 & 5:   *DRT* (Bond-Balow-Hoyt and Bond-Clymer-Hoyt)

bed. (There is a high correlation between bed-wetting and dyslexia.) In a very few weeks rebellious children started to make friends with the teacher.

Teachers who believe the are teaching a class of especially bright students will get a better performance and higher grades from that class. This phenomenon is known as the Hawthorne effect. To make sure the teacher's belief in the Delacato method had not influenced the rapid improvement of this experimental class, Sister Vivian designed an unobtrusive study which would also test to see if the improvement would eventually disappear. After the first year, the reading scores of both classes — the control and the experimental one — were recorded each year by testers who did not know anything about the original study. Teachers changed from year to year. A new principal took over. Almost no one knew about the original study. Yet, five years later, the experimental group retained its lead in reading scores over the control group. Sister Vivian gave the scores for each child individually and not only in terms of mean averages.

The question of whose reports to believe and whose to ignore would fill an entire chapter, if not a book. The answers lie less in the various studies, which are very hard to evaluate, but in all the independent brain research that has been consistently verifying the original premise from which Delacato developed his therapy.

Roger Sperry won a Nobel Prize for his work with patients whose brains had been split, either because of an accident or by surgery to stop uncontrollable seizures. He documented the specific functions of each brain hemisphere.

New methods of looking into the brain, Positive Emission Tomography (PET) scans can make pretty exact pictures of which parts of a person's brain are functioning when different activities are performed. These PET-scan pictures are so accurate that, for instance, if you play music to a person you can tell from his scan if he is just passively listening to the music — the right side (the symbolic) lights up more — or if he is writing down the score in his imagination — the left side (the linear and verbal side) lights up more.

Dr. Norman Geschwind investigated the relationship between left handed people, dyslexia and immune disorders — allergies and asthma. Similar studies are going on at Johns Hopkins University. Both studies are searching for the links in the male hormone, testosterone, which would account for more boys being left-handed, mathematically inclined and often more dyslexic than girls.

All these discoveries lend more credence to Delacato's work, simply because they are independent of it. They simply inform what he has been quietly doing to help children for the last 20 years.

One of the most frequent obstacles encountered when trying to persuade someone to use his methods is the objection to having someone — child or adult — get back on the floor and crawl or creep. "Well, I can understand what he is trying to do — but all the crawling business, that sounds really ridiculous!" There is nothing ridiculous about it. There is nothing more magical about it than the process by which, once we have found our way to a new address, we remember how to get there the next time.

The research which explains the need for these movements actually started during World War I, when neurologists kept track of the impact on soldiers who had been shot in the spine. Each injured vertebra affected a different segment of the soldier's skin. Delacato mentioned this segmentation in his earliest book on the subject. In the meantime, these areas have been studied more thoroughly, and a new word is appearing in some of the books on the brain and on anatomy: dermatome.

A "dermatome" is a well defined strip about an inch or more wide on the body surface. Nerve connections from each strip make up a bundle of nerves which enter the spinal cord at a specific vertebra. (This segmentation of the body comes from the early development of the embryo. The most common evidence of this is seen during a heart attack, when pain actually originating in the heart is felt in the left arm and hand. This relationship holds true in spite of the fact that in the course of the development of the fetus the heart migrates to a position quite remote from its original site. The same way, the pain from injury to the spleen is felt in the left shoulder. Pain from the back of the tongue may be felt in its segmental partner in the ear.)

The Encyclopedia Britannica probably describes it the clearest way: "Each of the nerves distributed along the spinal cord contains a sensory bundle that serves a well-defined strip of skin (a dermatome) about an inch or more wide on the body surface. Successive spinal nerves overlap, so that each place on the skin represents two and sometimes three dermatomes; this yields a segmented patter of strips over the body from head to toe. All dermatomes feed into a single relay center (the sensory thalamus) deep within the brain, where a precise three-dimensional layout

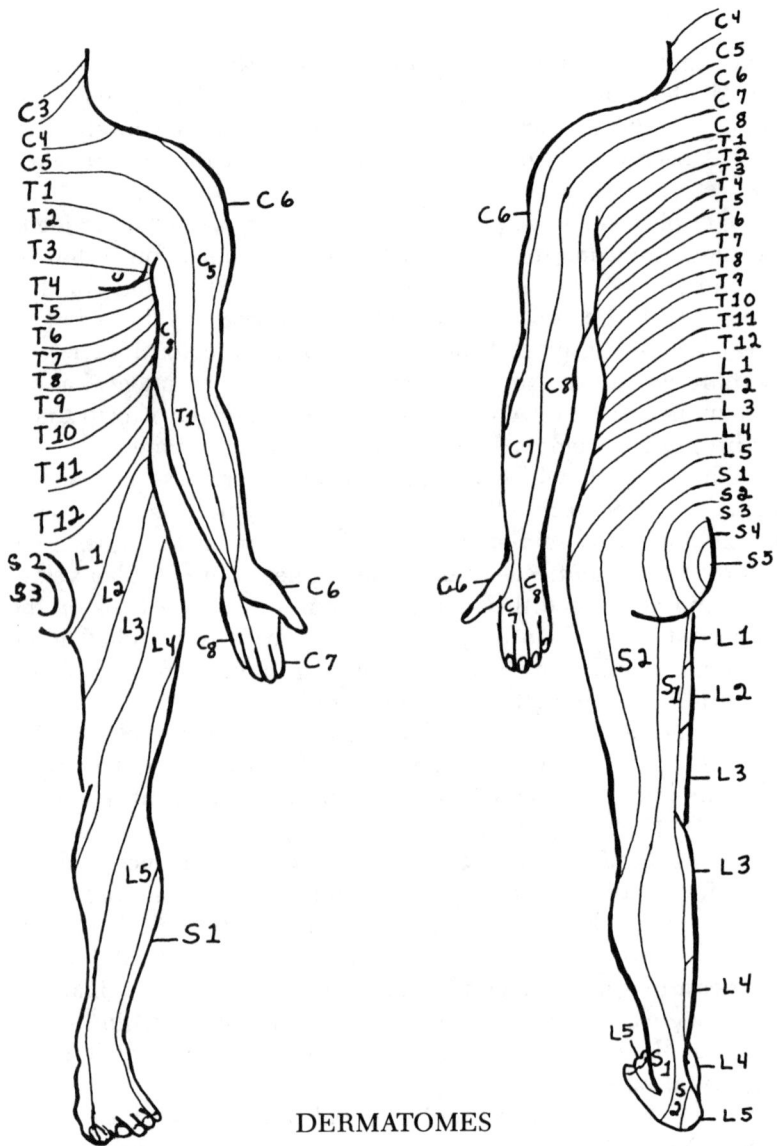

DERMATOMES

Nerve fibers enter spinal cord in these vertebrae.

C — cervical
T — thoracic
L — lumbar
S — sacral

Nerves overlap to some extent.

of tactual sensitivity at the body surface can be found. The neurons in this part of the thalamus (the ventral posterolateral) are specific to particular skin senses (such as pressure) and form small and precise receptor fields."

In other words, the impulses received from the nerve endings create a kind of holographic image of the body in the thalamus.

Now, what is the thalamus? The thalamus is a switching area, which routes impulses not only from the spinal cord, but from the cerebellum to the cortex. When a person goes through the crawling and creeping process, sensori imput from all the dermatomes are sending messages to this switching station so that all the other parts of the brain can get the correct information which they too will eventually process.

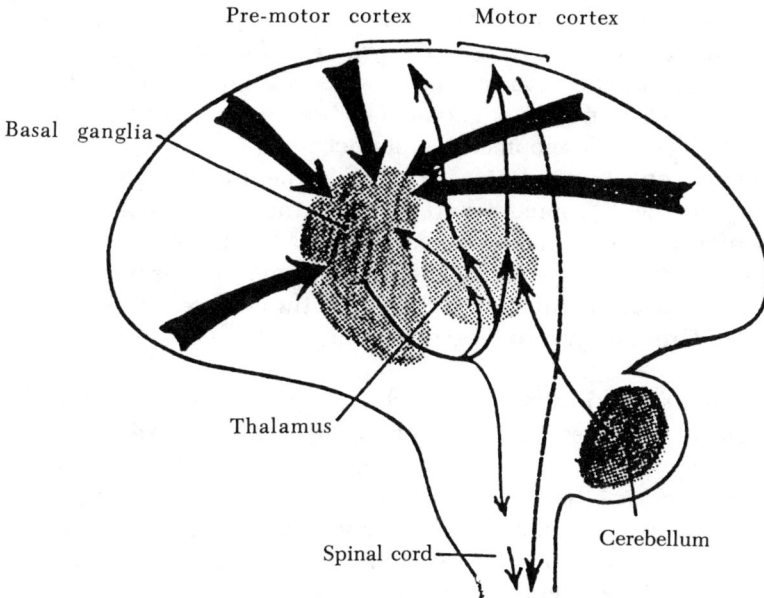

Tracing movement in the brain of the monkey.

Slowly, bit by bit, the brain is yielding up its secrets of organization. Putting the information to work is what matters most when you have a child who is not functioning.

Today, in spite of the earlier controversy, most remedial centers use recapitulation of neurological development when a child has learning problems.

Miriam Bender, at Purdue University, has developed a method, very similar to Delacato's, based on overcoming reflexes which the child has retained. This method also uses movements the child makes as he grows from infancy into childhood. A. Jean Ayers does a lot of work with vestibular stimulation — sensory integration which occurs even earlier than that learned through crawling. Head Start programs use multi-sensory stimulation as part of their regular program.

Some optometrists have become aware that this same total neurological approach is necessary when optometrists try to establish proper vision. This is especially true when one eye has become "lazy". One eye becomes lazy, not because there is something wrong with it, but because the images from the two eyes, for whatever reason, do not fuse. This is very annoying to the child, so the brain refuses to pay attention to one of the two eyes. Simply patching the stong eye, so that the weak one may be used more, will not undo the harm. These developmental optometrists may give vestibular stimulation on a trampoline, they may take the child back to doing infant movements, sometimes even stimulating each eye (or rather the visual cortex) by shining bright lights into each eye. They may utilize creeping. Only with such total involvement of the body can the two eyes learn to function together and the child see one image, not two. Crossed eyes, too, become straight with such therapy.

Thanks to the brilliant TV production of "Cosmos," in which Carl Sagan describes the brain as a library in which information is stored like bits in a computer, almost everyone now has at least some awareness of the functions of the brain. The concepts of right-brain function and left-brain function have become almost household words because of television shows such as "Twentieth Century" and Jonathan Miller's "The Body."

Nevertheless, the concept that somebody can actually influence what goes on in a child's brain by making him do certain developmental exercises, is just a little frightening to most parents. And how does a teacher explain to a visiting V.I.P. why she has a group of children rolling around or creeping on the floor?

One way of making it pleasant for a child to do his sensorimotor program is to creep along with him while he is doing his exercises. So what does a mother tell a neighbor who drops in unexpectedly and finds both mother and child playing tag on the living room floor, she says "I am teaching him to read!"? Of course she is not teaching him to read. That is a separate process. But she does make it possible for him to learn to read!

(For relatives and neighbors, there is a simple five-minute explanation in Appendix III.)

What about Dr. Geschwind's findings of the dyslexic man's brain which was radically different in the speech-processing area? The preceding pages are not in disagreement with this research. First of all, as Dr. Geschwind states, not all reading problems are necessarily associated with an injured brain.

Our brains change continuously with the functions for which we put them to use. A perfectly healthy man had an accident at age 16 in which he lost his eye. When this man died at age 40, the visual cortex into which the messages from the blinded eye would normally have been sent had shrunk considerably, and the space that normally would have been taken up by that part of the cortex had been filled up completely by the greatly enlarged visual cortex which received messages from the other eye. To someone not aware of the medical history of this man, there would have been clearly visible anomalies in this man's brain. So, when Geschwind is speaking of differences in the dyslexic man's brain, we have no way of knowing if the difference was there from birth, or whether the change happened because, for whatever reason, messages did not get into that part of the cortex which processes written language.

Man — as far as we can prove — has been studying the brain since 1700 B.C. (A papyrus, now in the rare book room of the New York Academy of Medicine contains the description and prognosis of two Egyptians wounded in the head, who had compound fractures of the skull.) For thousands of years, we have been able to map what goes on in the brain only by observing the results of an injury. Only recently have scientists been able to trace what goes on in a well brain. Only recently can we actually trace electrical impulses from their start to the cerebral cortex. As a result, we have learned more about the brain in the last 20 years than during all the thousands of years of study which went before.

Perhaps now the time has come for the pure scientists to find out, not only what happens when a child's brain is injured, but also what happens when a child gets well. Perhaps they should investigate some of these centers where other, equally dedicated men

93

and women have actually worked with dyslexic or otherwise brain injured children. Dyslexic children rarely have an abnormal EEG. PET-scans may pick up the pathology, but do not show where the fault lies in the organization of the brain. There are many more secrets to explore. The men who have dedicated their lives to the study of the brain have not done so out of idle curiosity. Dr. Norman Geschwind — who may have never heard of Carl H. Delacato — stated that finding of such distinct organic problems as the abnormal brain of the dyslexic young man may lead to the solution for the problem. Perhaps, in this case, the finding simply throws more light on a remedy that already exists.

Chapter 8

The Psychological Connection

L ittle six-year-old Arnold seemed to be chased by just about every child in the school yard. He had barely eluded one when another child seemed to materialize out of some other direction to hit him while he was still out of breath from being chased by the first. If he eluded the second one, the first had regained his breath and was after him again.

I was watching from outside the wire-mesh fence, having just observed the children in Arnold's first grade class, and I knew Arnold had it coming to him. He was always poking at the others, and then, if the child next to him took a swipe at Arnold, the teacher, not having seen Arnold's offense, would punish the innocent neighbor. Then, coming out of the classroom, Arnold had deliberately swiped a kid's sweater. And now, half the class was after Arnold, poor Arnold, who was running madly like a stag from the hounds.

Hoping to put an end to this situation, I called Arnold over to the fence. The other children, seeing a grown-up, stopped chasing Arnold and stood in undecided groups waiting for him and trying to figure out a new strategy.

Arnold, a handsome little boy, came over to the fence and stood with his fingers entwined in the wire mesh of the fence. "Arnold,"

I said, "why don't you go over there where your teacher is eating lunch? She'll protect you!"

Arnold took a deep breath to try to quiet his panting and looked at me with a strangely impassive face, as if he did not want to cry. "Oh," he said bravely, "they don't hit so hard!"

For a brief moment, there flashed across my memory a scene from the movie "The Wild One." Marlon Brando is on the pavement being beaten up by a group of angry citizens. Between bleeding lips he spits out, "My father can hit harder than that!" Then I saw Arnold's pale and sweaty little face again. He turned obediently and walked in the general direction of his teacher. The other boys, at a distance, eyed him and me carefully to see what was going to happen next. Halfway between where I stood at the fence and where the teachers now stood talking, Arnold picked up a kid's lunch box and kicked it into the sandpile—and the chase was on again.

I knew from my son, who was in Arnold's class, that this curious drama was being played out on that playground every day. It was a drama which I did not fully understand then. I knew that sometimes, when there is a pain which is so great that we cannot cope with it, we substitute a smaller amount of pain which we can handle. The psychologists have a term for it. It's called transfer of emotion. This is what makes sad movies so popular. We can safely cry there, when our own sadness is too deep for tears.

Hoping I could somehow break the pattern of violence which was taking place in the schoolyard, I invited Arnold to play with my son.

My son, though by no means an angel, was nevertheless a reasonably civilized six-year-old who had a number of friends with whom he managed to play without much more than a few verbal clashes. This was different. I took the children out, figuring the park would be a safe, non-threatening place for both children.

I had not counted on the animosity which had built up. Previously I had blamed the teachers for not stopping the violence; now I was getting a lesson in impotence.

I could never figure out what started it, but I would barely turn my back on those two before they were at each other! Not just a poke and a shove — that's pretty standard for six-year-olds — this was the kind of stuff of which Mickey Spillane would have been proud: A flying leap into the other child's stomach; a swift kick to the groin; angry, violent blows handed out with full force and fury.

Within 20 minutes, I loaded the children in the car and delivered Arnold to his mother.

A few months after that, Arnold left the neighborhood. I never did find out why he had to keep proving to himself that he "could still take it." What pain was it that he had to recreate over and over again by making himself the school's enemy who had to be beaten up? Was Arnold an abused child?

At the time we did not know what was wrong with Arnold. There is a technical name for it: scapegoating behavior, sequential to battering. These children develop a compulsive need to provoke punishment from everyone with whom they have contact. Sometimes this is only from other children; sometimes also from adults.

Violence against the child apparently causes the child to identify with the aggressor, and, therefore, he begins to develop a superego, or what we call a conscience. At the same time, a hurt child is an angry child, and the anger the child feels makes him also feel very guilty. He believes he is no good, and deserves nothing good. And now, he has to prove constantly, (1) that he is no good; and, (2) that he can still handle whatever punishment is being handed out to him.

There is another theory which is being explored at present and this shows how important research on the brain can be to modern psychology. Under stress the body manufactures chemicals that are very similar to morphine and they deaden pain in an emergency. These chemicals are called endorphins. It is very possible that, if a child is hurt too often, the body becomes addicted to the endorphins, the way it would become addicted to morphine, and the child seeks the painful stimuli to get another "fix" of endorphins. This theory needs further exploration.

This leads us to another clue which might have made us think Arnold was abused at home: Arnold did not cry. Any other child beaten as badly as Arnold was in the schoolyard would have run screaming and crying to the teacher. After all, Arnold was only six years old! Abused children are very often stoic. Often they are not allowed to cry at home — if they do, the beating gets worse. At other times, they have simply learned to disassociate themselves from what is happening to their bodies.

(There was also the possibility that Arnold was one of the hyposensitive children, who do not feel anything unless it is contact that would be painful to a normal child. Looking back on the situation, however, Arnold gave us no clues that might have led us to come to this conclusion.)

There seems to be so very little that a school can do when faced with the Arnolds of this world. In fact, so many of the children bring a heavy load of anger and fear into the classroom with them. Even with the best of intentions, the parents cannot meet all the needs of a child.

Abused or not abused, just growing up, becoming "civilized" and trying to cope with all the normal frustrations is difficult. Each child carries with him a certain amount of unresolved anger and, of course, brings this anger with him to school.

In a case as difficult as that of our little Arnold, a professional counselor would probably be needed to involve his whole family in some form of therapy. In the meantime, however, all that hatred which Arnold had managed to build up in the class needed to be defused. Just changing Arnold would not help much. It wasn't just what Arnold did that caused all the violence. Each child had found a convenient excuse in Arnold's behavior to let out his own anger. If Jimmy was angry at his brother at home, and the brother was too big to beat up or if Jimmy's mother would not let him do so, Arnold most certainly had given Jimmy enough provocation to take a poke at Arnold instead. Into that poke at Arnold went all the frustration that Jimmy had stored up since breakfast.

If the teacher could have found an outlet for all that anger by having the children draw a picture that is supposed to tell what is bothering them, or by having them write an angry story about their feelings, at least that part of the anger would have been discharged and would not have to be let out on Arnold.

Amazingly enough, using school activities for venting anger does not take time away from teaching. Sylvia Ashton Warner, in New Zealand, was able to teach reading far more quickly by teaching emotion-charged words than by following the prescribed primers. "My father is in jail" and "The goat ate my dress" seem to make an urgent impression on the child to whom these experiences had been very traumatic. Children experience great relief when they become aware that they are not the only ones in the world who have problems and angry thoughts. In psychotherapy, when a feeling is allowed to be stated openly, the energy that has been wasted in suppressing the feeling is now freed for use in doing more constructive things. And so the children, now less bothered by conflicting emotions, find it easier to concentrate on their schoolwork.

Of course, we can simply suppress all that anger. We can ride herd on the children and keep them all quiet and well-behaved. We can use behavior modification and keep any angry outbursts to a minimum. But the anger is still there. Though gone underground, it will show up in headaches, stomach aches, and other psychosomatic symptoms. A child can throw up because he has eaten something bad. He can just as easily throw up because he is frightened. Allergies and brain damage are often misdiagnosed as emotional disturbances, simply because these same signs can be the result of conflicting feelings with which the child is trying to cope. Once feelings are brought out in the open, they can be sorted out, and the conflict can be resolved.

In 1949 there appeared a book by Dorothy Baruch called "New Ways in Discipline." It is the forerunner of many of today's popular child-rearing books. In spite of this rather forbidding title, it is still one of the most charming and delightful of that type of book. Apparently this is not only my opinion, because the book is still in print after 30 years.

When the book was published, the world was just recuperating from World War II. The war had shown that frustration and the kind of rigid discipline used far too often in Germany can result in the kind of suppressed violence which will eventually explode and can destroy nations and peoples. Permissiveness in raising children had been shown not to work, either. Children tend to test for limits to the point where they, too, become involved in some kind of self-destructive behavior. During that same time it had been shown that psychoanalysis could reverse the effects of some emotional problems by bringing the original conflict to the conscious awareness of the patient. So Dorothy Baruch asked the next logical question: Why allow conflicts to build up to the point where they will have to go underground and cause emotional problems?

Obviously, the child has to be taught the skills to live with the rest of mankind. In the process, the parent has to say "no" to the child, and resentment is inevitable. Somewhere between harsh discipline and permissiveness, a new way had to be found.

Many other educators have used similar techniques since, but she outlined them very simply, and they are easily adaptable to a home or a school situation. There are four general principles involved:

1. Stop the destructive action.
2. Accept feelings and, if necessary, clarify them for the child.

3. Help the child find ways to drain off accumulated anger and hurt in ways that are not destructive to him or to others.

4. Try to fulfill the child's needs whenever possible so that the unfilled wants do not become overwhelming to him. This includes physical needs, nutrition, exercise, vision training, and so on.

In the school situation with Arnold, this might translate into the following action:

FIRST CONCEPT: STOP THE DESTRUCTIVE ACTION

The children must not be allowed to gang up on Arnold, even if volunteers have to be requested to patrol the yard or sit in the classroom.

Not only is Arnold entitled to physical protection when he goes to school, but the other children must have the emotional security that they will not be allowed to cause anyone serious harm. If they hurt Arnold, they will feel guilty. If Arnold is hurt, this will only perpetuate his problems: If he then gets extra attention from his mother or from his teacher, he will seek getting hurt again to gain more attention. He will also carry with him an extra load of hate mixed with the lasting feeling of "they're all ganging up on me." Until Arnold starts behaving better, the children must also be protected from him.

THE SECOND CONCEPT:
PERMIT FEELINGS AND EXPLAIN THEM.

Tom says, "I hate Arnold. I am going to burn down his house!" With a less wise teacher, the answer would probably be, "What a dreadful thing to say! Don't ever let me hear you say a thing like that!" At this point, Tom would think, "I guess I am a terrible kid, but the next time I think of burning down Arnold's house I will certainly not tell anyone!" And in the back of his mind will always be that terrible feeling: "What if I really burn down Arnold's house?"

The wise teacher (or mother) says, "Arnold must have really made you mad if you'd even think of burning his house down. I can understand that you would have such a thought, but I won't really let you do it!" (Stop action.) With an answer like this, Tom thinks: "Well, it's sure fun to think about it, but I won't really do it, so there's no harm done!" Tom can now easily forget the whole "Arnold" incident and not have the haunting feeling, for the rest of his life, that indeed he might set fire to someone's home. While in actuality the teacher cannot really stop Tom from burning down

Arnold's house, the child absorbs the statement "I will not let you do it" as his conscience. This statement will stand him in good stead when he is tempted to do something wrong in later life. "It is all right to think it, but I will not let you do it" becomes his own inner command.

THIRD CONCEPT:
HELP THE CHILD DRAIN OFF ACCUMULATED ANGER

To help Arnold get rid of his anger, there will probably have to be professional counseling. But unless the other children can find a way to get rid of what is bothering them when they come to school, they'll take it out on Arnold, and Arnold will be in the same fix as before. Why, even that sweet little Janet, who seems to be all the things little girls are supposed to be and who is always making peace when there is a fight, she too was quite willing to take a swipe at "that nasty Arnold." Are we going to send her to the principal's office, too? Janet, who had never had a chance to be anything but a "good girl" has some angry feelings hidden away!

Looking back at that incident in the schoolyard and remembering those teachers calmly eating lunch, I wonder if they did not tolerate this daily violence just for that very reason: It gave their class a chance to feel superior to someone and to let out some anger in a way that would not be punished. It's an old human custom. When there is tension, society usually comes up with some convenient victim for an outlet. In Roman times it was "bread and circuses" to keep the angry masses in line (the circus being no less important than the bread). If there were no foreigners to hate, there were always witches, or Jews, or Blacks, or some other convenient minority who could be used as a lightning rod.

In the schools, lacking these outlets, there is always some child like Arnold who will bear and even provoke the suppressed anger of the other children in the class.

There may be just as much anger in the schools of the rich as in the ghetto schools. But there are techniques, some of which Dorothy Baruch suggested, which are quite unobtrusive and which can be worked into the school curriculum.

A pile of modeling clay can be kept in one corner of the room. If the teacher sees that Arnold is obviously disturbed, she can allow him to work with the clay for a while. All the anger and the restlessness that is urging the child's muscles to move in that famous "fight or flight" readiness can safely be expended there. The child can punch and poke and pinch the clay until all that tension is gone.

Once the teacher sees that the child is calming down, she can ask him to get back to work and, given another minute or two, he will cheerfully do that.

There are other ways to deal with a child's anger, ways which can involve the whole class at the same time. If the children cannot yet write, having them tell stories works just fine. Mamma Bear, Papa Bear, and Baby Bear can have many uses in bringing out the children's conflicts. As they get older, poetry can help them give a name to their problems. Encourage angry poetry. The children may not admit to their anger except in such an indirect way. As a matter of fact, they may not even be aware of just how angry they are. But the hurts and the anger must be released before they can allow warm feelings to come to the surface.

As the children get older, there can be regular gripe sessions on paper. If a child is not willing to share his experience, his paper can be deposited in a sealed container and then burned ceremoniously at the end of the day. If that is not possible, just shred the paper carefully into the garbage. It is amazing what a relief it is to get something on paper and tear it up. The methods are endless and are limited only by the inventiveness of the teacher.

FOURTH CONCEPT: TRY TO FILL THE CHILD'S NEEDS

It may take a long time of venting angry thoughts before a child may dare to say — or even know — what he wants. (Psychologist Karen Horney used to say that psychotherapy was successful if the patient could finally say "I want.") As long as the angry thoughts are there and kept secret, the child may feel that he dare not voice a need, because how could someone so evil as to have such thoughts be deserving of something good?

Sometimes there may be physical need. Arnold does not know why he must always provoke the other students. If he cannot sit still during the reading period and bothers the others, perhaps there is a problem with his vision — not his eyes, his vision. This gives the school a good chance to talk to Arnold's mother. Talking about Arnold's vision is not threatening to the mother and can bring to light many factors that influence Arnold's behavior — physical and emotional factors that might be dealt with fairly easily. If it is indeed a visual problem, the mother can be shown how to do visual training with her child, and a new relationship can be started at home — and at school also. If it is true (and this is very possible) that Arnold is abused at home, counseling can be given in one form or another. Parents rarely want to abuse their children; they just want to be shown how to cope.

Remember, any kind of technique, but especially child-raising technique, is only necessary when you are stuck. When things go smoothly, you don't even have to look at a child-rearing book. Though these four principles also work very well at home, this doesn't mean you have to go around counting "Step One, Step Two, Step Three..." every time you interact with your child. Kids generally do what their parents tell them. It's genetically programmed into them. It is, however, also programmed into them that they must slowly grow away from their parents and find areas in which they function on their own. This includes coping with their own feelings and fulfilling their own needs.

If the child's behavior is not acceptable to you, usually a brisk "Cut it out!," a quick distraction, or a small bribe will keep his actions within acceptable limits. Save the techniques for those moments when the little monster's behavior will not yield to friendly persuasion and is slowly driving you to consider child abuse! Even then, you don't need to follow the techniques — Step One, Step Two, etc. — but keeping the whole process in mind certainly helps.

Suppose every time you hug your husband, there is this three-year-old creature, right smack between the two of you and pushing you apart! The first time it's cute; by the tenth time it gets a little irritating. So, instead of pushing him away roughly (which would make the poor kid even more jealous), you pick him up and give him a hug — both of you. Stay together, though; don't let him push you apart! (You have stopped his actions, and you have filled his needs.) Then you say to him, "You want to have Mommy all to yourself, and you want to have Daddy all to yourself!" (You've accepted his feelings and made clear to him what they are.) Now, the behavior modification experts throw up their hands in horror and say, "But you're reinforcing his behavior!" It doesn't work that way! After you have done this four or five times, the next time he sees you and your husband hug each other, he just sits there with a big grin on his face and says very distinctly, "I want to have Daddy all to myself!"

It really works. It works from the time the chubby one-year-old stands screaming in his crib. Say to him, "Boy, you're really angry, aren't you? Let's see if we can do something about that!" and take him out. (You reflected his feeling and filled his need.) After all, he's only a year old and can't tell you what he needs in any other way. Are you reinforcing his behavior? You're darn tootin'! You are teaching him to show you how he feels so you can help him get what he needs. By the time he is a little older, he will have the word "angry" in his vocabulary and can tell you what he wants without having to throw a tantrum.

(What can happen to children who are taken out of the crib only when they do not cry, was written up by the Schiffs in "All My Children." They become very disturbed adults. How can a person go through life with the certainty that he will only receive things when he does not ask for them?)

Dorothy Baruch's system works with teenagers. I've seen it at a ghetto teen club. A 15-year-old girl who looked and acted like a tough little prostitute let out a 10-minute-long stream of dirty jokes and obscenities into a tape recorder. We did not stop her or take the microphone away from her. We laughed with her and accepted what she was saying, and suddenly she quieted down and changed abruptly right in front of our eyes. In spite of all the harsh make-up she was wearing, there suddenly emerged a soft, vulnerable young girl. She told us how she had been hungry and desperate after a fight at home, and how the people at the teen club had fed her and comforted her. For a few moments, she allowed us to see what she really felt. For a little while she allowed herself to be free enough to let her defenses down and be gentle and open. Under the circumstances, there was little we could do to fill her needs except to accept her gentleness in a tough world. There probably was no permanent change in the girl, but given another chance, when the occasion was right, instead of assuming the tough streetwalker pose, she might permit herself to be gentle with someone who could respond equally to such gentleness.

When you allow your own children to show their feelings, you are likely to get a lot of unsolicited advice from the relatives. When you are holding a screaming two-year-old in your arms, it's likely to be Aunt Anna saying, "Why don't you put him in his room until he cools off?" What? And let him think his anger is so powerful and frightening that we have to put him in solitary confinement? Or your mother-in-law: "Why do you let him yell at you like that?" "But dear, dear mother-in-law, he is not yelling at me, he is just angry — angry as I get, and angry as you get — see?"

(For dealing with many kinds of behavior which could test anyone's patience, see Chapter 14.)

When you allow your children to express their feelings at home, you will get to wipe away a lot of tears. You will also get to see

104

a lot of anger, and there are many times when you wonder why on earth you have to put up with it. But chances are the children will control their feelings outside of the house if they can express them at home. At home, they'll know you will keep them from doing something destructive.

The sniper who shoots up a whole town from the church steeple is usually the person who never showed any emotion at home — or anywhere else. The kid next door who suddenly held up the bank is usually described as the kid who never gave anyone any trouble. "So relax, mother-in-law, he's going to grow up to be a gentleman, even if he hasn't learned to control his temper yet!"

If you allow your children to express their anger without thinking that you have to knock them across the room to teach them some "respect;" you will see a lot more of your children's anger than more conservative families will, but you will also get an awful lot more hugs and genuine affection.

SECTION I

THE TEEN YEARS

Chapter 9

Delinquency: The Learning Disability Connection

The fascinating fact about trying to solve the enigma of the delinquent teenager is that from whatever angle the subject is approached, you end up with the same conclusion. Judge Maurice Merten, then of the Oregon Circuit Court, was very emphatic when he talked about the burglars who come before him to be sentenced:

"They tell me that this is the first time they have ever done such a thing, and to go easy on them. That's a lie. If it were true, they would not be standing in front of me. They have all been in and out of trouble before, and they have all been battered, abused, are school dropouts and graduates of McLaren Hall (the juvenile detention center for the State of Oregon). These kids are a mess at 18!"

He is not being prejudiced. The fact is that today, because of the crowded jails and for humanitarian reasons, everything is done to try to keep children out of jail. There is almost no greater abuse of a child than to remove him from home and to incarcerate him. Children in summer camps suffer dreadfully from homesickness. To actually lock up a child, no matter how apparently benign the institution, can only cause deep, deep pain and confusion. And rather than feel the pain, the child becomes angry or forms a shell of indifference to protect himself. That mask of indifference may already be there by the time he enters the institution, and this pretended "cool" is interpreted by others as impertinence and only angers the authorities even further.

Allan Berman was raised in the streets of poorer Boston and had been close enough to delinquents to know about kids in trouble. He wanted to find a profession to help such kids, so he became a teacher. What he found was that teachers were authority figures for such children, and they would not let him approach them. So he went on to graduate school to become a psychologist. His first job was at the Rhode Island Department of Corrections. At the time, he knew nothing about learning disabilities, largely because little was known at the time. What he did find out was that all the efforts of rehabilitation being used seemed inadequate. 75% of the delinquents were repeaters; 80% of the delinquents had been in trouble with the law by the time they were 11 or 12 years old. Not only that, but teenagers have a reported suicide rate of 18,000 to 20,000 a year. (There are many more that are written off as accidents but which may actually be intentional "accidents.")

"Thousands and thousands of young people each year become alienated, asocial, are being arrested, put into institutions, arrested again and again. They start their desperate journey into delinquency at younger and younger ages, and more and more of them will never do anything else. They will either keep going in and out of institutions, for the rest of their lives, or they will kill themselves before they receive any meaningful rehabilitation or treatment."*

* Allan Berman, *Delinquent Youth and Learning Disabilities.* Nancy P. Ramos, ed., Academic Therapy Publications, San Rafael, CA 1977, p. 37.

As a graduate student, Berman had taken some courses in neuropsychology with Dr. Ralph Reitan. Reitan had developed a test for neurological functioning of the child, and Berman hoped these tests might explain the behavior of each delinquent. He knew it made no sense simply to say: "This child is a bad child." Now, in Rhode Island, Berman was also moonlighting as a consultant with Dr. Eric Denhof, who was treating a lot of learning-disabled children. With this kind of experience, Berman was now looking quite differently at the delinquents with whom he was working as a clinical psychologist. It seemed to him they were all learning-disabled. They behaved badly because they had problems; they were not "bad kids" to begin with.

When he went to the local judge with this theory, the answer he got was little different from what we got from Judge Merten in Oregon: "We've known that!" said the Rhode Island judge, "We know that these kids have problems in school. They're ratty! (That's the word he used.) They're ratty kids. They've been screwed up all their lives, that's what's been causing the delinquency. We just don't know why they're screwed up." When Berman suggested they were "screwed up" because of the learning problems, the judge got interested: "Well, that's a possibility, but ... where are your data?"

So Berman went back home, and continued to work, and went through all the hard work of getting a grant for a five-year study, a very thoroughly controlled study of juvenile delinquents. The researchers used several different tests and the results of each of them were these: 71% of the delinquent kids were on the neurologically impaired list, while only 23% of the control group were impaired. This control group had been carefully screened so they did not include delinquents who had simply never been caught. It was found, though, that the impaired kids who were not delinquent had slightly different learning problems from those in the detention center.

There were three different disabilities in the delinquent group. The most frequent disability was in visual perception. A close second was in auditory memory. This was an interesting discovery for Berman, because the reason most people get angry at the learning-disabled kids is that they won't do what they're told to do. In other words, it turned out that they were not wilfully disobedient; they forgot almost immediately what they were supposed to do. The third most frequent problem, was that there was a language deficit.

Now, these findings are so typical that it seems almost superfluous to print them. The incidence of learning problems in the jails are so high that they are practically taken for granted. The national reading average of adults in the jail population is at the fifth-grade level. That is the highest grade average I could find. Most statistics of jailed kids show a far lower reading level. These levels are regarded as functional illiteracy — the kids do not have the skills to earn a living.

Whatever detention facility you enter, the problem exists. The Clearing House for Offender Literacy says there are probably a quarter of a million individuals — both adults and youths — incarcerated in this country on any one day, who cannot read to survive! Nor is this a problem of our time alone. An 1898 yearbook of the New York State Reformatory in Elmira calls 18% of the prison inmates illiterate, and 44%, it states, could read and write only with great difficulty. This is a total of 62% compared with today's figures of 55% of offenders who read at fifth-grade level or below.

Neither is this a problem existing only in the United States. In 1976 results were published on a study made on the Isle of Wight, in Great Britain. It was felt that in a rural area, such as the Isle of Wight, none of the social pressures which could influence the delinquents of the city ghettos would be a factor in creating delinquency.

What they found was this: The delinquent kids were almost uniformly two grades behind in their reading achievement!

This is a very important clue. These kids were not stupid. As a matter of fact, they were bright enough to be pushed through the school system in spite of their problem. But they were always just a little behind their classmates, and their frustration must have been overwhelming.

To suggest that school factors are the only ones to predispose a kid to getting himself into trouble, would be ridiculous. However, Daniel Offer, Richard C. Marohn, and Eric Ostrov did a very thorough study, which was detailed in a book called "The Psychological World of the Juvenile Delinquent". They found that delinquents tended to have certain types of personalities, though being such a type would not necessarily lead to crime any more than would having a learning disability. However, the statistical graphs at the end of the book showed that the only factors consistently of statistical significance, were that these children were having problems with learning.

It seems that of all the many, many factors involved, this is the straw that breaks the camel's back. A child who is functioning well in school can get enough satisfaction, both from the teachers and from his own sense of achievement, to see him through all kinds of problems at home. Faced with failure in school day after day, year after year, without a chance of escape, the child must find ways of proving himself, and usually this is possible only in an antisocial situation.

Let's presume that an adult were to go out and play tennis and get beaten in every match. He most certainly would give up tennis and take up something else at which he was more successful. It's human nature. Yet, we expect these kids to continue with their schooling and experience nothing but failure year, after year, after year!

We must give these failure children a curriculum at which they can succeed — and many of these children have great talents in other directions. Unfortunately, even artists and mechanics, cooks and gardeners, all of whom need a special kind of intelligence, must be able to take a driver's license exam, fill out job applications, and be able to read all the instructions on the many tests they have to take in their lifetime. We have no choice. We must find out why these kids are not functioning and fix whatever the problem is.

Richard Compton, in Colorado, examined 444 delinquent kids and found that 203 of them had visual problems, 118 had auditory problems, and 175 had language processing problems. Also 303 had sociological problems and 235 had psychological problems. That means there were over 1,000 problems among the 444 kids, and almost every kid had to have more than one problem.

These problems should have been caught and fixed long before the kids got into trouble, and that trouble often started with truancy in school. From the kids' school records, they discovered that the learning problems had been discovered even before the truancy, and it is pathetic that they were not remedied at that time! (Techniques to accomplish this are discussed in Chapter 7.) Once the child is already in a juvenile detention center, to give him more drills of the type that did not teach him in the first place, is to add insult to injury.

Frank R. Vellutino wrote a book on dyslexia and, again, there were countless factors involved; auditory and visual, and each of these broke down into several components. Statistically, the most significant were intersensory problems.

Now what is an intersensory problem? The chapter on the neurological connection between the two sides of the brain (Chapter 7) was concerned mainly with the connection between the two sides of the brain. The chapter on the time connection (Chapter 6) discussed the various growth spurts of the brain. During these spurts, further and further connections are made between the various areas of the brain. If some of these connections were not established during the younger years of the child, the child does not outgrow the problems; rather, their impact becomes more and more evident.

Research into the various areas of the brain was started during World War I, when a few soldiers survived head wounds and it became evident that these wounds had a devastating effect on various functions of the body. More was learned during World War

II when the chances of survival for these wounded soldiers became greater. It was not until the Korean War, however, that the M.A.S.H. units were able to save more and more soldiers with head wounds and there were a great number of such injured available for study. These soldiers had been screened and tested carefully before they entered the army and, as a result, a great deal was known about them which could be used for comparison when they were retested after their injury.

At the time, scientists had already carefully mapped the various areas of the brain which control the different functions of the body.

Now a new fact emerged. A soldier might have been shot in the visual cortex and have become totally blind. Yet, when he was tested, his I.Q. would have remained constant. He might have been shot in the auditory cortex and lost his hearing; yet, when tested his I.Q. would have remained constant. In fact, there were only two specific areas of the brain that, when hurt, caused the I.Q. to drop as much as 25 points.

These studies gave a whole new insight into the functioning of the brain. Messages through the different senses — vision, touch, hearing, and so on, are sent in the form of electrical impulses to the specific area of the cortex concerned with that particular sense. These impulses are then relayed, so to speak, to another area, in which they are interpreted so they have meaning. From this area they are shunted even further to these I.Q. areas. There, apparently, all the input is checked against all the other information the brain might have stored, and from all this further information the person draws his conclusion as to what to do about the particular messages he has just received.

Scientists have measured the blood flow to these association areas and found that when an I.Q. test is given, these are the areas receiving the most blood flow.

Dr. Norman Geschwind calls these areas "the association area of association areas." It is not quite proven, but there are enough data from different experiments to create the hypothesis that these are the areas in which the intersensory connections are made. Without this intersensory transfer of information, we would be simply reactive organisms and could not make any intelligent decisions.

Very young infants have not yet made this kind of cross-modal connection. If you observe them carefully, you see that they can see, or they can listen, or they can move, but the infants essentially cannot pay attention to any of those activities except one at a time.

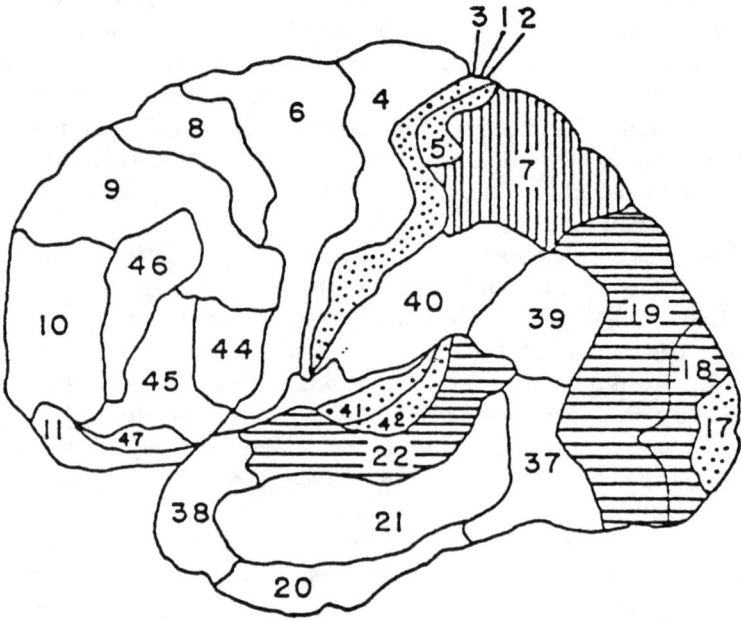

Cross-Section of Brain

Areas 40 and 39 of this cross section of the human brain are believed to be the most recently evolved areas of the back of the brain. These are the areas which show significant increase in blood circulation when I.Q. tests are given, and which when injured, will cause a drop in I.Q.

Area 17 is the primary reception region for vision. Number 18 and 19 are visual association areas. Auditory recption areas are 41 and 42, while 22 is the auditory association area. Touch receptors in 1, 2, and 3 are associated in area 7.

It is only slowly, as the brain grows, that they can associate a voice with the appearance of Mother or show signs of excitement when you bring a bottle. By the time a baby is a little over a year old, he can shake his bottle and decide from the weight and the lack of noise that the milk is "all gone!" That is already some pretty sophisticated intersensory judgment!

Now if for some reason, either because of an injury or simply because of lack of experience (stimulation), these early associations were not made, the connections in the "association area of association areas" cannot be made either. The computer cannot compute what was not fed into it to begin with!

Now some very interesting things can happen when, for one reason or another, the association between one sense and another is not made. The brain compensates through a connection with another sense.

We saw this in the children in Dr. Burr's office, who, when they were not wearing their glasses would make loud noises, using their voices as a sort of sonar to locate themselves in space. You would think this sort of accommodation would solve the problems. Unfortunately, little boys who make a great deal of noise are not welcome and get scolded a lot. What's more, this compensation has not solved the children's vision problems.

Unfortunately, the children have learned to rely on this hearing way of orienting themselves to the point that, sometimes even when they are given glasses, they refuse to use their eyes.

A friend of mine used to teach at Fairview Hospital and Training School, one of the centers for retarded children in Oregon. Because the teachers were aware that some of the kids could not see, they used special funds to buy eyeglasses for them. After a while, however, the staff just gave up; the kids simply would not wear the glasses. The inability to see was in the brain and not in the eyes.

At the State Reformatory in Green Bay, Wisconsin, a different approach was tried. The young men whom you could see creeping on hands and knees, back and forth, back and forth, were not going through some medieval torture or put through some unusual modern form of punishment. These were the "creepy-crawlies," who voluntarily allowed themselves to be put through a sensori-motor program under the guidance of a gentle woman, whom they could have easily overpowered.

The result of this program was that for 102 offenders who participated, the average rate of reading improvement increased fourfold. In other words before the program their reading improvement after one month in school had been only one-half month's improvement. After the program, they had improved almost two and a quarter months in one month. In six months of work, they all had improved a year's worth in reading. Another important aspect, though, reported by Warden Elmer O'Cady that those delinquents who started the program with an impulsivity problem were much improved. They now tested as normal and had a much longer attention span.

What had happened in that bare room that caused these changes? The men had gone through training which involved giving them a chance to catch up on the critical aspects of their sensory input to the brain which they might have missed in their earlier years. They were allowed to crawl, to creep, to hop, to skip, to learn balance, and to learn to tell right from left. In short, their brain was given all the information they needed to process incoming information correctly.

Even though these kids were all over 16 years old, the same kind of input discussed in the chapter on the neurological connection was being given, and improvement was made. The brain continues to make adjustments until we die, and as long as it continues to do so, changes can be made, as long as they are in the proper sequence of normal development. Of course, this program is not a panacea. It is ideal only for those who are in need of such neurological reorganization.

Ruth Hawkes, who organized the program in the Wisconsin jail, writes, "I felt, after working in our program for a few months, that I did not need to test the children to prove which ones needed this kind of help. I could look at their eyes. It is certainly not good clinical evidence, but the pupil was always large and made very little adjustment to light changes. It was a starey eye ... sometimes did not appear to focus properly or quickly enough ... was often cloudy looking, as if there was a barrier behind the lens. The remarkable part of it was, that after several weeks to several months on the program, the cloudiness went away. Often, in evaluating a child, I made a written reference to the changes in eye appearance. The eyes became a communicating device, not just a vehicle for sight. And even more remarkable, the improvement in reading abilities was matched to the eye focus and clearing change."

114

Because today we are able to trace quite accurately just where the impulses go that are received by the brain, there should be and probably eventually will be some research done, as to just why this reorganization of the brain occurs.

About twenty years ago, the team of Glenn Doman and Carl H. Delacato would first move the limbs of brain-injured, paralyzed children to simulate crawling and creeping, hoping eventually to teach them to move by themselves. They were delighted to find that some of them finally were able to creep on hands and knees by themselves. Many of them had crossed eyes which aimlessly moved around the room. And then, one day, one of the nurses mentioned to the team that since these children started creeping, their eyes had started working together! Since the intent of the program had been to get the children to move, and no effort had been made to get them to see, at first no one paid attention. However, when the improvement of the vision became permanent (and this happened as they worked with more and more children), the nurse's findings simply could no longer be ignored. They put the creeping children on a glass table and, sure enough, the moment the children crept, their eyes worked in cooperation with each other. Almost by accident, the ability to form intersensory connections had been discovered!

The actual confirmation as to what is happening in the brain may well be established at a later time. In the meantime, it is pathetic that we have to wait until children end up in trouble with the law before we do something for them.

It does not matter whether you call them learning-disabled, children with intersensory problems, or MBD (Minimal Brain Damaged) children. What is important is that something be done quickly. Dr. Doris H. Milman, of the Downstate Medical Center in Brooklyn, New York, did a long-term study and a 12-year follow-up of 73 such children who had been labeled MBD children.

Only 6% were free of psychiatrically disabling symptoms! 80% had personality disorders, and 14% were classified as borderline psychotics. Personality traits consisted of passive-aggressive, 40%; inadequate, 49%; schizoid, 44%; paranoid, 15%; and impulse disorder, 16%. In addition, 14% showed antisocial behavior; 34% anxiety; 67% learning disabilities and other signs of minor neurological impairment. Nevertheless, 84% had graduated from high school and 27% had gone on to college. (These findings are very similar to the ones in Offer's study of the "Psychological World of the Juvenile Delinquent"!) Even if the youngsters do not end up in jail, this sensori-motor therapy should be given a chance. It is not that these kids do not survive; it is just that the price paid for this survival is unnecessary pain, a horrendous waste of energy, and a waste of human potential. In the meantime, because it is not always possible to do this, it is important to remember that many of the young people who have reading and writing deficiencies have very fine compensatory skills. Some are simply right-brained people in a left-brained world. Mechanical and perceptual skills of symbolic nature are their strength.

Football players, for instance, are very good at calculating how fast a ball will reach a certain spot, calculating rapidly the strength of the kick and the speed and direction of the wind. They are not known, however, for being particularly good at academic skills. At the University of Oregon, when a foreign language is required for graduation, they are often taught Chinese as their fulfillment of this requirement. Most of us who are dominantly left-brained (the left hemisphere is where linear and rational skills are stored), could not learn to read Chinese in a million years. The right-brained football players have less trouble memorizing the many symbols of which this language consists.

Chinese children, on the whole, have fewer reading problems than children from other parts of the world, probably because of the right-brained orientation of their word symbols. The writing of the Japanese, too, is right-brained. The Japanese have two kinds of writing: a symbolic one, called Kanji, and one which is alphabetical — like ours — called Kana. If a Japanese has a stroke on the right side, he can no longer read the symbolic language but can still read the alphabetic one. If his stroke is on the left side, he can read only the symbolic characters.

When it is not possible to give a learning-disabled child the help he needs, we must give him a curriculum at which he can excel. A child needs a sense of worth and a taste of success. Once he has tasted that, he will not have to go out and steal hubcaps, break into the neighbor's toolshed, or continue to provoke the local law establishment until there is no choice but to put him away.

Chapter 10

Offender Behavior: The Nutrition Connection

While Allan Berman pioneered his study of the learning disabilities of the delinquent, he found that among the students whom he used as the control group for his study, 23% had learning problems quite similar to those of the delinquents. Nevertheless, these youngsters did not end up in trouble with the law. Why did these learning-problem kids behave themselves while the others were just asking for trouble? While Berman was still hoping someone might come up with further studies to shed light on this question, in another corner of the United States, Alexander G. Schauss was busy finding other pieces to fit into the puzzle.

The search had started back in 1970, when Schauss, then a young probation/parole officer with the New Mexico State Courts, was in consultation with his colleagues about a particularly difficult case. The 15-year-old delinquent in question was a fairly tall, very fat young man, with curly hair and swollen features. He was a particularly obnoxious character. He had been in and out of the courts, had been warned, had been put on probation, had been warned again. It was no use — this fellow was always getting himself into trouble. Finally, since they no longer knew what to do with this very unpleasant young man, they decided they had no choice but to put him in jail. In court, however, the boy's lawyer pleaded that he be permitted to send his client to a doctor for a medical evaluation.

A few days later, the phone rang in Mr. Schauss' office, and a woman with a heavy Austrian accent identified herself as the young miscreant's doctor.

"How marvelous of you people to send this young man to us! He has a very rare disease, called Klinefelter's syndrome." Klinefelter's syndrome is a rare inherited malfunction of the glands which normally produce the male hormone. The resulting deficiency of this hormone causes generally female characteristics and gives the patient the appearance of a eunuch.

The symptoms of the disease had made the boy feel so embarrassed and awkward that he had to keep proving his macho image by outdoing his friends and getting into more dangerous scrapes than the others did.

Alexander Schauss, with his usual scientific curiosity, did some research. Then, armed with the facts, he urged the court to send the young man to a specialist familiar with this particular problem. The specialist prescribed a hormone treatment. Not only did the boy's physical characteristics change so that he became an attractive, masculine-looking male, but his entire attitude and outlook on life changed. He is now married, has completed four years in the U.S. Air Force, and, at the writing of this book, is attending college.

The incident sparked Alexander Schauss' interest in the biochemical makeup of offenders. His findings have been so important that they are having an impact on the treatment of criminal offenders all over North America. Criminologists in Australia, New Zealand, England, West Germany and many other countries have invited him to share what he has learned. Through one man's efforts, a new chapter in the history of criminology is being written.

One of the areas which fascinated Schauss was the nutrition of the delinquents. The interest had been aroused almost by chance. He had been investigating a juvenile rehabilitation center because, against all expectations, kids stayed there for only about three months before they were allowed to go home. In all the other rehabilitation centers in the state, the kids stayed for 18 months before they were judged fit to leave. To his surprise, he found that this center, unlike the others, served only fresh, unprocessed food and banned all refined sugar, coffee, and tea.

Intrigued by the possible relationship between food and criminal behavior, he decided to do a scientific study of just what the typical chronic delinquent was eating. What the study showed was appalling. In case, after case, after case, breakfast for these kids was cold cereal, the kind that is almost half sugar to start with. Not content with that, most of the children added more sugar. On the average they ate up to 2.14 ounces of sugar before they even went to school! At school they managed to eat candy bars, mints, and glazed donuts.

Then, at lunch, there was a bottle or two of soda pop. The rest of the lunch, too, was loaded with more junk — catsup and relish, for example, both of which are loaded with sugar — and, to top it off, some sweet dessert.

After school, there were snacks of ice cream, candy and more soda pop; after dinner, more sweet desserts and usually another can of pop before bedtime.

Later random surveys by Schauss found that some of these delinquents eat as much as 450 pounds of sugar a year. The average American usually consumes the already high amount of 115 pounds.

These findings were very similar to some studies made by Barbara Reed of Cuyahoga Falls, Ohio. Reed had found that of 743 criminal offenders whom she had studied, 82% had atrocious diets. She had taken this study one step further: When these criminals were put on probation, she also gave them some advice on how diet would affect them. In 1977, she was able to report to the McGovern Senate Select Committee on Nutrition and Human Needs that not one single person who had gone on a nutritionally designed diet and stayed on it was back in trouble with the law. A later follow-up of the group showed that only 9% of her caseload were re-arrested — when the normal expectation of recidivism was 30%.

Alexander Schauss knew that if he was ever to convince the penal system that there needed to be a change in the way criminals were "rehabilitated," he needed some scientific proof. None was available at the time, so Schauss conducted a 21-month-long study of 102 adults who were on probation for misdemeanors. Sixty-eight of these were put on the regular counseling program. The other 34 were given six separate sessions — each only about half an hour long — during which they were given basic lessons on what chemical imbalances occurred if certain foods were eaten. They were told of the impact of blood sugar fluctuations on the brain and told that if the blood sugar was low, a person might make decisions he would later regret.

The men and women on this study were also given a questionnaire to uncover whether they had the most common symptoms of hypoglycemia.

It was found that, just as in Barbara Reed's study, 85% of them had such symptoms. Not only that, but in 25% of chronic offenders, there was a family history of diabetes.

Now, the offenders who got the nutritional advice did not know very much about the biochemistry of the body, but they knew they were not functioning well, so they followed the advice on how to eat better.

Within one month, they started to report almost a total change in their perception of life. They no longer needed to get involved in "exciting" activities. They did not want to hang around with people who could get them into trouble. Some of them even moved out of their neighborhoods. They reported having more energy and tried harder to do something constructive with their lives.

Schauss decided to extend the study. Were there other kids who ate equally badly, but who did not become delinquent? And, since he was also aware that many delinquents had learning problems, he used a matching group for study from the special education classes in the school district. The students in this control group were in these classes for having such problems as hyperactivity, learning disabilities, and behavior disorders.

The juvenile delinquent group was also carefully, and randomly, chosen. (A study is not considered scientifically accurate unless the subjects are chosen at random from a specific group). Each delinquent had to have been arrested at least three times in the prior two years, and one of the offenses had to be a felony and not just a misdemeanor.

With the delinquency factor as the only major difference, the two groups were then matched by age and sex, and they all came from approximately the same social background. The same questionnaire was used with both. Most questions were about nutrition, but there were also some about social and possibly genetic influences: "Do you eat your meals with the rest of your family?" and "Is there a diabetic in your family?"

On the whole there were few differences between the groups. Delinquents tended to eat alone, and they smoked more. The eating habits, however, tended to be the same. In both groups, the kids showed a preference for pizza, steaks, and hamburgers. Soda and colas were favorite drinks.

The one and only truly nutritionally significant factor emerging from the study was this: The juvenile delinquent group drank twice as much milk as the control group! Over the years these findings have been confirmed by numerous correctional institutions who investigated the eating habits of delinquents.

When I first learned about this correlation of the vast amounts of milk consumed by delinquents, I remembered with sudden vividness a scene from the movie "Rebel Without a Cause," in which James Dean brilliantly portrayed a disturbed teenager. I don't remember any of the prior scenes, but this one stayed in my memory because of the desperation made evident by a simple act: James Dean, having just experienced something frightening with which he could not cope, enters his parents' house, heads straight for the refrigerator, grabs a carton of milk and with big thirsty gulps, almost without stopping, drinks the entire quart. Now, looking back, I realize that the character was, no doubt, written with a living model in mind.

When one becomes interested in these kinds of correlations, all kinds of tidbits crop up that tend to lead to some fascinating conclusions. Carl Delacato, when working with autistic children, automatically takes them off milk and wheat, and he has the parents report if there are any changes in behavior. Though this is only part of their therapy, in many cases the improvement is startling.

The other day, I had a meeting with my school-nurse friend, Jeannie Morris, to discuss her experiences with abused children. Almost out of a clear blue sky, she opened the conversation with this: "You know, when we see cases in which a child soils and wets his pants at the age of 10 or 11, the thing we find that helps most is to eliminate all milk! That seems to solve the problem more than anything. And you know, encropresis at 10 — that's pretty awful!"

Of course, it is awful, awful for parents, because we have always implied that there is anger against parents involved in such an act, and awful for the child, because he is being shamed for the act. And, also, it's just a big mess!

If it seems this information does not really belong in this chapter, it merely indicates how overlapping all these factors are — how nutritional problems can lead to all kinds of emotional disasters, which are later blamed for the child's delinquency.

There is another reason for bringing up Jeannie Morris' conversation. Lendon Smith suggests giving magnesium to stop bedwetting. Alexander Schauss states that too much milk consumption interferes with magnesium availability. He also found that the diet of the delinquent kids, more so than that of the non-delinquent, was lacking in foods rich in magnesium, such as meat, fruits, and green vegetables. Magnesium is especially important for muscle growth and nerve tissue development. Nerve tissue development includes the brain, and when we are talking about the brain, we are also talking about emotional stability and learning.

When we, at this point, return to Lendon Smith's statement that the one food the child "must" have every day is the very food to which he is allergic — in this case milk — we have again come full circle on the impact of nutrition on behavior.

Schauss did not stop his research. He had discovered a whole new subject needing study. Further research was needed in evaluating the importance of calcium, phosphorous, and magnesium ratios. He investigated factors of toxicity (minimal and subclinical poisoning) which had been known to change human behavior. Lead poisoning has a measurable effect on intelligence and behavior. In some of the "bad kids" he dealt with, lead exposure was considerably higher than normal and at more dangerous levels. Schauss felt that the impact of this poison was sufficient to cloud the judgment of the delinquents. He arranged for those kids to have the lead eliminated with the latest chelation therapies. Excess minerals can be pulled out of the body by finding ways to attach them to another substance, which is then eliminated through the colon or through the sweat glands. These therapies must be directed by an expert in the field, because if they are not done correctly, they may do more harm than good. Schauss also found that high intracellular copper levels and low zinc caused many children to be overactive, and that's a sure invitation to get someone angry at you. Many with these imbalances also tended to crave drugs.

To measure the minerals in a person's body, Schauss investigated a technique called hair trace mineral analysis to see if it would help pinpoint the metabolic problems of the offenders he was trying to help. About a tablespoonful of hair (one gram) is cut from above the nape of the neck and sent to a chemical laboratory for analysis. The analysis will tell if the chemical elements present in the hair are within standardized normal limits. There may be a deficiency or there may be so much that the element becomes poisonous. Inversely, abnormal ratios may point to the possibility of specific diseases which are usually associated with these abnormal ratios. The technique is not yet a complete diagnostic test, but Schauss has found again and again that it is a valuable screening tool for hemotoxins affecting human behavior.

By comparing thousands of samples from the heads of both delinquent and non-delinquent men and women, Schauss was beginning to develop a fund of information from which he could draw all kinds of conclusions. He found, for instance, that in every case in which someone had exhibited extreme, prolonged violence, there was clear evidence of some kind of chemical imbalance.

His findings are beginning to pay off, but far too slowly. Here in the small city of Eugene, Oregon, the probation department came across a strange and tragic case. Here was a boy who had been in and out of the juvenile justice system since he was five years old. At 14, he was still tiny — barely 98 pounds and slightly built. The child was so violent that the staff began to believe they had another Charles Manson on their hands. He was also exceedingly bright, which made matters worse, because it was easy for him to manipulate not only his friends but also the counselors, his many foster parents, and members of his own family. Then fate provided him with a new probation counselor, Wil Willhite. Wil Willhite had followed the research of Reed and studied with Schauss. Willhite took one look at the child's record, packed his research under one arm and the child's record under the other and took the matter to court. It took almost three years of legal battle, but finally the court ordered a hair analysis for the boy. When the results came back, there was no doubt — the ratio between zinc and mercury was abnormal: The child had mercury poisoning.

Money was provided by Children's Services to pay for the chelation therapy to pull the mercury out of the boy's system. Unfortunately, the destructive spiral in which the boy was caught had gone on too long. The father, who had agreed to take the boy to keep him out of jail, became so angry at him that he backed out at the last minute, and the boy had to go to the state reformatory. Here was another proof that he could not rely on adults to help him! At the detention center the doctor in charge examined him and, since he could find no overt signs of mercury poisoning, refused to have the boy sent to the nearest town for chelation therapy. All this, even though the funds had been allocated. At the same time, with Oregon's economy in a crunch, Wil Willhite was assigned to other duties and could not follow up on the situation. At the writing of this book, the boy was about to leave McLaren Hall on probation.

Only the future will tell whether the boy has strength enough to surmount the odds against him.

Slowly — very slowly — similar influence of this type of research is being felt all over the United States. In Baker, a small town just outside Baton Rouge, Louisiana, Judge Bryant Conway gives those convicted of drunk driving a choice between the usual sentence and a period of probation, during which they have to have blood tests and a hair analysis to find out what nutritional therapy they need to help them stop drinking. Counseling and Alcoholics Anonymous meetings are also part of the sentence. At first, Judge Conway was under fire for trying this new method of getting drunks off the road. But, before long he was able to report that of 20 adult offenders tested, these tests have uncovered toxic metal poisoning in 12. Therapy of these offenders is converting many skeptics. As Alexander Schauss says, the research in this field is so persuasive that, sooner or later, the entire judicial system will make use of it to change the treatment of criminals.

Of course, there are other health problems for the juvenile delinquent besides nutritional ones. In New York City, Dr. Iris F. Litt, from the Division of Adolescent Medicine at Montefiori Hospital cooperated with the juvenile detention facilities. She took advantage of the time the children were in jail and gave them complete physical examinations within 24 hours of their admission. She found that 50% of the children suffered from physical illness, not even counting dental or psychiatric problems. Of 31,000 children who were seen under the program, 3,700 were suffering from hepatitis because of illegal drug use. Two thousand were sent to the infirmary and 400 to Montefiori Hospital. The program discovered many pregnancies that the children did not even suspect. They also found heart defects and congenital endocrine disorders.

It is hard to conceive of the misery a child must feel, finding himself behind bars, lonely and frightened and ill!

There are probably as many causes leading a child to get himself in trouble with the law as there are juvenile delinquents, and Alexander Schauss knows this. Of all these causes though, the one condition which could change a child's behavior — and the one that could be most easily changed — is a poor diet.

In spite of all that is known today about nutrition, the schools still teach nutrition with materials put out by the very companies that put out the junk foods. Many industries are beginning to show genuine concern for the health of the children, nevertheless, it is still a constant fight — one that has to be won separately for each school district — to get the junk-food vending machines out of the schools, and we have known for a long time now that poor nutrition can cause irritable, hyperaggressive behavior! It can cause sleepiness and laziness, and it can cause horrendous appetite and weight gain. (Weight gain may not seem like much of a medical problem, but to a teenager, being fat can be a devastating experience.) One of the side effects is impulsivity, which will cause discipline problems. Junk food can actually cause mental confusion, which in turn makes it very hard for a child to learn and to make intelligent decisions.

Juvenile detention centers are appalling in the food they serve the youngsters. These children, most of whom crave sugar, feel punished if their meals do not include desserts and sweets. As rewards for good behavior, they are allowed to buy candy and soda, and so the nutritional tragedy perpetuates itself.

When Wil Willhite organized a nutrition workshop for the local and, I might add, excellent Juvenile Department, everybody from the counselors to the cooks attended — everybody but the administration. As a result, there were only minimal changes in the diet at the detention facilities.

George von Hilsheimer ran the Green Valley School for throw-away children, children who had been given up as hopeless, and for most of whom attendance at this school was the only alternative to going to jail. When he attempted to use — among other methods — nutrition to help these children, his school was ordered closed because he had "practiced medicine without a license."

There will eventually have to be laws in every state, just as there are now in California, saying that nutritional counseling does not constitute illegal practice of medicine.

Diet counseling and a special food allowance should be given to institutions and foster homes. There should probably be rotating diets in any institutions dealing with "high-risk" kids. The major culprits in food allergies — wheat, milk, corn, and eggs, would be served in rotation; only once every five days. This would help prevent allergic reactions. It takes a little more planning, but it costs no more and it might solve a whole lot of emotional problems. (See also Chapter 3 on allergies.)

Not only should there be a change in the diets in the institutions, but when the child is returned to the family, the family must be told how important nutrition can be and shown how easily and inexpensively good nutrition can be achieved. If the child returns to his former habits of bad eating, in time there will be a recurrence of his behavior. If the child suffers from poor nutrition, chances are that the diet causing it is usually the fare of the whole family. The rest of the family may have the same or similar problems. The clash of temperaments of people who are all at the end of their strength can be devastating, both to the child and to the parents.

Chapter 11

The Sexual Abuse Connection: When To Suspect The Child Has Been Sexually Abused

A 12-year old girl suddenly becomes an avid student. She goes to all the extracurricular activities after school and can barely be persuaded to go home in the evening. She will do anything to avoid going home. Whenever her mother is not at home, her stepfather is lying in wait for her.

Every time a seven-year-old girl returns from her monthly visits with her divorced father, she throws up. The concerned mother believes that maybe the excitement and the strange food is too much for her. It is not until the mother moves to another town that the truth finally comes out: The father and his new wife had been using the child to make pornographic movies.

A couple adopt two brothers who were known to have been neglected. The younger is five, the older eight. The moment the older comes home from school, he wets his pants. At school he is dry. The new parents are loving, but they can now understand why, so far, no one has wanted to keep this child. Then, slowly the little one starts to talk. The older tries to shush him up. Both children have been sexually abused. Bit by bit, under the guidance of an adoption counselor, the new mother allows the boy to ask questions. At first he asks the questions as if the experience had happened to someone else. Sometimes it is only one question a day, usually as she tucks him in at night. Finally, after two months the children are allowed to join a support group of other sexually abused children. But help comes too late. The brothers, in spite of all efforts by counselors and parents to stop this practice, find unsupervised moments during which they have sexual relations with each other. When one of them attacks another child sexually, Children's Services steps in and separates the brothers. One of the boys remains in a foster home. The older is found killing and mutilating the pets of his adopted parents and is institutionalized in a jail situation where theoretically, he is to get psychiatric help. And the future?

In another case, in a small town in Montana a 14-year-old girl is seduced by her priest. How could she dare tell anyone? Who would believe her words against a priest's? That girl eventually became a delightful, secure, competent woman, a talented actress, mother of two children out of one marriage and a third out of a very successful second marriage.

These are just some of the people in my immediate acquaintance who have experienced sexual abuse.

The U.S. Department of Health and Human Services published an issue on "Perspectives in Child Maltreatment in the Mid '80s." In it, David Finkelhor, Associate Director of Family Violence Research Program at the University of New Hampshire, cites various studies. He concludes that while these studies cannot be generalized, it is fair to say that anywhere from 9% to 52% of women and 3% to 9% percent of men had experienced some kind of sexual abuse and unwanted advances before they were 18.

We do not know why there is such a surge in sexual and incestual abuse. Perhaps it only seems so because there has been a greater rate of reporting such abuse. Incest certainly has been a prime concern of mankind since the beginning of history. It is clearly spelled out in Leviticus 18:6-16: Stay away sexually from blood relatives. Freud did not dare believe that such things occurred to his patients and tried to convince most of them that they had hallucinated the entire experience. Whether he knowingly repressed the truth — that his patients' memories were real and incest had actually occurred, or whether his moralistic upbringing made it impossible for him to believe that incest could actually happen, are still being debated.

Whatever the truth, the unfortunate result is that many young women have been told that these incidences were simply figments of imaginations. To a woman who is already incapable of trusting another human being because her early trust had been betrayed, this can be the final destruction of her tenuous hold on reality.

If the situation was reality for the child, whether there is proof or not, in therapy it must be treated as reality because the child experienced it as such.

There are laws against incest in most cultures. There are such laws in most of the states of the United States.

If there were not a considerable number of people doing such things, why would there have to be any such laws? These laws do not simply enforce old taboos. Consanguinity — the name geneticists call incest — creates a kind of genetic Russian roulette. Accurate statistics of incestually conceived children are hard to find, for the simple reason that the genetically caused defects may well have aborted the fetus. A 1967 study of 18 children born of incestuous mating (6 father-daughter, the others brother-sister), showed that five were dead by six months of age, two were severely mentally retarded, one had a bilateral cleft palate, three were of borderline intelligence, and only seven were free of pathology. Of the control group only one child was defective. Studies of large samples of inbreeding in the population show a definitely higher incidence of loss of child during pregnancy, mortality during the first year, later age when the child first walked, lower visual and auditory accuity, lower intelligence and greater incidence of physical defects.

Sexual abuse cases — along with other abuse reports — become endemic in areas where there is a sudden increase in unemployment. The breakup of families also increases the chances of such abuse. While in those cases the excuse is that this is not real incest, the betrayal of the child is just as great. Even the Bible says that the sexual union of a stepfather with a stepchild is a great dishonor.

Our children seem to mature earlier and in their early teens are breathtakingly beautiful. Most dress in the latest charming styles and in their very innocence imitate sexually attractive women before the children really know what it is all about.

Whatever the reason for the increase of sexual abuse, this chapter does not focus on that aspect, but on the behavior of the children after the abuse and how this behavior will spiral the isolation and the mistreatment of such children.

There have been many books about incest within the last few years. Some of them read like — and possibly are — nothing more than legal pornography. A few have been written about the psychological impact on the child and possible therapy, but nothing has been written about how their behavior after the abuse will lead to their being abused in many other ways. It is this aspect which will be explored here.

In the Journal of the American Medical Association, Barbara Herjanic and Ronald B. Wilbois say this:

"The psychological impact of sexual abuse depends on many factors, such as the age of the victim, the number of occurrences, the relationship of the abuser, the psychosocial situation of the family, the amount of physical trauma involved, the reaction of the parent or guardian, and finally the treatment received in the emergency room or the physician's office.

"A child's reaction to sexual abuse may range from apparent indifference to acute states of anxiety, or withdrawal and depression. A few seem to relish the attention and will actively seek out sexual partners. Some children engage in sexual activities in imitation of observed behavior at home, but may be subject to severe punishment when discovered. Often the child is more disturbed by the reaction the behavior brings forth than from the actual sexual activity itself." (In a child abuse case, no matter what the legal implications, we try to help the child. We must not approach the case with preconceived ideas. If the child is devastated, this must be recognized. If the child shrugs it off, the experience should not be turned into a major trauma.)

In the children's section of our library — supposedly a quiet and safe place — a man exposed himself to a little girl. The mother was furious, but a calm librarian quietly asked the little girl: "And what did you do then?" "Oh," the young lady — all of six years old — said calmly, "I told him the bathroom was upstairs!"

We must be very careful not to superimpose our adult outraged reaction on the reactions of a child and create problems where the child does not experience them. (Had the child been frightened, a way to reassure her might have been to say: "It's a little scary, isn't it, if someone does a dumb thing like that! I'm glad you told me!" This opens the door to further talk about the fright and never disputes the child's feelings.)

Even the low estimates of studies indicate that one out of five women had some kind of unwanted sexual experience in early life. If this is correct, there are many people who might think there is something wrong with them that they do not experience any lasting guilt from the encounter. On the contrary! They have coped with the trauma as they did with any other kind of bad experience. Eventually we all have to decide to get rid of the burdens of our childhood and get on with life.

When we talk about sexual abuse we must define the term. Is it sexual abuse if the father gives a bath to a two year old girl, a six year old girl, a ten year old girl? Is it sexual abuse if a six year old boy sleeps with his parents — even if the sex act is not performed in his presence? Is it abusive if an eight year old boy is allowed to walk into the bathroom and watch his mother taking a bath? Indeed, is it sexual abuse if parents never let their children see them in the nude? What becomes traumatic depends very much not only on the age of a child, but on the particular personality of a child. Even if no violence is involved in a sexually charged situation, some very subtle behavioral changes can happen and some impact may not be revealed until many years later.

The most lasting damage occurs in those situations where violence has been involved. Long term incidences involving family members or actual father-child incest cause great harm.

Many children have survived terrible situations and remained comparatively unscathed. The difference between most shocks and that of sexual violation of the child is that nobody talks about it. If a child breaks a leg, a cast is put on the leg, and there is a sign-the-cast party, and everybody makes a big fuss. The child hobbles around for a few weeks and talks with everybody about the terrible accident, and by the time the cast comes off, the emotional impact of the experience will have been talked out — abreacted is the psychological term — and the emotional wound will have healed along with the physical one.

In the case of sexual abuse, no one talks about the incident. The child is usually either afraid to talk, too ashamed to talk or not allowed to talk about it, because even if a family member knows about the abuse, the child cannot be allowed to go around the neighborhood discussing the experience!

A further complication is that we tend to treat children who are known to have been sexually abused in a different way. We are so afraid to add to the trauma that we overprotect them. We tend to blame all their misbehavior on the sexual assault and are afraid to give them the limits they so desperately need. If the limits are not set, the child will continue to test the adults. An adult who does not enforce limits will not seem strong enough to these children, who are now searching for someone to protect them from further harm.

We also tend to overlook problems which have nothing to do with the sexual abuse. The smaller boy of the two brothers mentioned at the beginning of the chapter had all the symptoms common to the sexually abused child. He had a lack of space perception and a lack of a sense of self. This kind of de-personalization is common among such cases. In this child's case, however, testing showed this lack to be clearly the result of neurological disorganization. No doubt this was caused by early neglect— it was known that the child had been kept in a playpen, was rarely allowed to move about and explore, and rarely picked up to be touched and cuddled. Though the child is, at the writing of this book, receiving some psychotherapy, he may never get therapy for the sensory input which he missed, abused or not abused, he needs to function well. Incidentally such therapy would speed up the healing process.

There are no two cases exactly alike.

What makes it so hard to detect if a child's "bad" behavior has been caused by sexual abuse, is that by now we know some of the typical behavior resulting from sexual abuse. This same behavior can be caused by a great number of other things. A study at the Child Abuse Prevention Center in Hennepin County, Minnesota shows that 30% of the children involved had already shown behavior problems before the abuse!

I talked about this problem with my friend Jeannie Morris, who is a district nurse for the Springfield, Oregon school district. It came as no surprise that her experiences with abused children, sexually or otherwise, fell right in with what national statistics had already proved. Nevertheless, statistics are numbers, and children are a one-at-a-time reality.

Jeannie Morris is the first to receive reports from the teachers whom she herself has taught to detect tell-tale signs. It is then her difficult task to investigate the family, to see if the child's symptoms are actually sex related.

One of the symptoms, particularly in younger children, is a regression to behavior that the child has already outgrown. The child, for instance, may start sucking her thumb again. Now if at home Susie is undergoing a frightening experience with which she cannot cope and then comes to school sucking her thumb, she will also have to face the teasing from the other children. Chances are that since thumbsucking is a habit for which children get ridiculed at home also, the child will become overwhelmed by the feeling of having no comfort anywhere. This is the total neglect syndrome which is so common in incest situations.

The "forbidden games" may give the child sudden fear of the dark, fear of leaving the house, or fear of staying overnight at the baby sitter's. Far too often, these fears are ridiculed and ignored. If the adults don't accept the child's feelings, how can he explain to them what is really behind those terrors? The child himself does not know what to make of this secret behavior for which he has not even a word in his vocabulary.

Often there is a return to bed-wetting, another behavior which will cause problems for the child. Instead of being able to turn to the mother for comfort, the mother too becomes an angry adult or, even worse, a punishing adult. The child has lost another possible ally.

In school, the child may suddenly ask constantly to be allowed to go to the bathroom — a tell-tale sign that something is wrong. If she has a knowledgeable teacher, she may get sent to the nurse. The nurse, suspecting abuse, may in turn refer the case to a doctor, passing on to him her observations and her suspicions. Unfortunately, the chances are that the teacher thinks Susie is pulling "a fast one." The teacher is already harassed by a bunch of active youngsters who are trying to manipulate her, and so she may not allow Susie to go. What may be seen as a challenge to the teacher's authority may well be caused by a vaginal infection or urinary inflammation. In boys, there may be pain on urination, penile swelling, or discharge. If Johnny knows it hurts to go to the bathroom, he may wait too long to go and wet his pants. Instead of a haven from the threat, school too becomes a frightening place, where he is ridiculed by the other children.

There may be other signs. There may be a kind of sex play that the child normally would not do at that particular age. There may be a sudden seductive behavior toward adults. Sometimes the child masturbates in public. These behaviors are not necessarily a sign of emotional disturbance: Whenever children learn something new in one situation, they try it out in another setting.

The same thing holds true with sexual experiences. Uncle Jimmy taught Johnny to masturbate him. Now Johnny is doing it in school, the same way he would show off that he learned how to ride a bicycle.

The reaction from the teacher or from the outraged parents of the other children comes as a terrible shock to Johnny. At this point, Johnny's experimentation, which in another area would be considered quite normal, is being regarded as an emotional disturbance, or even worse, a sign that Johnny is a bad, bad boy. Johnny is getting mixed messages about what is good or bad, and so he starts to doubt himself. The lack of self-esteem which is so common among sexually abused children is made worse by their being punished for behavior for which they are rewarded in secret.

If a child is older, the school nurse may get reports of sudden personality changes. These changes are often the same as those which may warn of impending suicide. In the older child, sexual abuse can trigger sudden violent hostility in unprovoking situations. There may be a sudden aggression and, at the same time, withdrawal from the group. Grades may suddenly decline, and there may be hints that the child is thinking of suicide or may actually be making suicidal attempts.

All this "acting out" behavior by a child is symptomatic of depression, whatever the cause. Immediate intervention is necessary as the child's aggression can lead to further problems. If the child is smaller than the other children, he'll get beaten up. If his violence lands him in jail, the anger will only increase and add to his other problems. If his schoolwork deteriorates, there will be further recriminations at home, more pressure from the teachers, and, instead of getting the help the child needs, he is being beaten down even more. Drugs or suicide can easily be the next step.

There are no easy answers. A teenager in the Springfield high school was called into the office for counseling because he was acting strangely. It was one of many such sessions. This time the boy ran out of the counseling session, hid in the bathroom and shot himself. No one knew he owned a gun.

Schools can only attempt to help. In many states there are laws requiring suspected abuse to be reported. The nurse may report her findings to the doctor; unfortunately, while he has to report the abuse to the state, he may not report his findings back to the nurse. This means she has no feedback as to whether she was correct, nor can she pass on the information which the teachers may need to help protect the child in the future.

Running away from home is a particularly common reaction to incest when children are in their teens. If these runaways are caught, they are considered status offenders and put in detention.

If they are lucky, it is a benign institution or a halfway house. Though a foster home may be better than jail, there is less chance in the home that the children's problems will be evaluated by a psychologist. If they do end up in jail there may be further violence and, often, rape. Even more frequently they are sent back on parole into the same incestuous situation from which they tried to escape in the first place.

The blame for such a faulty decision cannot be put on the judge. The child, out of that fierce sense of loyalty which is characteristic of such children, will not reveal the true reason for running away. Even if the courts are aware of the incest, they hesitate to prosecute such cases because it is known from experience that this loyalty makes the child a poor witness. Where does this loyalty come from?

In looking backward, adults who have been sexually or otherwise abused as children find it incomprehensible that they did not complain to anyone in order to escape from the situation. Children, of course, have no way of comparing their life situation with any other and they may not be able to imagine that a better way of living exists. When the parent is the abuser, not only is the actual abuse the problem, but another even more devastating condition exists: The child finds himself caught in a bind in which he hates the most loved person in his life.

There is a curious psychological reality that children who have a mother who punished them severely are more dependent and clinging than those with a gentle mother. The family bonds which must eventually be broken so children can grow up and function on their own, are far harder to break for these children.

Research has shown that monkeys who have been reared by a punitive mother have this same dependency. This holds true for real monkey mothers as well as for those horrible wire-mesh and bottle surrogate mothers which the scientists make for infant monkeys so they could observe them in controlled studies.

The earlier the abuse starts, the stronger the dependency. The very young child does not see one mother who is both good and bad. He separates the mother into two beings, a good one and a bad one. When a two-year-old refuses to hold still for being dressed, and the mother wrestles him down, bending over him with an angry distorted face, he cries in despair, "I want my Mommy!" That nasty old witch who is fighting with him has nothing to do with his loving Mommy, from whom he gets smiles and hugs and good food.

When the child is older he does see the punitive person and the loved one as one and the same. Hating the person you love creates such guilt that the child suppresses the hate. However, as the result of the internal conflict he will forever doubt his feelings. He will never again be sure just what things really mean to him.

Of course, such confusion can result from incidents other than incest. In the case of incest the violent anger is coupled with such tremendous need that the emotional scar may never heal.

The sexually abused child who runs away from home and is not caught has little choice but to make money as a prostitute. This is unfortunately true both for girls and for boys. Even if the children are taken in and "kept," the price of freedom is continued sexual slavery. This is particularly true of girls, because boys can turn to more violent crimes to make a living.

At a meeting of the Oregon Chapter of the National Organization of Women, Judge Helen Frye was very angry: "But what happens to little girls who are battered and neglected? How many women do you know that are rapists, robbers, assaulters and murderers? Besides the occasional woman who drives a getaway car or participates in other forms of aiding and abetting, most battered or neglected girls grow up to become prostitutes, alcoholics, drug addicts, chronic depressants or battered women." Teenage prostitution is rampant in America, Judge Frye told her audience. She cited a study from the University of Washington by researcher Jennifer James. It showed that of the teenage prostitutes interviewed, 47% had been raped and 62% were sexually abused at some time during their childhood. Most teenage prostitutes were victims of incest, abuse, or neglect. They ran away from home and into the arms of pimps who delivered them into the arms of "Johns."

"These," Judge Frye said, "are the little girls who are programmed to say 'Yes Sir!' and 'No Sir!' instead of learning to think for themselves."

Men used to tell a joke which went something like this: "How come a nice girl like you is in a profession like this?" And the prostitute answers, "Just lucky I guess!"

There is nothing lucky about the situation in which these girls find themselves. To make money as a prostitute, you have to be very astute and worldly-wise. Those children are still too young to handle their own affairs well. They are prime candidates for every form of violence, and every "trick" could lead to their death. V.D. is rampant, and in spite of birth control pills and devices, there is always a chance of getting pregnant. The program of Dr. Iris F. Litt, who did medical examinations of jailed juveniles in New York

City, found that many of the girls were pregnant and did not even know it.

What money they make tends to go to drugs. They are so depressed by what they experience that they need drugs just to face another day. The trouble is that these girls are forced to go with men who cannot possibly give them the kind of love they so desperately need. The guilt these children feel makes them believe that they are not entitled to a better life.

This does not mean that all sexually abused girls end up as prostitutes. Jeannie Morris, as Springfield's school district nurse, teaches a class in child care to the high school's teenage mothers. These students, whose sexual abuse was never suspected by the school, often volunteer that they have been sexually abused. Usually half the class has had some such experience.

It is not that their babies are incestually conceived, but in running away from an unbearable situation at home, they have turned to a boyfriend for solace and ended up pregnant. They do wish to get married, and many of them eventually do, even if not to the father of their first baby. While the teenager may be willing to give up her baby, the grandmother and grandfather will step in and say, "You can't give up my grandchild!" It is a very understandable sentiment, and in theory it sounds good. Unfortunately, many of them would be better off giving the children away because the mothers — often not more than thirteen years old — are now in a very precarious situation. If the baby is then raised in the grandmother's house, there ensues a power struggle between the mother and the grandmother, who is often young enough to have had the baby herself.

We have an added problem here. Children of teenagers simply have more developmental problems than those of more mature parents. Breeders would not dream of breeding a horse before it is fully mature. So, in addition to having a responsibility for which the young mother is simply not ready, she is burdened with a child who is harder to raise.

Of course, the 13-year-old is not very good at taking care of the baby, even a healthy one, and so the grandmother says, "Here, let me do it!" Before long the young mother has the feeling of being totally incompetent — even in such matters as raising her own child. This is true not only in Springfield but all over the United States. The same drama is being played out wherever there are illegitimate children. Often this conflict escalates to the point where the child is taken away from both mother and grandmother and, of course, it is the baby who suffers. So the abusive cycle continues from generation to generation.

Only recently have there been hot-lines for children to call to get help. Even so, why did these children — in case history after case history — not talk? Part of the reason for this silence seems to be the innate feeling that sex or anything sexual is a very private matter. Is it because for the survival of the species it was imperative that sexual intercourse take place in hiding? Sex would absorb all of the attention of the participants and leave the partners defenseless against any enemies who might be lurking about. Sex would have to be carried out in complete seclusion. Perhaps it is simply that in our culture sex is rarely discussed in front of children. If it is, it is done so by innuendo or with a feeling of secret relish which the child nevertheless picks up.

If a little girl says "I want to marry Daddy," this "marry" does not have the same sexual connotation as if it were used by an adult. A child who wants to possess Daddy (or, if a boy, Mommy) wants his love and attention — no more than that. Nevertheless, when a father makes sexual contact, the child may feel uncomfortable but may take the guilt on herself, because she feels she has captured Daddy's attention and now feels just a little superior to Mommy.

(Psychotherapists find that in almost all cases in which a patient is haunted by a memory, if the patient digs deep enough, there was a situation about which the patient felt, rightly or not, guilty at the time.)

Of course the child is not guilty in incest cases, but this feeling of guilt seems so universal that prisoners who had been tortured often later report having felt that they were guilty somehow and deserved the mistreatment.

The seductive parent fosters this feeling of guilt by all manner of means. If possible he bribes the child, even if the child had cooperated just to please him, and thus he makes her an accomplice to be manipulated more easily in future incidents.

To a child, mother and father are not just people. They are sort of super-human being whose every announcement carries a special weight. Mother, who even if she works, is around more, tends to be taken for granted a little. She is treated as if she were a convenient piece of furniture made especially to cater to the child's need. The father on the other hand, partly because of the deferential tone with which the mother refers to him, and partly because he is not always around, takes on the importance of a god.

Very often children feel that in taking over the sexual role in the family they are actually keeping the family together. Only when the father starts to abuse another child do they finally talk. The child makes the father promise to leave the others alone. When the father breaks the promise, she tells on the father. In the case of the Haynes boy, who had been kidnapped and used sexually, the boy did not come forward until his kidnapper had abducted another boy and he wanted to protect that child from a similar fate.

I don't believe there is jealousy involved in such cases. It is far more likely that the children could tolerate the abuse as long as they felt there was importance and meaning to their self-sacrifice.

Both Bruno Bettelheim and Victor Frankl have reported incident after incident from their experiences in a concentration camp which proved this human ability to withstand hardship: but only as long as there was a purpose to the suffering. When the children feel no longer useful, they can also no longer tolerate the situaton.

Very often, too, children have no idea that these sexual practices are different from what happens in other families. When they are young, they do not really comprehend what it's all about. They can no more accept the knowledge of sex in a conscious way than they can accept the fact that there is no Santa Claus before they have reached a certain age. (Even teenagers who have been taught all about sex still feel very often that other people do it, but not Mom and Dad.) And so, because the child keeps silent and does not object or talk, the abuse may go on for years.

Most often even the abuser does not realize how much the child suffers under the situation.

Once the children become old enough to understand that they should have told a long time ago, they are hopelessly enmeshed in guilt and can no longer do so.

It is almost symptomatic that sexually abused children blame their mothers for not protecting them and not the actual perpetrator of the abuse. Psychologists have a field day, saying the mother subconsciously set the child up for abuse. This may be true in some cases, but how can you blame a woman for not suspecting sexual abuse of her child when until recently no one dared even breathe of such a thing. She has been told to love, honor and obey her husband, and now how could she even suspect him of such a crime?

Nevertheless, even if the mother is caring, the children feel betrayed. There is a sense of total neglect or abandonment because the children feel they are being used and have no one to talk to.

These children suffer from a feeling of getting no support, not realizing that their own behavior has spiraled their isolation.

Another question, one which is even more puzzling, is this: How did these children survive the incest situation at all, especially if there was pain and violence involved or if, as is often true, the incest continued for years?

There seem to be several survival mechanisms built into the human animal. One which we have already discussed, is that we can tolerate a great deal if we are convinced that there is a purpose to our suffering. The second one is that we are able to withdraw or to split our feelings from what is happening to us. We deny the reality of our bodies.

I recently talked to a young woman who had been part of a child abuse team in Indiana. We discussed how the children somehow managed to disassociate themselves from the frightening things which were happening to them. "Oh yes, of course," she said. "Someone recently showed me a study which showed how incest creates split personalities. And my only reaction was, 'So what else is new?'"

A fascinating insight into just how deep this split can become is shown in the biography of the hypnosis of a young woman who, as a four-year-old, had been used in the rituals of a satanic cult.

During the rituals she experienced not only sexual violation but macabre scenes of ritual horrors which would have terrified an adult. The little girl, in moments of abject misery, maintained an outward calm. She managed this by literally withdrawing into some kind of warm core within herself to which she clung for dear life. Sometimes, to give her comfort, she actually hallucinated an imaginary companion. This could be another little girl or even her favorite teddy bear. The actual fear and terror she experienced did not come out in tears and in screaming until 20 years later and then only under hypnosis. Many of the incidents she relived under hypnosis — incidents too outrageous for the psychiatrist to believe without further proof — have since been verified.

Similar defense mechanisms help many of the abused children to maintain a calm and unruffled outside. While they cannot push away all the disturbing awareness, they put it into a corner of their mind so it does not interfere with their ability to survive.

This outer calm keeps others from suspecting the abuse. A case that most clearly illustrates this spiraling nightmare of a child caught in an incestual entrapment, is brilliantly told in Charlotte Vale Allen's memoir, "Daddy's Girl."

Charlotte Vale Allen describes herself as having been a hyperactive little girl. To the mother, left alone while her husband was in the army, she was no doubt a difficult, sometimes irritating child. Because of this, there was also no doubt more than the usual friction between her and her mother. The child, like most hyperactive children, probably heard more than her share of "Don't do this!" and "Get away from there!" Like most hyperactive children, she frequently experienced anger and perceived her mother as not loving her. That this hyperactivity was caused by neurological dysfunction seems to be confirmed later when, after she was tested at school because her grades were poor, it was found that she was actually seeing double! The same visual perception problem (for which she was later treated) was quite likely the cause of the many accidents she had as a child. She complains of falling constantly, knocking food over at the table, or having accidents on her bicycle. In short, she was constantly creating crises for her mother. The mother, of course, would explode in resentment at this child who never gave her a moment's peace. When the husband returned from the army and still did not fill the mother's needs, the child interpreted the woman's attempts to escape from the home as further proof that the mother did not love her. As a result, when the sexual abuse started, little Charlotte did not dare tell her mother. Had she been a quiet, soft little girl, the mother might have had a more loving relationship with the child and it would have been far easier for both of them to share their feelings.

Once the sexual incidents started, the father manipulated the little girl — first with bribes and later with dire threats. She lived in constant fear that should she tell anyone, both she and her father would go to jail — a jail he had described to her in terrifyingly exaggerated detail.

Now the child made it even harder for the mother to approach her. Charlotte wished desperately to throw her arms around her mother and ask for help and protection. Yet, when the mother asked her in deep concern why she was so silent and unhappy, the child repulsed the advance with a hardness born out of a desperate attempt to suppress her tears: "I'm all right! Just leave me alone!" And the mother would shrug and wonder at the strange, hard child who was rejecting her at every turn. Overwhelmed by the emotional entrapment at home, Charlotte would not allow the concerned school psychologist to help her. When her visual problem was detected it was presumed to be the cause of her school failure and her depression. The real reason, the emotional turmoil created by the incest, was not suspected. Not until many years later did she have the courage to share her problem — and even after she was able to find caring friends to help it was years before she found ways to remove some of the emotional scars.

All children, in a sense, are prisoners in the home situation into which they were born. Sometimes there is a relative, a friend, a counselor who can rescue a child from an intolerable situation. Charlotte Vale Allen's hyperactivity and later her visual problem did not cause the incestuous situation. These conditions, over which she had absolutely no control, created first her difficult relationship with her mother — who might have helped — then misled the counselors into a wrong diagnosis of her problem, so this avenue of escape was also cut off. As a result, she too was caught in that terrifying isolation, that total sense of neglect which is so devastating for sexually abused children.

In sexual abuse cases it is never the child's fault, although the defense attorneys still try to prove that it is. In Indiana in 1982 a judge released a sexual offender on the basis that the five-year-old victim had acted "seductively!" Apparently the temptation to seduce children is so great that the question of what kind of children are sexually abused has been studied rather carefully and from many psychological aspects. Not very much information is available at this time, because the incest problem has not really been officially recognized until recently, and the causes seem to vary so. However, Robert K. Davies, who is now the medical director at Fair Oaks Hospital in Summit, NJ, studied the medical records of patients who were admitted to the Psychiatric Inpatient Unit of Yale-New Haven Hospital between 1968 and 1977. He was looking at the I.Q. scores and the electro-encephalographs (the brain wave recordings) of 22 patients who had been either the child or the younger member in a case of sexual abuse by a family member.

Of the 22 former victims of incest, Davies found that 17 had an abnormal EEG. This is a 77% incidence compared with a 20% incidence of all the patients admitted to the hospital unit. It compares with estimates of 5% to 30% in the general population. In addition, of 13 subjects tested, 5 showed dull normal I.Q. scores and 7 showed problems in perceptual motor tasks, concrete thinking, and word-finding. Furthermore, impulsive behavior was reported in 18 of the 22 patients, and feelings of unreality (depersonalization) in 12.

The impulsiveness, but especially the depersonalization, may well be a result of the incest, as the children seek a way to escape from the reality of their daily horrifying existence. Davies, however, suggests that these neuropsychiatric handicaps make the children very vulnerable and so increase the chances that someone in the family might take advantage of them. They find it more difficult to resist incestual relationships. He notes that such EEG abnormalities are frequently associated with disturbances in cerebral mechanisms in the temporal and limbic regions of the brain. Disturbances in this part of the brain make the children feel physically insecure and increase their demand for closeness. Given an unhappy marriage or an insecure family situation, the temptation for incest may become too strong, and the father may not be able to resist breaking the taboo.

There seem to be some interesting connections here between the EEG abnormalities and consistent reports of epileptic seizures in teenagers who have been sexually abused. In most cases, there seem to be no brain-wave abnormalities recorded, and the seizures are considered "hysterical," that is, emotionally caused. Some American Indian tribes considered seizures the sure sign that there had been an incestuous relationship. Freud reported similar cases. Which came first, the sexual abuse or the tendency toward epilepsy, is a difficult question to answer.

New techniques of CAT scans can actually show what part of a brain is active when a person with a multiple personality changes from one personality to another. As stated before, sexually abused children tend to escape into another personality to be able to survive the situation. Could these actual changes in brain function cause the seizures?

Are some children more likely to get sexually abused than others? Probably. The soft, the gentle, the more hungry for touch. Usually in the early stages of sexual abuse, contrary to popular misconception, there is no violence involved.

Nevertheless, we are only talking about percentages. A certain number, not all children, are slightly higher at risk. The actual responsibility for the act lies with the adult, not with the child, no matter what the circumstances. Childhood sexuality is totally different from adult sexuality and can in no way be interpreted as actually demanding sexual fulfillment from an adult. It is up to the adult to set the limits.

Are there adults who are more likely to abuse children sexually? Alfred Kinsey was instrumental in arranging for the research which provided the information for the book "Sex Offenders" by Paul Gebhard, John H. Gagnon, Wardell Pomeroy and Celia V. Christenson. While distinct emotional patterns became evident in rapists and exhibitionists, no obvious profile emerged on those who were in jail for incest. Prior sexual abuse of the offender was not in the picture. From this research at least, there was no way found to spot ahead of time someone who might abuse a child incestually. Incest has been considered the vice particular to the poor, but has been found to exist in all strata of society.

Are we making any progress in solving the sexual abuse problem? We are beginning to talk about its existence — that is an enormous step forward. For children and adults who had been abused, we are providing agencies and hot-lines where they can go for help. That is another step. Often when the frightening secret is brought out in the open, the incest victims feel so relieved that out of that feeling of relief they will discontinue therapy. Nevertheless, the scars are not eliminated until the anger and the fear and all the unshed tears have been released.

Psychologists are becoming more aware of the possibility of sexual abuse and will mention such possibility early in the therapy and save much time by letting the patient know that it is all right to discuss the problem.

Hypnosis has been found to be of great value in working with incest victims. Under hypnosis the emotions which were repressed at the time are allowed to be lived out. First the patient relives the experience — as a child — and is allowed to cry the tears that were not shed at the time. All this in a hypnotic trance. Then, when the grief and the fury have been aired, the person is allowed to look at the situation consciously and with adult awareness. It is only then that the incest victim can see objectively what has happened in childhood and decide to discard what has been, in order to live a full life.

If the feelings of love, guilt or anger are not relived, sorted out and finally consciously discarded, often through long and gentle therapy, the adult may experience all kinds of psychosomatic side effects. These symptoms may include headaches, frigidity and tremendous alienation and depression. Suicide attempts, or at least suicidal thoughts, are almost universal in incest victims.

Are we doing anything about the social situation that places children in such grave danger? No, we are not. We are teaching children to be aware of the possibility of unwanted sexual touching. We are starting all kinds of programs which have never been really tested as to their impact. In teaching them that there are "private" zones on their bodies not to be touched, are we also frightening them away from sex altogether?

We don't know. We are teaching the children to say "No" to unwanted touch. That is fine. But that sort of thing should not start in special sex abuse prevention classes, it must start at home. What happens when the child says "No" to Mother and gets slapped in the face? This is a very difficult problem to solve and no child should be taught to say "No" unless the parents are also given counseling.

We are teaching the children to defend themselves. Self defense skills are great, no harm in teaching those. But teaching the child to defend himself against a much stronger and larger adult is ironical and could be even more dangerous for the child than if he did not try to defend himself. We must be careful also to teach them when not to fight!

Where are the hot-lines for the adults who find themselves tempted to use a child sexually? Do sex education classes and pamphlets spell out that you can hurt children, both physically and emotionally, if you attempt any kind of sexual contact? If we teach young people that children are not stupid, that they will not forget, are we simply putting ideas into their heads that children can be used for sex? Our society provides no psychiatric help for potential offenders. We pay attention to them only after the crime has been committed. Are such services too expensive? It costs $80,000 a year to keep the older of the two brothers mentioned earlier in this chapter in an institution. What it costs to undo the damage done to one child could pay for many social services.

We know that unemployment increases child abuse. Yet we refuse to create "make work" programs to take up the slack when the economy is down. The ultimate cost is staggering.

The Institute for the Community as Extended Family in Santa Clara, California is providing an in-depth, professional and self-help treatment program. It has trained professionals to assist children and their families all over the United States. It is a beginning toward solving the problem. But unless we start tackling the basic underlying malaise of the times, such programs will barely make a dent in the underlying problem.

145

Chapter 12

Drug Abuse: The Metabolism Connection

The drug offenders who were being treated by Alfred F. Libby and Irwin Stone in 1977 were no different from other drug addicts all over the world. They were scrawny, they had no appetite, there were raw ulcers on their skin, and their gums were swollen and bleeding. These were very sick people who looked as if they were in the advanced stages of scurvy.

And these were not old men! They were young men in their twenties and early thirties. They had been on drugs for 10, sometimes 20 years. Ten or twenty years! Some of them had started taking drugs when they were only 11 years old. It was marijuana at 11, heroin at 13, 15, 16. These figures were not exceptional. Usually they started with marijuana, alcohol, barbituates, or LSD, or with sniffing glue, paint or gasoline, and later went on to heroin. What had started out as a lark for a weekend high, slowly turned into a daily habit from which they suddenly found they could not escape.

This was the common experience at all the drug detoxification centers. What it meant was this: An 11-year-old had been on marijuana!

We still see kids like this today. They're not even in junior high, smoking with their friends on the farthest side of the schoolyard.

Their voices have not yet changed, and from a distance it is hard to tell if they are boys or girls. If you talk to the principal, you usually get the answer, "Well, there's really nothing we can do about it. Most of them get it from their parents; if not from their parents, from an older brother or sister!"

We're not just talking about inner-city schools or about the schools of the very wealthy, where kids get money from home. Even in small towns, this is the everyday world in which our kids live. You can see those kids smoking a quick one before they go to school in the morning: These are the "stonies". Depending on to which group or subgroup the kids belong, the term is used derisively or as a badge of honor.

The crime rate, because these kids, by hook or by crook, have to make money to support their habit, is of course tremendous. People heaved a big sigh of relief when the nation was told that a drug called methadone would be given legally to drug addicts and that this would result in a great reduction in crime. In some ways, people were thinking only in terms of finances and their own security. Nevertheless, it was a step in the right direction. The addict was no longer being "punished" by a cold-turkey withdrawal period. The concept of the drug fiend was being replaced with the concept of someone who was very ill.

Still, by and large, few people understood what an addict's life was like. Each addict lives on a roller coaster of ups and downs. It is not even that the drugs give him such a tremendous high; it's that, to begin with, he feels so terrible. Some addicts, of course, originally were simply pressured by friends to try the drugs. Once they started, they were dealing not only with the depression from which they might have tried to escape in the first place, but with the additional drug withdrawal crash.

Alcohol withdrawal — the hangover — has its own similar set of symptoms: Hypersensitivity to noise and to light, and nausea. All these symptoms make life more unbearable for a child who is already at odds with the world. Amphetamine withdrawal is even worse. The child wakes up with a feeling of utter despair, from which it is hard to arouse himself to face another day.

Let's presume someone gives an 11-year-old an amphetamine — the kids call it an upper. He's been warned about drug abuse, but this is not drug abuse in his eyes. He's been given a simple little pill, something like the baby aspirin his mother gives him. He is, after all, only 11 years old and, rather than fight his new-found friend who seems to be taking a sudden interest in him, he takes the pill and swallows it. Now he feels great. Suddenly, even if it is the middle of winter, he feels as if it were springtime. He experiences the same delightful excitement as when he knows that his birthday will come the next day. Instead, when that next morning comes, he finds himself sitting in his mother's rocking chair and crying his eyes out. And he doesn't even know why he is so sad! He is only a child and has no way of putting two and two together. He has no way of relating the feeling of despair to the little pill he ate the day before. Besides, maybe he was smart enough to know that he should not have accepted the pill, and so he does not dare tell anyone how he feels.

The effects of alcohol on human beings have been known since almost the beginning of history. Morphine addiction has been seen in the United States since the wounded were given morphine during the Civil War. Heroin addiction has been seen in this country since 1880. Amphetamines became glorified during World War II, when the Germans gave benzedrine to their fighter pilots to give them reportedly "super-human" endurance.

After the war, benzedrine and other amphetamines were freely available, and it was not until some time later that they could be had by prescription only. Students experimented with them, even studied for tests under their influence, not knowing what later experiments showed — that rats who learned very quickly when on amphetamines could no longer remember what they had learned once the drug had worn off. And so the kids flunked their tests in spite of the benzedrine.

By the time amphetamines were put on the "prescribed" list, it was too late — the drugs had gone underground. From amphetamines the kids went on to harder drugs, not even to get back the high, but just to counteract the drug-induced depression they felt. To cut the rising heroin addiction, finally, in the 1960s, methadone was used for drug withdrawal. Those addicts who wanted to quit the rat race of trying to support their addiction turned to a controlled methadone program — only to find that they were becoming equally addicted to that.

What had gone wrong? Libby and Stone explained it this way: On drugs, addicts lose their appetite for food. The less they eat, the more quickly their body becomes deprived of normal amounts of proteins and other nutrients. All the addicts they tested suffered from hypoaminoaciduria, which is an imbalance of the proteins of the body such as doctors find in severe cases of starvation. Libby and Stone discovered something else. The drug addicts seemed to have one thing in common: They suffered from metabolic dysfunction. Without treating this malfunction, most attempts to detoxify them and, what was more important, to keep them off drugs were doomed to failure.

Most humans, unlike most animal species, don't have the ability to make their own vitamin C. (Some few can manufacture their own. Among these were the few who survived on board those ships on which most sailors came down with scurvy.) A certain amount of vitamin C is needed to maintain the chemical balance of the body. When there is stress — on humans or on animals — this balance is upset by the body's mechanism that gets the body ready for fight or flight. If an animal is under stress, it returns quickly to its normal state of health, because it can restore its vitamin C requirements. The human being cannot do that and feels the full impact of the stress. He depends entirely on his diet for the extra vitamin C he needs.

The typical nutrition information we were exposed to in school followed the guidelines of the National Academy of Sciences' National Research Council. The Council recommends that a person needs only one orange a day to get his supply of vitamin C. The attitude is that, if you eat any more than 100 milligram of vitamin C — the equivalent of an orange — then you are wasting money, and the only result is that you have expensive urine.

Libby and Stone found that none of the addicts who came for treatment, though they had been given more vitamin C than the proverbial orange a day would provide, had any spillage of vitamin C in their urine. (They also showed very low amino acids in the urine, which is a sign of starvation.) The results were so consistent that today many detoxification centers no longer even bother to go to the expense of performing these tests.

Interestingly enough, George von Hilsheimer, independently of these studies, writes that of the delinquent children — not addicted, just delinquent children — admitted to his Green Valley school, 99% did not show any spillage of vitamin C. More than 80% did not show any spillage after loading with three grams of vitamin C per day for two weeks. In fact, he states that most of his children do not spill even after six weeks of this additional amount of vitamin C given in divided doses three times a day.

Alexander Schauss, however, in studies with delinquents all over the world, found that giving therapeutic doses of vitamin C with bioflavonoids for one week will eventually allow vitamin C to spill into the urine, which is a sign that the body has begun to saturate its various tissues with this essential nutrient.

The treatment of thirty addicts in a pilot study by Drs. Libby and Stone consisted of giving them increasing amounts of vitamin C just beyond the point at which they developed diarrhea. This point is called bowel tolerance and varies from person to person. After the addicts received vitamin C at that level for two days, the amount was cut down to the point at which the diarrhea symptoms disappeared. Then, after 10 days at this level, which varied but was approximately 45 grams a day, the dosage was reduced to a maintenance level of 10gm a day. In addition, the addict was given predigested protein and a therapeutic vitamin-and-mineral supplement.

Schauss, who worked with addicts during the 1960s and 70s and studied their biochemistry, found that it is possible to detoxify an addict in 10 days and to do so with almost no withdrawal symptoms. He also found, however, that it was better to spread the detoxification procedure over a 21-day period. This extra time permitted the detoxification center to give the addict additional emotional support. Most of the addicts had been on drugs for many years — years during which their one aim in life had been to find a way to get that next fix. It was not sufficient to show addicts that they could feel well even without drugs, they also had to be helped to find new goals for themselves. They needed a new challenge, a reason to stay healthy, in short, they needed something to live for.

One of the advantages of giving vitamin C for detoxification is that if an addict then tries to shoot up, the effect is no greater than if he were shooting water. (The vitamin C can be given in juice. Alexander Schauss recommends that sodium ascorbate, rather than ascorbic acid, be used, because the ascorbate form is less acidic.) Vitamin C in large doses has been found to have a pain-killing effect. Apparently, the vitamin C molecules attach themselves to the opiate receptors in the brain — that is, they fit into the spaces which would normally have been occupied by the molecules of the addictive drug — and so they block the drug's action.

Vitamin C, when used to ease withdrawal, does three things: It blocks the action of the drug, it takes the pain away, and it replenishes the body's exhausted supply of vitamin C. The multivitamin and mineral supplements help reduce and alleviate withdrawal symptoms such as restlessness, hypersensitivity, and cramps. These side effects are often due to subclinical nutritional deficiencies. Rather than forcing an already exhausted human being from one addictive drug to another (as giving methadone), using vitamins for withdrawal purposes helps to build up his health to the point where he is well enough to function. Addicts, so ill that they had no longer been able to eat, were able to do so after three to five days, at which time the frequent protein supplement feedings would be discontinued. There was one added advantage to the therapy: Should the patients, for whatever reason, start getting on drugs again, they would no longer face the terror of a repeated addiction, but would know what to do to pull themselves out of that otherwise hopeless spiral. Schauss has found that many, many street addicts — men and women who never make it to the inside of an official detoxification clinic — have learned this technique, not only by word of mouth, but also from reading his book, "Diet, Crime and Delinquency" (Parker House, 1980).

Parents who normally have no reason to concern themselves with these matters, often stand helplessly by when they see their child caught up in that spiral of ever-increasing deterioration. Even in the early stages, all talk and all warnings will fall on deaf ears. The more parents talk, the more the child will hide what he is doing. There may be a few visible signs until the secondary signs appear: The child starts to steal. He has to have money from somewhere. Even if there are no arrests, no automobile accidents — and usually there are — the child may disappear for a length of time and then return, ill and exhausted. The parents take him back, build him up a little bit and, before they know it, he is back with his old friends and back to taking drugs. The parents feel not only concerned but betrayed and finally they have little choice but to call juvenile hall or to kick him out.

Families in many cities have gotten together to form groups called "Tough Love". They feel that the shape-up-or-ship-out approach is the only way they can save their children who have become involved in drug use. To make such a firm commitment is a very hard step to take and a risky one — sometimes though the only way to stop the child short. The trouble is that you cannot expect the child to shape up, without showing him how. Even the best (and often most expensive) detoxification centers usually make special financial arrangements. There is little time to lose, as brain damage can occur, especially when drink and drugs are mixed.

With what has been learned from the severe cases of addiction, hopefully enough information has been gathered to reverse and even to prevent addiction of other children.

Drs. Libby and Stone have a theory that some humans are born with an error of carbohydrate metabolism which puts them at high risk of becoming addicted. This metabolic error is a liver-enzyme disease: Hypoascorbemia. It prevents the liver from processing vitamin C in our diet in the same way a normal liver would. Already at birth, these children suffer from subclinical scurvy. The disease is asymptomatic — it has no obvious signs — therefore doctors do not recognize it. If this theory is correct, a routine checkup on the vitamin C spillage in the baby's urine should be an inexpensive way to warn the parents that the child will need extra nutritional care.

The amount of vitamin C necessary to prevent scurvy is not the same that it takes to keep an individual feeling really well. The need varies tremendously with each individual. When the amount of vitamin C a person needs has saturated the various tissues of the body, the rest is thrown out with the urine. The point at which this spillage occurs indicates how much vitamin C a person requires. In some people it occurs at 200 milligrams (mg.), some at 2,000mg, while in a few it does not reach that point even at 5,000mg of vitamin C a day. The amount, of course, can vary with the amount of stress a person experiences at any given time.

There is a whole new aspect of nutrition which must be considered. As important as it is to add vitamin C to a child's diet, this should not be a hit-or-miss supplementation. If large amounts of vitamin C have been given for a stretch of time, stopping the vitamin C suddenly may cause scurvy, because the body is used to eliminating much of the vitamin and has to adjust to the lower dosage. If the mother has used too much vitamin C during pregnancy, this may cause scurvy in the newborn unless he also receives additional doses. In a diabetic child, the extra vitamin C may cause wrong readings of the urine tests which determine how much insulin the child needs.

The trick is to find a doctor who is willing to work with the mother to do tests of this kind, because levels vary during the day and during periods of stress. (For information on simple tests, see Appendix, pg. VII)

A whole area of research in preventive medicine is opening up in this field, and there is really no reason why such tests for nutritional deficencies should not be used in the doctor's office as routinely as a yearly diabetes check up. It is certainly a test which would be indicated for the stonies who hang around in small groups, taking a hit on their joints.

Chapter 13

Delinquency: The Genetic Connection

When a child first starts to use drugs, a little here, then a little there, the damage is usually not that severe. At least it is not visible. The parents generally do not suspect it, and so nothing is being done. (PCP, sniffing, or free-basing can cause immediate severe harm, and mixing drugs and drink can have totally unpredictable consequences.) There will probably never be a way of proving it — how do you prove that a child "would have" taken drugs — but at that period of time, even a minimal amount of nutrition therapy might stop the child from getting hooked.

The question of why one child will become addicted and not another, is a fascinating one. Some children, of course, will just experiment along with the others and get hooked. The child who intentionally seeks drugs is obviously not content with his normal state of feeling. He needs to run away from the routine, the restlessness, the depression.

Depression in childhood has been studied only in recent years. It was presumed that healthy children are happy and elated, and adults were supposed to be neutral. Actually, normal children have tremendous emotional ups and downs; much more so than adults do. They laugh easily, they cry easily. During certain periods of their lives, they seem to be more weepy than during others, and these mood swings occur at the same age period over the entire range of the population.

Psychologists, then, have been faced with the problem of defining just what is a truly depressed child. The main answer, they believe, is that a depressed child is one who is increasingly unable to enjoy certain kinds of pleasure. The child who seems to react neither to joy nor to unpleasantness is the one who's in trouble.

To escape this kind of "nothingness", the youngster will tend to "act out." To "act out" is the psychologist's way of saying the child misbehaves. The subconscious imagery of this expression is very much to the point. The instinctive human drive is to explore and to experience. The inner drive seems to be that once a skill has been mastered, there is an urge to learn something new; that once a feeling has been experienced, another one needs to be explored. The child, whether to escape hurt or to avoid being overwhelmed by his own anger, may have taught himself not to feel anything. The need to feel, however, is still there, and so, to break out of the terror of nothingness, the child "acts out." He breaks the laws for the thrill of it. He uses drugs to get the "high" he can no longer achieve. Before long, he is in trouble with the law and finds himself behind bars. (Suicidal thinking and actual suicide behind bars is far beyond any normal expectation.)

What many of the recent studies on depression do not take into consideration, are the physical health factors involved. As a result, the picture we are getting from the psychologists is not really complete. Psychologists do take into consideration that there is justified depression, such as after the loss of a loved one, or after abuse. The "justifiably depressed" persons, those who have good reason to be sad, are distinguished from those they call "clinically depressed."

Actually, what the psychologist sees as "clinical" may be a case of long-standing depression. An infant monkey removed from his mother shows actual changes in his brain chemistry. This change in the brain causes "nonaffective" reaction in the little monkey — that is, he has no emotional changes to either good or bad situations. These are the same symptoms which the psychologists describe as childhood depression. (It is the same kind of flat reaction — that seeming noninvolvement in life — that is seen often in snipers, whose anger suddenly explodes in utter violence.)

155

We are on the verge of great discoveries in these areas. Some of these discoveries come from a test developed by Bernard J. Carol. He found, as a result of many studies, that if a person has a "depressive" personality, when you give that person dexamethesone at night, the cortisol level in the blood is no different from what it was the night before. In a person who may have other problems but who is not depressed, the cortisol level in the blood and in the urine is lowered. The test has been used to tell a doctor whether a patient is depressed, manic depressive or might be sad for a specific reason. This knowledge then helps the doctors decide how to treat the patient.

Another fact which emerged as a result of these studies is that the tendency toward depression is often inherited. Bernard J. Carol found that people who show a lack of cortisol suppression when dexamethesone is given, tended to have someone in the immediate family with some kind of manic, depressive, or otherwise antisocial behavior. The researchers even found the gene that is the carrier of the trait. They named it P.C. Duarte, in honor of the city where it was found. Shortly after, the University of Rochester and University of Toronto reported that they had found the genetic marker in the DNA that indicates a tendency toward depressive illness. (Now remember: This is only a tendency. If the genetic influence occurs on both sides of the family, the tendency, of course, is stronger.)

Since we already know that alcohol problems, diabetes, and hypoglycemia — all illnesses relating to adrenal malfunction — tend to run in families, this should not come as a surprise. People do not like to admit there was a black sheep in the family. Doctors can't always rely on what is being told to them, but parents should be alert if there is such a history in the family. That doesn't mean the child should be told he's turning out to be just like Uncle Charlie, but it does mean the child's nutrition must be watched especially carefully and that he should be protected a little more from frustration than other children.

Of even greater importance, especially in the way we treat those kids who have become caught in drug abuse, is another discovery. The patients tested by Bernard J. Carol had also been given antidepressive drugs. Whether they were given those drugs or not, there was no difference in the result of the dexamethesone suppression test — the cortisol level still remained high in the morning. This indicated that the drugs, though they may have improved the mood of the patient, did not affect the underlying cause of the depression. As a result, the scientists searched further and deducted that this type of depression was related to a dysfunction in the pituitary-hypothalamic-adrenal axis. When that function became normal, the depression was also gone.

While the scientists still do not fully understand depressive illness, this research has led to a new approach in helping the children who become addicted.

One of the reasons these matters are so complicated is that our bodies are run, not simply in a mechanical way (the way, for instance our muscles move our arms and legs), but are controlled by constantly varying chemical interchanges. These interchanges occur in simple ways in our digestive system. The adrenal glands' function is far more complicated. They receive their messages not only through direct nerve stimulation, but also through chemical stimulation. The adrenals make at least six separate chemicals — probably more — and these are being studied at present. We know some of their functions, which are aimed at specific areas in the body. There is a constant change and fluctuation of the amount and the kind of chemicals which they release. Just which one is released depends on the amount of other chemicals present in the blood at the time. If one goes up, another goes down.

Dexamethesone (another name for cortisone) is a hormone from the adrenal cortex. Cortisol, another such hormone, is the stuff that gives you "butterflies" when you are about to make a speech. Once you get on the podium, you are suddenly very calm: Another hormone, adrenalin, has just readjusted the chemical balance of your body. Theoretically, giving dexamethesone should lower the amount of cortisol in the blood. If this does not happen, we know there is something amiss in the way the chemical messages are sent or received.

The adrenals affect the pituitary gland and, in another way, the pituitary gland stimulates the adrenals. The pituitary is also controlled by the hypothalamus, which is part of the limbic system in the brain. This is why the scientists link depressive illness not just to the adrenals, but to the entire pituitary-hypothalamic-adrenal axis.

The hypothalamus is the part of the brain — part of the limbic system — against which incoming messages are checked to see how a person should react.

The difference illustrated in the famous joke about the optimistic and the pessimistic child occurs in this part of the brain: The pessimistic child was put in a room full of wonderful toys and games

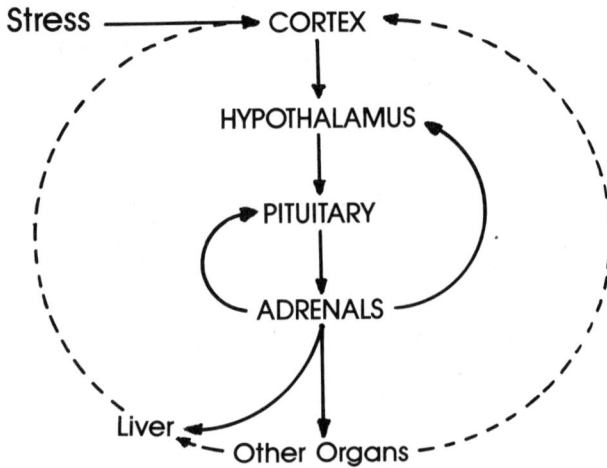

Malfunction of the self-balancing chemical control of the hypothalamic-pituitary function can make a child experience stress in situations where no stress is felt by a healthy child.

and was left there alone for a while. At the same time, the optimistic one was put in a room full of horse manure. An hour later, the first little fellow, in spite of all the beautiful toys, was sitting in a corner pouting. When asked why he was so depressed, he answered, "Well, what's the use of playing with this stuff? Someone will come and take it away sooner or later." The child in the room full of manure, however, was found whistling and singing and shoveling the stuff around with great good humor. When asked why he was so happy, he said cheerfully, "Well, with all this shit, there must be a pony somewhere!"

One child's hypothalamus reacted with the information already stored from prior experience with "Terrible situation, something will go wrong any minute!" The other's hypothalamus computed "Fantastic! Something good is about to happen!"

Each child's hypothalamus sends it electrical message to the pituitary which, in turn, squirts out a different chemical to stimulate the adrenals of the child. The reaction of each child is different, because the adrenals control the amount of sugar — through the liver — which is released into the blood. This in turn affects the function of the brain, and we get into a spiral of cause and effect: The amount of sugar or the lack of it in the brain affects the function of the brain and causes further changes in how the child thinks. And this thinking, in turn, reaffects the hypothalamus.

After a while, it becomes hard to tell which came first — outside circumstances or the distorted kind of thinking caused by lack of sugar in the brain. (With the new brain-scanning techniques, this too has been confirmed to happen in depressed persons.) It is easy to see that if, because of outside circumstances, the hypothalamus keeps receiving messages which indicate constant disappointment, the entire system gets overworked and things get out of kilter. As if all of this were not complicated enough, it has been found, during the last decade or so, that the brain is not, as believed earlier, just a network of electrical way stations. It is also a gland in its own right: It manufactures chemicals like the other glands in the body. There is enough information for an entire book — several books.

Now, what does all this mean to someone dealing with an addicted youngster? Just knowing there are genetic tendencies toward depression will change a counselor's attitude. The dexamethesone suppression test is not totally reliable in cases of mild depression and need not be given. But an awareness of the lessons learned through the study of this test is very important. A family history might in some instances give some clues, but can not be relied upon for accuracy, and might frighten the family and the child because they might believe they are destined for problems and live out a self-fulfilling prophecy. All these new discoveries, all these complicated studies give the counselor one advantage: He need no longer make emotional judgments about the morality of the addict. He can simply go on the assumption that there are underlying metabolic factors involved and then go ahead and see what can be done about treating these.

Dr. Janice Phelps, a pediatrician in Seattle, does just that. She has taken this recent research to help the addicted children and young people with whom she deals. Since much of the addiction is a flight from depression, she not only treats the withdrawal symptoms, but keeps the child from going back to drugs by treating the underlying depression which caused the child to run to drugs in the first place.

Dr. Phelps describes this kind of depression as "adrenal exhaustion syndrome." When an addicted child is brought to her, she first gets him through the withdrawal period. She gives some methadone, but only for the first three days. At the same time, from the first moment on, she starts to build up the body. She gives massive doses of vitamin C, though not as much as Libby and Stone used in their pilot study. She gives vitamins and minerals and insists that all sugar and refined carbohydrates be eliminated from the diet. In addition to this, she takes into consideration the kind of adrenal-pituitary-hypothalamic problems the addictive persons tend to share: She gives adrenal hormones, and support for the thyroid and pituitary glands.

In 10 days the withdrawal period is over, but the child continues to receive nutritional support, though on lower doses. As a result of the body's equilibrium being restored so quickly, none of the addicts had to take methadone for more than three days and therefore did not become dependent on the methadone. Within a short time, the addict is back to normal health, without the constant craving which other former addicts have to endure.

The ex-addict will have to be fairly strict about the kind of food he eats, but that is a vast improvement over having to depend on a drug like methadone for the rest of one's life. Unlike a drug, which creates a physical dependency, this form of nutritional treatment helps heal the body. Even the hormone system will become healed to the point where its normal balance is restored. A day, a week, even an occasional month without the vitamins or hormonal support will not start a return of the craving.

It must be remembered that the adrenal exhaustion syndrome can be caused purely by stress. In the child with an inherited tendency toward depression, the point at which the stress will trigger the depression simply is reached far sooner.

When a child, for whatever reason, has become caught in the drug trap, nutritional support is absolutely necessary to break the hold of the craving. Otherwise, once the child has reached this stage of depression and is "acting out", no change of surroundings, no amount of counseling will help. Children at this stage "flunk" foster homes. Their behavior is such that no one wants to put up with them. (Nutrition in foster homes is notoriously bad.)

Once the child feels better physically, he becomes more approachable, and his behavior can be changed. No moral judgments have been made. The young person has become master of his own life again. He does not have to think of himself as weak or evil. He has a metabolic problem, which he himself can keep in check.

There is still need for a further prescription. It's a prescription for some love and laughter; for hard, meaningful work; and for occasional wild excitement. These are the messages which will help the hypothalamus give the right instructions to the pituitary and through those to the adrenals to keep the body functions properly balanced. The messages which come from the brain must be positive and satisfying!

If at all possible, the root cause for the stress which caused the depression must be found. If the problem was related to learning disabilities, these must be cured. If it related to sexual abuse, the child must be protected and receive emotional therapy. If the problem was otherwise family related, there must be some family counseling.

Even if we are able to restore the health of the child who had been addicted, we cannot expect the family to take the child back with open arms. Apart from mistrust, there is a huge backlog of anger. The parents have experienced great anxiety and frustration because of the child's behavior, but they usually also feel great guilt that they might have done something to contribute to the problem. As a result, no matter how much relief is felt that the child is now well, there is great resentment.

Just explaining the metabolic connnection to the family, and especially to the child, will take the element of despair and guilt out of the entire threatening situation. Since there tends to be a genetic influence involved, both parent and child must face the fact that there is a possibility of relapse and both must be taught how to guard against it. Both parent and child must be allowd to vent some of the accumulated anger — in the presence of a protective, impartial counselor. A good relationship at home is important also to maintain a good metabolic balance.

If you look at only one part of the child's body, only one part of the child's life, you see only one aspect of the problem. That's why it is so important for all the different experts to get together and share what they have found. It would be wonderful if we could order a prescription from the pharmacy not only for vitamins, but also for laughter, and for quiet happiness, for excitement and for relaxation. We can only hope that once the child is back on his feet, he will be able to find his own way to get these — without having to break any laws.

SECTION   II

JUST GROWING UP

Chapter 14

The Developmental Connection:

"I was an insufferable child.

All children are perfectly insufferable."

—George Bernard Shaw

Not all children are perfectly insufferable, but all children do go through some perfectly horrible stages. As a matter of fact, I could not think of anything more dreadful than a child who is always perfectly angelic.

In our neighborhood, there was a little girl who was so perfect that if the rest of us mothers had a problem with our children, we would go to the mother of that perfect little girl for advice. That woman was practically a legend in her time and seemed to have answers for everything. There was, however, one occurrence which shook everybody's faith in her methods. When her second child, a little boy, was born, there was nothing she could do with him. The child was a veritable little devil, and even a year of child therapy at UCLA failed to change the child's disposition.

I'm convinced that every mother on the block experienced some small satisfaction that the lady was not infallible. I'm also ashamed to say that while I felt sorry for that little boy, I was delighted that I no longer needed to compete with that woman's mothering. As a matter of fact, I can picture no sweeter revenge than this scene: The friend who used to cluck disapprovingly when your three-year-old threw a tantrum while her infant still cooed peacefully in her arms, now stands helplessly by as hers, now also three years old, lies screaming and kicking on the floor. That is poetic justice!

No matter what you do, most one-year-olds will try to take a bite out of you, most two-year-olds will kick you, three-year-olds will throw a tantrum or two, and you can almost bet, that the four year old will call you dirty names. The stages of bad behavior a child will exhibit are so predictable that it is a good thing nature built parental love into our subconscious, or there would be even more child abuse.

Today, when men and women are beginning to share equally in the raising of children, it might be a good idea to have "Child Development" as a required subject in high school. It is appalling how very few people know anything about the subject; at times, it seems as if we were still in the Dark Ages.

In April, 1980, in Salem, Oregon, 31-year-old Clifford Stein beat and starved his 15-months-old son, David, because the child would not keep his eyes closed during evening prayers. In court, Stein testified that his son finally died on May 5, after being beaten with a willow switch for 45 minutes — every two or three hours — from noon to midnight that day. For the last two weeks of David's life, Stein said, he confined the child in a bedroom and would allow him only water.

At the age of 15 months, children, unless they are asleep, are unable to keep their eyes closed for any great length of time.

Also in May, 1980, not two hours by car from Salem, a social worker went to check on how a young couple was getting along with their newly adopted infant. She found, to her horror, the mother was beating the six-month-old infant with a willow switch! When the social worker suggested a different way to handle the situation that had brought on the punishment, the mother listened patiently. Then, just as patiently, she explained that, according to material given her by her church, it was "God's will" that the child be taught immediate obedience to her parents.

She then showed the social worker a copy of an article entitled "Why Daddy Likes to Come Home from Work". It seems that Daddy likes to come home from work because his children obey instantly. If they do not mind on the first command, they are beaten with a switch and told that God wants Mommy or Daddy to punish them if they do not obey. After the beating, they are comforted, and presumably, from then on, they will be nice, God-loving children. the author of this piece of literature tells of a time when their three-year-old daughter had misbehaved during dinner, but the parents had been lenient and did not punish her. The parents later repented that they had not followed God's command. So they woke the three-year-old out of her sleep, explained to her why she was about to be hit, spanked her, comforted her, and put her back to bed.

I have no word for such insanity. It boggles the mind. Presumably, this kind of training teaches the child to obey quickly, and, as a result, there will not be any constant nagging or more violent blowups later.

This was —I hope— a misconstrued version of James Dobson's theories of raising children, which he detailed in a book called "Dare to Discipline." Dobson suggests, among other things, that you do not spank the child with your hand, because otherwise the child might flinch every time you lifted your hand! Use a belt or a willow switch instead!

(A recent study of 11 murderers showed that each one of them had been beaten by a parent with some implement such as a rope, a piece of wood, or a belt!)

Actually, apart from the viciousness of hitting a child with an object, this business of spanking a child and then routinely comforting him afterwards sets up a beautiful sado-masochistic pattern: "After I am hurt, I will be loved." In addition, this rigid adherence to immediate obedience does not take into account human fallibility.

I have seen this sort of thing at a department store. A young mother was driving two little boys around in a shopping cart. It was one of those small shopping baskets, designed to go through the narrow aisles of a crowded store. Both these little fellows waited quietly and patiently while the mother picked her way through racks of clothes. Somehow, we kept meeting each other, off and on, during a shopping spree which lasted almost an hour. Finally, as the mother started her way past the checkout counter, the older child, not yet five years old, started getting restless. She told him to sit down. He did, but then he got right up again. She immediately took him out of the cart, put him over her knee, ordered him to put his legs down, and proceeded to spank him. Other customers looked on, presumably pleased with the fact that these were well-behaved children whose mother knew how to keep them in line. What they did not realize, was that this little fellow had been sitting in a wire cage for almost an hour! An adult would not be able to accomplish that feat, much less a little boy, whose legs need moving and stretching!

This kind of rigid demand for compliance also does not take into account the fragility of the human child. An illness or a cold can affect a child's hearing, and he may not have heard. More often, children become so deeply involved in what they are doing or thinking that they do not hear what goes on around them.

Even more, these simplistic concepts do not take into consideration the common lack of knowledge as to just what to expect of a child at any given age! It seems that a list of expected behavior patterns during a child's growth should be handed to every new mother as she leaves the hospital. From 50 years of observation done by the Gesell Institute for Human Development, we know pretty well what to expect at each age, both the good and the bad behavior. Their findings have been backed up by other child research all over the world.

Under the auspices of the Los Angeles Adult Education Department, parents and their preschoolers used to meet in the parks for special child development classes. At first, the mothers observed while the teacher played with the children. Then, while someone baby-sat, the mothers met with the teacher to discuss problems and to learn the rudiments of child raising.

I shall forever love our teacher, Elizabeth Alexander. At the beginning of the class, I went to her and groaned, "I thought I was a good mother, until he turned three!" She gave me a warm, mischievous smile and said only this: "Wait, it gets worse!"

(Actually, three and a half is the more difficult period in a child's life. Mine must have been a little advanced!)

Mrs. Alexander taught us some of the findings of the Gesell Institute. A child goes through various predictable phases of equilibrium and disequilibrium. The newborn infant, for instance, exhibits certain kinds of behavior which are extinguished after about 10 days. He will make walking movements when held up. He can swipe quite accurately at a target object. He can hang on to a finger or to a stick to support his own weight, and he can, quite accurately, mimic some expressions on his mother's face. All these skills will then go underground, so to speak, for a time and will not emerge again for several months to a year later. It is now believed this same "going underground" may be true for most behavior and as well for social skills.

After the child has matured to an advanced form of behavior, he seems to slide back to a more babyish form of dealing with people. As a result, just when you are patting yourself on the back as to what a wonderful job you have done, raising such a perfect youngster, who smiles and is pleasant and generally seems to be able to cope, look out: There comes another phase!

Since this is not a book on child development, I cannot go through all the phases of development; I will deal only with some general principles. (There are behavioral charts from the Gesell Institute in Part VII of the Appendix which show just how predictable some of this behavior actually is.) This chapter will deal with those behaviors that, statistically, have been known to cause the greatest number of abuse incidents. It would be wonderful to have a simple answer for every situation that has you tearing your hair and wondering if there isn't some way to send him back where he came from. It's not that easy.

What I wanted to teach my child is not necessarily what you want to teach yours. What he needs to be taught depends on the society into which he is being raised and in which he will have to cope.

If the following pages seem a little haphazard, so is child raising. No two children are exactly alike. Not only that, but each child is constantly changing. During the first few weeks, you can see this easily. Every time the infant wakes up, he seems to see a little more, do a little more. As he gets older, the changes happen at longer intervals. First every few months or so; later, every half-year, and still later, the changes occur year by year. Sometimes, the child seems to be one thing one day and something totally different the next. Curiously enough, within these changes, each child maintains his own personality.

Not only does the child change, but so do you. What seems to bother you terribly one year may seem totally unimportant the next. Glenn Doman says that to love a child is to enjoy a child. If you enjoy having him around, he feels loved. And so, for his sake as well as your own, you will have to set some limits to his behavior so that you can enjoy being with the child.

If in the next few pages you can find a few ideas you can use, that's great! If not, try something else, and maybe by that time the

child might have passed on into a smoother phase, and, for a while
— that is until he reaches the next stage of development — you may
have a model child on your hands!

Reprinted from *Hi Mom! Hi Dad!* © 1977 by Lynn Johnston,
with permission from Meadowbrook Press.

Crying

"How can there be a baby with no cryin'?" goes the song, and
yet more children are murdered and battered because they cry! The
papers are full of horror stories of infants thrown against a wall,
tossed out the window, and "tranquilized" to death.

Dr. Benjamin Spock, whose book has been the bible for mothers
during the last 40 or so years, states that there is usually much
evening crying from the infant's third to sixth months. The question
is, always, just what is "usual?" If the child shows a great deal of
fussiness, is it normal or is there some other problem needing further
attention? If a child seems to cry too much, the doctor might
prescribe a few drops of phenobarbital, and that's it. Far too often
this does not work, and the baby continues crying.

There may be many reasons why some babies wail constantly,
but somehow the neighbors always seem to blame the mother.
"What kind of a mother is that! There must be something wrong!"
Colicky infants are exhausting, and the causes for the colic vary

tremendously. If the mother breastfeeds, it could be an allergy to something the mother ate and that affects her milk. There might be extra emotional tension in the home, to which the baby is reacting. Possibly the house is too cold. There is a recent theory that if the crib is too cold, the baby cries instinctively, because the crying helps raise his temperature and insures his survival. (Prewarming the bed with a hot-water bottle might help.) Yet for years, mothers have been told to let the baby cry it out, because otherwise they might spoil the child.

Many factors interact. The baby might have inherited the mother's hypoglycemia, and that usually means there are other nutritional deficiencies involved. Some of the many other possibilities are described in Chapter 1.

As the child gets a little older, he will cry when he is frustrated. He does not have the adult self-control that you barely manage in moments like these. He's only three and has few polite ways to tell you he is unhappy. So, hang on to him anyway and let him scream out his rage and frustration. It shows him you understand and accept how he feels, even when you can't give him what he wants. At that stage he is usually quite easily distracted, and if you draw his attention to something else, the storm will blow over.

This sort of screaming is quite easy to take compared to what is to follow at age four, when screaming gives way to whining — and that stage is enough to make anyone's hair curl.

Whining is somewhere between crying and demanding. It is actually one step advanced from just crying. It will go on for anywhere from one to two years and demands almost superhuman self-control from those in charge of the child. If ever there was a child who is courting disaster, it's the whining child! The weird part is that all the threats in the world will not stop the whining. It finally yields to the griping stage, which is quite tolerable, but in the meantime, when he whines, try giving a name to his needs: "You are angry and tired, and you want your own way. I can't give you what you want, but maybe we can do something else that makes you feel better. Any ideas?" This does not spoil the child; it helps him get a little faster to a later stage, during which he can cope better.

There are endless variations: "It sounds to me like you're at the end of your rope. Need a hug?" Or: "I have a feeling you need a little attention, but I'm busy right now. Here, sit next to me at the table and help me with...!" This entitles you to a "Supermother" star and, if it works, keeps you from going crazy.

If it doesn't do the trick and the whining gets worse, perhaps the child does not feel well. If you continue to give names to his feelings, though, before long he can tell you if his ears hurt, or his teeth, or perhaps that his pants are too tight. Hang in there — before long he will have moved out of this phase and — after a little respite where he seems quite mature — into the next problem!

While there is no reason to give in every time a child cries, don't feel that he should not be comforted. Sometimes, however, the child does not want to be comforted and needs to fight the problem out by himself. If he knows that you will not laugh at him, call him a crybaby, or otherwise berate him for babyish behavior, he is more likely to show up for comforting after he has weathered the storm.

Crying is not something one does for the fun of it, nevertheless, we tend to feel the child cries to spite us, or to annoy us, or to get his way. There is a definite reason for crying, or it would not be part of the human mechanism. Crying helps to establish a new chemical balance in the body. Recent research shows that tears which are wept when we peel an onion have a different consistency from the ones we cry when we are sad. This indicates tears are a way of getting rid of some waste products that are created when the body is under tension.

When you are sad, your throat seems to restrict, often very painfully, until the tears finally come. There is much need for research in this direction. When a child is not allowed to cry, the effort of keeping from crying creates terrific tension in the child, and that tension, in return, causes further physical and emotional problems. It is amazing how quickly tears seem to dry up when the child is encouraged to cry it out. Tell him not to cry, and the crying gets stronger and more desperate. (It is an old actor's trick that when an actor wants to cry, he will tell himself, "I am not going to cry!" and, before long, the tears come!)

The need to cry never really goes away. It remains all through life. Small tensions will build up and cause terrible depression if there is not a release through crying at certain intervals. This accounts for the extraordinary demand for sad movies or plays, to which one can go to cry and let out a great deal of sadness without being socially ostracized. It accounts for the great popularity of spectator sports, where thousands of people can go and scream and yell to their heart's content. But there will be a great deal less of unspent tears and screams and yells which need to be screamed in

169

later life if you can tolerate your child's tears and your child's anger.

It is one of the great tragedies in juvenile detention centers that there is really no place for the children to cry it out. Crying is not "cool." Besides, crying really does not do much good unless there is someone to hold and comfort you.

If you can teach your child not to be afraid of crying, now, or as an adult, you will have saved him many problems!

> *"We got married yesterday!*
> *. . .and NYA, NYA, NAA. . .*
> *I didn't suck my thumb!!!"*
> (Inscription on a greeting card)

Thumb Sucking

Surprisingly, a great deal of abuse, both physical and emotional, centers around thumbsucking. Surprisingly, because if you let the child suck, he will eventually stop of his own accord.

We have become a little more enlightened and tolerant of thumbsucking in the last 40 years or so. It is not so long ago that in order to break — even infants — of sucking their thumbs, mothers did horrible things to their children. Some used devices as simple as cardboard tubes into which the baby's arms were tucked at night; they prevented him from being able to bend his elbows and so to find his thumb. Metal prongs were fitted on the thumbs to make sucking painful. Even if the hands were just wrapped in heavy bandages, I don't understand how the mothers could listen to the babies' heartbroken cries when they could not find their comfort!

Thumbsucking is such a fundamental urge that some children suck their thumb even before they are born. The urge to suck is part of the survival reflex. The baby would not survive if he could not nurse or drink his bottle.

As a result, sucking has become associated with the pleasurable feeling of drinking. And so if things go wrong in a child's life, if mother just keeps talking on the phone and is paying no attention to him, he learns to go back to his thumb to console himself. Somehow, then, we see that if a child over three years old is sucking his thumb, we wonder why the child is so unhappy. It's as if he were carrying his sadness around for all the world to see. And so a thumb-sucking child becomes a sort of threat to the mother.

If an infant has been allowed plenty of sucking, chances are he will give up the habit without any great effort and in due time. The less fuss made about it the better. If, however, the whole thing bothers you, and you have to fight the urge to yank the thumb out of his mouth, you might tell him gently that he is, after all, a big boy now, and he will suck his thumb less and less.

During the withdrawal period, provide him with lots of chances to get satisfaction through the sensations he gets in and around his mouth. Foods that require lots of chewing, such as a crust of bread or some bagels, are wonderful for that. He's probably too young for peanut butter, but he may like a piece of mild apple like Golden Delicious. Don't be surprised if much of the food seems to end up on the child's face. Young children have tastebuds on the outside of their mouth around the lips. These become less sensitive as he becomes an adult.

In addition to giving foods that let him suck and chew, you can provide what is known as trigeminal stimulation.

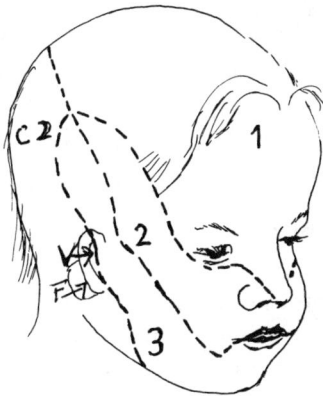

Dermatomes of the head are enervated by the trigeminal nerve, so called because it has three branches. Head sensations are sent through the trigeminal nerve, and in the area of the outer ear by the vagus and facial nerve.

The trigeminal nerve has three main branches: Under the chin, under the cheeks, and over the eyes. Stroke these areas — first very gently, then with a deeper pressure. Do this a few minutes at a time, two or three times a day. Wash his face, first with a warm washrag, then with a cold one. Also gently stroke and rub his lips and the area just around them. This will satisfy his need for oral stimulation and, within a few weeks, the thumbsucking should stop, or at least, become a very rare occurrence.

Reprinted from *Do They Ever Grow Up?* 1978 by Lynn Johnston, with permission from Meadowbrook Press.

Exploration Phase

The most dangerous period for a child who has potentially abusive parents is the time between two and four years. During the first year, the child does not move around very much, and after the fourth year, he manages to manipulate the parents somehow or to get out of the way. Actually, starting about the middle of his second year, the child presents a whole new set of problems to the parents. The toddler is suddenly a mobile little thing, with a will of his own, they can no longer pick him up and just set him down where they want him to be. He has discovered the world and is determined to explore it.

Delacato says, "Man is a hunter, a hunter for new sensations!" and as the child seeks his place in the world, the parent has to stand between the child and all the dangerous situations into which he seems to propel himself with uncanny speed.

The frustration of the parents is understandable, but I am appalled by how many parents discipline their children by slapping their hands when they touch something forbidden! Children overlearn easily. Not only do they learn it is not all right to touch the vase on the table, they also learn it is not all right to reach out and to explore. After all, the child does not know the vase can break, the window curtains will pull off the rod, and the garbage is meant to stay in the can. All he hears is "no" and he feels a sharp sting on the hand.

From this he deducts that hands should not be used to explore, and from that, logically, that one should not explore anything. This may have been a very good lesson when people lived under a tyranny of sorts and life was great if you just kept quiet and did not rock the boat. It does not make for a creative human being who lives in a democracy, where the government needs constant care and challenge to survive.

Will the child go through life touching everything in sight if you do not stop him now? Of course not! Once the child has learned what a smooth glass vase feels like, he will be able to tell with his eyes what it is and will no longer have to touch it. At the explorer stage of development, it is easier to make the house "childproof." If necessary, remove the child physically from the danger spot while you say, "No, you are not allowed to touch that." At this point, someone will object: "Ah, but you have to stop the child from touching the stove, or the hot tea kettle!"

At the hospitals, more child abuse incidents come to light in which a parent had deliberately burnt a child "to teach him not to get burned." I had a 90-year-old friend, whose eyes still brimmed with tears when she told how her "loving" mother once held her little hand against the teapot and burnt her fingers so that she had blisters on them. All this to teach her to stay away! It did not teach the child that tea kettles are hot; it taught her that her mother would deliberately hurt her!

It is amazing how quickly a child can learn to be careful. Gently show him how to approach a stove or a hot tea kettle — very, very, slowly, to see if it is hot. That way, the child can depend on his own reflexes to draw back when it gets too hot. After all, the tea kettle is not always hot, the stove not always turned on.

What you want to do in the long run is, (1) keep the child safe, and, (2) teach the child to explore with caution. Generally speaking, then, have only safe things around, or things you do not mind having broken. After all, children must learn that things not handled gently do break.

If the child continues to get into trouble, look for unsuspected sensory problems. Can the child feel hot or cold? Does he understand your warnings, or, if he reacts, does he react to the tone of your voice but not to what you are actually saying? Does he not see well, so he has to touch more than once or twice to "see" with his hands? Many of the possible problems, how to discover them, and how to handle them are discussed in Chapter 5.

Toilet Training

There is a picture book for children showing respected members of the community— a postman, a lawyer, a doctor (a woman doctor!), Grandma, a gardener, a fireman, and many more — all happily sitting on the toilet seat. Shocking? No. It's a superb little book, half of it written for the parent, the other half for the child. It's Allison Mack's "Toilet Learning!"

"Toilet learning" is an alien concept in our culture. It seems we "teach" our children everything except going to the bathroom. That, we "train" them to do, as if they were some species of wild animal.

It is not surprising that of the very young abused children who end up in the hospitals, 50% turn up there because of incidents related to toilet training. What is this thing about dirty diapers that creates such violent anger?

As in other areas of child raising, often the abuse and violence is simply a repetition of what the parents have experienced in their own childhood. But there seems to be more to it than that. Experiments have been made recently to see how smells affect emotions. One of the smells which arouse violent anger is the smell of urine. Again, whether this is innate (part of our animal heritage) or related to having been abused during toilet training is not entirely clear yet. It could be either.

There are facts concerning our reaction to the smell of a child's feces that make me believe it may well be an instinctive, not a learned, reaction. When I was still very young, I had many baby sitting jobs which included changing a child's diapers, and I certainly did not relish the chore. When I finally had my own child, the smell of his bowel movements caused absolutely no revulsion in me. What caught me completely by surprise, however, was that one day, when I volunteered to change the diaper of a neighbor's child, the smell almost made me throw up. Suddenly, I could understand the anger of the caretakers and the abuse with which generations and generations of children were toilet trained — there is that word again!

Reprinted from *Hi Mom! Hi Dad!* © 1977 by Lynn Johnston, with permission from Meadowbrook Press.

Generations after generations of Europeans and well-to-do Americans were brought up by strangers — Nannies, or some young girl who had been given the job of looking after the baby.

With today's economic demands, we are experiencing a repetition of this tragedy. If a mother has to go out to work, the child is cared for by a stranger, to whom this smelly business of changing a diaper becomes a revolting procedure. Suppressed anger can cause abrupt movements when the child is being handled, and toddlers and, especially, infants are very fragile creatures. It does not take much to cause them pain, or even to dislocate a joint.

When every diaper still had to be washed by hand, it was very important to toilet train a child as early as possible. Today, there are diaper services and disposable diapers, and, of course, washing machines. So, theoretically, it should not matter too much whether a child is toilet trained a few months sooner or later. But old cultural pressures still hang on, and it seems important to comply with the standards of neighbors or relatives.

Having a back yard where a child's wet training pants can drip safely on the ground, would take a great deal of tension out of toilet training. Unfortunately, if a family lives in a tenement and can't afford a diaper service, teaching a child to stay dry becomes more urgent. If a child lives in a fancy home, with thousand-dollar rugs and expensive furniture, and is being raised by a nurse who risks being fired if the baby should soil the furniture, his "accidents" can also trigger a catastrophe!

To a very young mother, the six months or so during which there are toilet problems may seem like an eternity. This does not make for easy toilet training of a toddler. It helps if the mother is in her thirties, when she knows that in another year she will have forgotten completely what all the fuss was about and won't even remember what it was like to change a diaper! At that age, "future" time has already lost some of its terrors, and the present goes by much too fast. It is easier at that stage to be philosophical about giving the child some more time to learn to go to the bathroom by himself.

One of the tragedies of today's life styles is that if the mother is not at home with the child 24 hours a day, she cannot learn to read the child's signs indicating he is ready to learn to go to the bathroom.

It is fairly easy to see when an infant has to have a bowel movement. He gets red in the face, starts to push and grunt. When that happens, many mothers find it convenient to place him on a potty seat and so save a diaper. This practice, admirable as it seems to the mother-in-law and to the neighbors, may actually slow down later toilet training. The training that has been achieved so far was mother's doing, not the child's. When the child later has accidents, the mother is outraged and believes the child dirtied himself on purpose. This, then, becomes an even more emotion-charged situation for her, because we have been taught by the psychologists that if a child wets himself or smears his feces, this is a form of aggression against the mother. While this may be the case in some rare instances, I find the concept rather ludicrous. What is far more likely is this: the infant has learned that when he wets, mother shows up to change his diapers. If he moves his bowels, even more attention is forthcoming. This is something which occurs long before the child can make any deliberate decisions, even before he can consciously control his body processes! In Germany the common folkname for what is called "peepee" in this country is "ein kleiner Wunsch" — a small wish! What we call "potty" or "BM" is called "ein grosser Wunsch" — a big wish! Both processes are a natural reaction of the body that will bring the desired result: Someone will come and pay attention. The Freudians would call this a subconscious expression of the wish "Mother, please come and look after me."

The awareness of an infant is uncanny. When I had to dash off to work — it never failed — he had to have his diapers changed! While a child seems to give fair warning when he is about to have a bowel movement, it is far more difficult to read the signs that a child has to urinate. Pediatricians have learned to keep a diaper handy, because with boy babies, the moment you expose the little penis to the cold air, out comes the urine, in a nice, curved stream. (Male pediatricians have also learned to keep an extra supply of neckties in the office, just in case they do not manage to get out of the way in time.) Actually, this phenomenon which lets the bladder empty when the cold air hits the penis helps in toilet training later: When you take the child to the bathroom and stand him next to the toilet, as soon as the cold air hits him, out comes the urine! Then you can pat him on the back and tell him what a clever fellow he is! Just be sure you don't let his pants down until he gets up close!

As in all cases of teaching a child, it is very important to give a name to what is happening. The child may not be able to talk yet, but when he grunts and gets red in the face, tell him, "Oh, you have to go wooshwoosh!" (or whatever the code name is in your family). How else will he be able to tell you he has to go when he is finally ready to be "trained?" He needs to become aware that the feelings he is getting from the lower part of his body are related to going potty.

The children who are most likely to be abused because they are having trouble with their toileting skills are the hyposensitive children, who get no input from their sensations that something is about to happen down there. For those children, a lesson in naming the different parts of the body is a good idea. During bathing, and later while you dry them, play games with them to help them become aware of their body, even the parts they can't see.

The child wants to learn to go to the bathroom, just as he wants to learn to behave like you in other ways. First, however, he needs to know enough so he can tell you. Then he must know enough to take his pants off in time not to have an accident. He will have an accident or two before he learns just how long he can control his bodily functions before he has to stop doing whatever fascinates him at the moment and make a mad dash for the bathroom. Occasionally, he may lose control because he has been out in the cold and got chilled. At other times he may be affected by some food allergy. If the parents do not understand this, even if his name does not appear on a child abuse list, they will shame him, and the sense of failure may stay with the child even into adulthood.

If there seem to be too many "accidents," double-check the chapters on allergies and on nutrition. Occasionally, a child refuses to go to the potty except in a corner somewhere. That's not the most thrilling situation to live with, but knowing it will not last forever, you might put a potty in the corner for him. If that does not work, try newspaper — and try to keep the neighbors out of the house, unless you have some very knowing and intelligent friends who will put up with the situation until the phase is over.

Many of these special toileting problems are related to fears. The child may have been quite good about going, but then suddenly refuses to go to the bathroom by himself. If the child can talk, he can explain, but many do not talk at that stage, and then they are in trouble. (See the "Fears" part of this section.)

Punishment in this case, or in the case of any other toileting problem, rarely works, and even if it does, it only creates problems for the future. Psychologists say "Tell me how you were toilet trained, and I will tell you who you are." During this stage of development, the child not only learns to go to the toilet, which he will learn eventually anyhow, but also learns a generalized set of attitudes and feelings, feelings about his own body and about his relationships with adults. The good old standby "When you get older, you'll do it in the toilet, like everybody else" works fine. He may not understand fully why this has to be so, but it is comforting to him to know you have faith in him, and it certainly will be of comfort to you. It is the kind of consolation which goes a long way.

Don't think a two-year-old is too young to understand this concept. One little fellow, just turned two, had seen the baby chicks grow until they looked almost like hens. "When the chickies grow up, they have more chickies!" he volunteered. And then, without prompting, he added, "And the rooster lays eggs, too!" "No, not the rooster," corrected the mother. "Just the hens." The little man nodded his head wisely and said in an almost exact imitation of his mother's gentle voice, "When he gets older, he does!"

Bit weak in zoology — but this attitude of implicit faith in the child's future, whether it relates to toilet training or to other matters, is a good one for a child to take into a difficult and uncertain world.!

Bed-wetting

Bed-wetting! Whole books have been written about bed-wetting. The anxiety and the anger created when a child is dry by day but still wets the bed at night is as ridiculous as it is universal.

The abuse of the child who is not dry at night can take many, many forms, even if the child does not end up on the official child abuse list. If you see some small child dragging a wet bed sheet to hang it on the line, that may be his punishment for wetting the bed again. Even if the neighbors neither care nor know, he is told the whole neighborhood will see his shame. Thank heaven for washing machines and automatic dryers! You would think this would eliminate some of the tension surrounding this "accident," but it's not true. Even if the mother just makes the child change the sheet, there is that aura of punishment and shame connected with the transgression.

Even today, in our enlightened society, a 6-year-old boy was tied, naked, to the toilet and left there for days. When the child continued to wet his bed, he was given less and less water, and finally none at all, and died of dehydration!

This is not a horror story. This actually happened in Oregon. Not only that, but this is one of many incidents of a similar kind all over the United States.

Even if the child should not be physically abused, how will he get rid of that small secret feeling: "I am such a bad person, I still wet my bed. And what if the others find out?" He will keep the feeling of being unworthy and bad into adulthood, even though he may have forgotten what it was that made him so ashamed. As much as 7 % of the population, mostly boys, wet their beds until the early teens. Since this symptom is sometimes connected with an immature neurological development, and more often with hypoglycemia and allergy, chances are that there are other problems. To add the shame of bed-wetting to those other problems, really makes life very difficult for the child.

And it's not easy for the adult. No matter how kind the mother is, or the nurse or maid, it is a pain in the neck to have to change the sheets every day. It is a disgrace to have to send the child to a pajama party with a plastic sheet! That small anger builds up, and the problem can take on horrendous proportions in the mother's mind, no matter how often she tells herself he will not still wet his bed on his wedding night!

Psychologists used to say that bed-wetting was connected with hatred of the mother. Perhaps it was the other way around. The bed-wetting made the mother so angry, that the child ended up hating his mother! When I was young, we used to have a joke about the man who went to a psychiatrist because he wet his bed. After two years in analysis, he meets his best friend, who knows all about the situation:

"How's your analysis going?"

"Oh, fine, just fine!" Marvelous!"

"Then you no longer wet your bed!" says the friend.

"Oh, no!" comes the answer, "I still do, but now I know why!"

The secret lies in knowing how to find the real reason and then to cure the problem. Most people today accept the fact that if there is an emotional upheaval in the child's life, he may revert temporarily to bed-wetting. But if this continues, then what?

There are several approaches today that seem to work, and which one will work on a particular child will have to be found: first by observing the child and then by trying the procedure that seems the most likely to work. If one doesn't, try one of the others.

Imipramine, a mild antidepressant, has been known to work. Fine if it does, but better if you do not have to resort to drugs, especially — as in the case of imipramine — the leeway between the effective dose and an overdose is very small. Each year approximately 1000 children under five have required emergency treatment for such an overdose. Many children return to bed-wetting

180

when the drug is discontinued.

Dr. Lendon H. Smith gives magnesium to help stretch the bladder. The bladder is made up of long, smooth muscles, and the magnesium permits the muscle fibers to be more elastic, so the bladder can hold more urine. He also suggests that hypoglycemia can keep the blood sugar so low at night that the brain is not functioning properly and the message "You need to get up!" simply does not reach the child's cortex.

Dr. Broda O. Barnes, who says hypoglycemia is a syndrome resulting from low thyroid function, reports he can stop bed-wetting by giving the child thyroid pills. To see if low thyroid function may be the cause, take the child's temperature under the armpit as soon as the child wakes up. If the temperature is consistently less than 97.8 degrees, such treatment should be tried, but only under a doctor's care. Signs point more and more to the fact that allergies may be the cause of bed-wetting. (The allergies, too, may be part of the thyroid deficiency syndrome.)

Bed-wetting, of course, is normal and can be expected for a while after a child is dry during the day. Nevertheless it is important to try if some diet changes will make a difference. More and more evidence is being accumulated showing milk allergy or some other form of allergy to be the culprit. Eighty percent of the children, most studies agree, can stay dry at night when the offending food is removed. Of the other 20%, about 16% were helped by a device which rang a bell if the child started to wet, and no help was found for the rest of the children.

Dr. Doris Rapp tells of a family in which the younger boy was found to be allergic to milk, and the mother removed all milk from the house. The four-year-old sister was a bed-wetter, and as soon as the milk was removed from the diet, she stopped wetting her bed. Unfortunately, the little girl liked ice-cream, and when she ate some, the milk in it affected her bladder, and she wet the bed again and got a thrashing from her father! No one had told the father that in cases of milk allergies which cause bed-wetting, there have been found actual changes in the mucosa of the bladder.

Children generally do not wet their bed on purpose, certainly not when they are asleep.

Occasionally some little one will stand happily in the corner of a bed and proudly pee right into the center of it. That's a different matter. And in spite of what some Freudian-oriented mother may think, it's not because he is angry. To him it's a fascinating experiment, an early study of cause and effect (and rather a sign of intelligence on the two-year-old's part). If, of course, the mother shows signs of horror and dismay, junior has at least received some attention, and instead of this procedure of peeing into his bed in a glorious stream being a simple experiment in physics, it might well become an attention-getting device. A good washing machine and a sense of humor are a must on these occasions!

Temper Tantrums

Temper tantrums! Show me a child who has never had a temper tantrum and I'll show you a child who's in trouble. There are few things in life more glorious than a full-fledged, let-it-all-hang-out-and-scream-bloody-murder temper tantrum.

It's also very tempting to beat a child who is having one. It's even more of a temptation to lie right down next to him and throw one also! Here is this little monster, whom you love and for whom you will gladly do anything, and the "anything" you are doing for him is not enough. There he is, screaming and yelling in utter disregard of all the rules of civilized behavior!

How to cope with tantrums is anyone's guess. It depends on the time and the place and the state of your own raw nerves. Here are a few ideas to consider. You might be able to come up with a couple of your own.

Beating the child at this point is a totally useless method. The child's screams will only turn from rage and frustration to cries of utter despair and hopelessness.

If the child is in a place where the behavior is an embarrassment to you or to the people surrounding you, hand your shopping cart or whatever merchandise you are holding to the nearest clerk and remove yourself and the child from the area. Nobody is going to blame the child for his behavior; you are the one to get the dirty looks!

When you are in a safe place, sit down, and as calmly as you are able, wait for the storm to subside. Depending on how you were raised, his tantrum may make you feel either totally incompetent or very angry. If this kind of behavior or any expression of anger was taboo in your own childhood, it may arouse a great deal of anger in you. If you are able to empathize with the child, it may make you feel helpless. In either case, you will feel much better if you think of all the money you will save when the child will not have to have primal therapy when he gets older. In primal therapy the therapist teaches the patient to make contact with feelings which were repressed when he was little. Your child is having his primal scream right now.

When he comes out of the tantrum, blow his nose, cuddle him a little — not too much or you will be reinforcing the behavior — and then go back to whatever you were doing. Do not give him what he was trying to get with the tantrum; but on the other hand, do not treat him as if he were an outcast. At this point, he is probably exhausted and spent and not quite sure that all of this effort was worth it. Go on with whatever needed to be done. In the future, you will probably try to avoid situations that might bring on such a rage.

There is no need to worry that you might be raising a problem child: Unless you give in to him in order to stop him from screaming, this type of behavior will not happen very often. If it does, you might have to consider it a kind of emergency crying. This means that either his blood sugar is too low or his nerves are particularly raw because of some nutritional deficiency or allergy. (Double-check Chapters 3 and 4.) The trick is to be able to distinguish whether the temper tantrum has a nice, gutsy I'm-mad-and-the-world-had-better-do-what-I-want-it-to-do! quality or if it is indeed, a case of emergency crying.

A couple of gutsy temper tantrums are good for the child, because he learns that even if he gets angry, the world does not fall apart. However, if mother gives in to him at this point, it fosters his feelings of being omnipotent. If he is stronger than mother or father, who is going to protect him from the imagined and the very real dangers which surround him? This is a very frightening thought for a child. When he feels he has won, he has to keep provoking the parent until the parent finally puts his foot down and whacks him one. Now everybody has lost. The child has been abused, the parent feels guilty, and the child may even feel that it is he who has controlled his parent into controlling him. A nice, gutsy temper tantrum requires a nice, gutsy mother with calm nerves to wait out the storm.

An emergency crying situation, however, means that the child is totally out of control. His system has received an overload of stimulation, and he is at the end of his rope. When this happens, nothing you can do will calm the child, and it becomes important to keep track of just when this sort of thing happens. Often at 4:00 in the afternoon he'll come tearing up the street from his friend's house, and you can bet dollars to donuts that it wasn't anything his friend did but that the child's blood sugar had fallen too low, and anything could have set him off.

If this happens more than once or twice, you may have to decide to call him in at 3:30, feed him, and hope he'll be alright now for about two hours. You might also check his nutrition and start treating him for hypoglycemia. If the tantrums happen only away from home, in supermarkets or in — it never fails — libraries, you may find he is hypersensitive to noise, or to the lights, or to too many people, and keep visits to these places to a minimum.

Sometimes, the child simply has experienced too many frustrations. Whatever the cause, when the tantrum is over, try to give his anger a name: "You want to have all the candy behind the counter. It makes you very angry that you can't have it. When you get a little older and learn not to scream, then we can go back to the store again."

If the tantrums last beyond a reasonable time and seem totally out of proportion to the things that provoke them, suspect a cerebral allergy, and start keeping track of what the child eats within a certain period of that behavior. I've seen a child, who had been playing quietly, get absolutely violent within minutes of having eaten a banana. While rye bread is not usually on the list of most likely allergens, it can make a child, and even an adult, very cranky. Be especially alert in reading the labels of 7-grain breads or of different kinds of granola, which may include a grain to which the child reacts badly.

Occasionally, a child holds his breath during a tantrum and turns blue. This is very frightening, and the child is often suspected of doing it on purpose. The advice used to be for the mother to just walk away. That's very easy for a doctor to say. He knows that when the carbon dioxide level in the child's blood becomes high enough, the breathing will start again. But that's advice which is hard to follow, especially when it happens for the first time.

Contrary to the belief that children do this on purpose, when this happens, it is generally a sign the child's breathing mechanism is immature; otherwise, the breathing would restart before the child turned blue. Gently stroke the outside of the child's arms from shoulder to elbow and the outside of the child's legs from the hip to the knees. This should stimulate the breathing mechanism to start again. When the breathing starts, you can walk safely out of the room, because you don't want to give the child attention for tantrum behavior. Nevertheless, if this sort of thing occurs even once, it is advisable to find ways to stimulate the child's breathing efficiency.

One way to do this is to pour cool water over the child's chest after he has been in a warm bathtub. You will notice he will take a deep breath from the shock of the change in temperature. It's the same kind of thing that happens when you turn on the cold water after a hot shower: You take a deep, gasping breath. It's a reflex of sorts which insures that when a child comes out of the warmth of the mother's womb into the cold air, he will start to breathe. Some mothers throw cold water on their child when the child turns blue. This may work, but the action has a quality of punishment to it — and it leaves a mess to clean up afterward. A piece of ice placed briefly on the chest would probably do just as well if the arm and thigh stimulation did not work. Punishment is not the question in a case like this, though you certainly don't want to reward this kind of situation by showing great solicitude.

During the weeks after such an incident, continue giving the stroking stimulation of the arms and thighs on a regular basis for five to ten minutes a day, and if the child is old enough to do exercises, encourage such games as jumping rope or jumping on a trampoline. (A bed will do just as well.) This is similar to aerobic exercise and will stimulate the flow of blood to the brain, help the child oxygenate better, and generally help his breathing. It provides marvelous input to the vestibular system of his ears, which is terribly important for the integration of all the child's senses. Besides that, it is so much fun!

Very often, bad behavior happens when the child is about to come down with a sickness (see Chapter 2). Viruses can affect a child's behavior as much as a week or two before he actually gets a fever. With a little experience, you will learn the difference between the kinds of tantrums. The slightest frustration will set the child off in those pre-sickness days. You may be able to humor him along, but the most important thing is to remember that the temper tantrum is not really aimed at you.

185

Dirty Words

At my neighbor's house, the older of two brothers came crying to his mother that the younger one had called him a dirty name. "Never mind," his mother told him. "Just don't pay any attention to him!" And so the 7-year-old Andrew went back and played peacefully with his 4-year-old brother, Carl.

The next morning, however, when the mother was combing Andrew's hair, she pulled too hard, and the boy let out a yelp and called her the same dirty name — and he got his face slapped so hard you could see the fingerprints on his cheek for days.

This same charming lady had washed out Carl's mouth with soap when he came home with a new word he had just learned from some teen-age boys who had moved into the neighborhood. The immediate result was that Carl taught this exciting new word to all the other kids on the block.

Reprinted from *Do They Ever Grow Up?* 1978 by Lynn Johnston, with permission from Meadowbrook Press.

Dirty words are omnipresent. They not only seem to be part of the human make-up, but even the monkeys have them. Washoe, the famous chimp who has been taught sign language, invented his own dirty words. They were not part of the trainer's vocabulary. Washoe had spilled something on himself, and the trainer pointed to the mess Washoe had made and taught him the sign for "dirty." That very afternoon one of Washoe's trainers did something to annoy Washoe, and the chimp signed furiously, "Dirty Jack! Dirty Jack!"

Deaf children have their signs for dirty words, and the mothers of deaf children get just as upset as the mothers of hearing children when their kids "talk dirty." As in all other aspects of raising your children, you must teach them about language in a way which is comfortable for you. My sister, who is adamant about using dirty language, had it all figured out. When her son was four, which is the age for dirty words, every time he used the expression "Jiminy Cricket!" she would get angry with him. As a result, we would hear "Jiminy Cricket!" here and "Jiminy Cricket!" there, all day long. However, I don't think he ever used anything worse in his life!

Before you hit, or get mad, better find out first what the child is doing by calling you a "dirty name." My own little monster was three and a half when he came into the kitchen, stood smack in front of me, and said, "Dummy!" Figuring that it was my maternal duty to teach him not to call people "Dummy," I said, "Hey, wait a minute, you're not supposed to hurt my feelings!"

Little did I know he was not really calling me a dummy, he was just testing how one should react to being called "Dummy." His friends, most of whom were four years old (the name calling stage) had called him that. After that, every time they called him "Dummy," he'd come running home in tears: "They're hurting my feelings!"

Unfortunately, I had taught him the wrong lesson. From then on, if he called me "Dummy" I'd say things like, "Oh, Dummy, Rummy!" and make a joke of it. But the damage had been done, and it took a long time before he could foil the teasing of his friends.

(When he was 15 though, I am glad that I had learned my lesson. When he once called me "Stupid," I did some quick calculating, figured that sooner or later someone would call him that. How would I want him to react then? So with all the calm I could muster, I answered serenely, "It's a good thing that my self-concept does not depend on your opinion of me!" It worked. Besides, you have never seen a more squashed kid!)

Children learn dirty words in a special way because of the emotionally charged situations during which they hear them. It probably has something to do with the fact that at such moments the adrenalin is high, and recent research has proved that adrenalin sharpens the memory. (For the same reason, people remember exactly where they were when they heard that some shocking event occurred — such as the bombing of Pearl Harbor or the killing of President Kennedy.) The first words autistic children learn are often such emotion-charged words.

Janice Delacato tells the charming story of a little boy, six years old, who had never spoken a word in his life. One day, the mother waited in vain for the child to come home after school. A counselor usually dropped him off. Finally, after a tension-filled half hour, the boy and the counselor arrived. Even though the child did not talk, the loving mother knelt in front of him, took off his coat and hat, and gently inquired how his day had gone. The child looked at her calmly and said in a clear, loud voice: "The fucking car didn't start!"

The counselor turned red — but the mother was delighted!

To treat "dirty" words as if they had some special magic seems totally medieval to me. So when my son came back with that very explicit language that his friend Carl had been so quick to share, I explained to him just what the words meant. I told him that this was "army language" and not to be used in public, especially in front of ladies, but that as far as I was concerned, a word was just a word, and he could cuss in front of me as much as he wanted. However, he'd better watch his language in public, I said, or someone might clobber him. I figured that sooner or later, if he had to go into the army, some sergeant would cuss my poor kid up and down, and I did not want him to go into shock.

(As a matter of fact, my son's language, after a few days of some very peppery words remained exceptionally clean — that is, until he came home from college. There, he said, even the professors use the four letter words that most kids today pick up in kindergarten.)

I am not saying we should allow the indiscriminate use of dirty words. There is a great need for taboo words so we have some way of letting off steam without actually getting violent. We must, therefore, create a taboo around something. The child must be given the skills to be angry without being offensive. On the other hand, if too much attention is paid to the use of dirty words, the child will have been handed a weapon. It is great to be able to cause a small uproar just by using a simple little word. Unfortunately, the price the child pays for the use of this power is usually too high. So while we have to set limits, as long as we are aware of the universality of the use of forbidden language, we are not likely to get upset by its use to the point of abusing the child.

Fears

My baby brother was just about tall enough that, standing up in his little crib, he could reach the light switch, and he had just discovered that when he pulled it down, the lights would go off. I remember standing there, probably all of four years old — and terrified of the dark. What was in the dark? I wasn't sure, but it was probably the Big Bad Wolf. And each time my adored baby brother flicked the lights off, I was scared! I tried frantically to think of some way to stop him, but I had been under strict orders not to scare my little brother with "The Big Bad Wolf." But the little boy simply would not stop flicking the light and kept plunging my world into dark. Finally, in desperation, I blurted out with all the self-control I could muster, "When you turn out the light, the Big Bad Rabbit will come!"

Fear has been used for generations and generations to try to control children. Perhaps it was considered more humane than beating them up. Some parents still control their children by threatening to call the policeman, others threaten to and even actually lock them in a dark closet. Big brothers terrify the little ones with tall tales of monsters and then threaten them with those monsters. (Governments still do it by threatening the citizens with the big bad country across the frontier. Religious leaders do it by threatening hell and damnation.) Fear is a great method of controlling others.

My little brother never did stop flicking the light switch. He was not afraid of the Big Bad Rabbit, because there was no fear of the dark in his emotional vocabulary at that particular stage in his young life.

Fears and childhood go hand in hand: They, so to speak, "come with the territory." They come at fairly predictable times and slowly disappear as we grow up. "It is the eye of childhood, which fears the painted devil!" says Shakespeare. Growing up, in essence, also implies overcoming the fears we have inherited from our ancestors as a form of protection to assure the survival of the species.

The infant startles at loud, sudden sounds. Arms fling up and he starts to cry. The startle may have been just enough to scare away an aggressor, and the cry would have brought mother or father to help. This startle reflex is there at birth and, in a normal child, disappears as the child gets older.

The infant is not afraid of the dark. Only when he gets old

enough to creep on hands and knees across the floor, does he hesitate at doors which lead to dark rooms and beat a hasty retreat.

Nature's timetable includes not only the fearful periods but also the shapes these fears take. At three and a half it's bugs and flies; at five, lions and tigers or some other wild animal. This seems a rather ridiculous thing considering there are very few lions and tigers in our modern cities.

Parents who would otherwise never dream of beating or abusing their children are often driven in despair to physical violence when a little one stands in his bed screaming that there are bugs under the bed and nothing can convince the child otherwise. Dealing with these irrational fears is a huge problem. Sometimes, leaving on the light will help; sometimes, that too has no effect. Punishing the child for such fears can lead to the same kind of split personality we find in sexually abused children, because the fears become hidden so deeply they may remain underground and cause all kinds of irrational problems when the child becomes an adult.

Whether something needs to be done about the fears depends on whether the child — and the parent — can manage to live with them.

In old-time Russia, if a child had too many fears or constant nightmares, he was taken to the village witch. The witch would light a candle in a darkened room and carefully pour a tablespoon of oil on top of the water inside a special bowl. The child would then be asked to tell what shapes he saw in the design the oil made on the water and would be encouraged to talk about what he saw. After a few sessions of the sort, the fears would usually vanish.

Witchcraft? The ritual simply allowed the child to make contact with the information coded in symbolic form by the child's brain.

We know today that the human being stores the information he receives in two ways. The verbal and rational commands are stored mainly in the left side of the brain; at the same time, the same information is stored in visual or symbolic form in the right side of the brain. (This is an inherited, predetermined location. In almost all newborn infants, when they are exposed to music, the right hemisphere of the brain is stimulated; if they are allowed to listen to someone talking, it's the left side.)

The symbolic information stored in the right brain is rarely made conscious in the adult unless he is dreaming, near sleep, or engaged in some artistic function, such as drawing pictures. Children still use both sides of the brain quite readily, unless the rational demands of the left side of the brain have been emphasized too strongly by the parents.

The parent has to become a veritable detective to find out what's behind these fears. Very often, two-year-olds, just as they are being toilet trained, become afraid of the bathroom. One little fellow I know, insisted on being accompanied there, because there was an "Indian" in the bathroom. Since no one had told him there was anything frightening about Indians, this was rather puzzling. Still he dragged his mother to the toilet every time he went.

When mine was that age, he did the same thing, only he was afraid of the "ground hoggy!" Now, why he should be afraid of the ground hog in the bathroom and not a lion or a squirrel or an owl, or any of the other animals in the books we read to him, was a complete mystery. Finally, after months of being dragged to the bathroom by a determined tot clutching at my little finger, I took a good look at the ground hog in the one book which showed one. I found that this ground hog, peeping out of his hole, looked like a round face coming out of a dark triangle! (Remember the "Indian" in the bathroom? In that child's book, it too looked like a round face, surrounded by dark feathers!) And then I realized that my son must have seen his father in the nude! The penis must have looked like a small, round thing surrounded by dark hair! When I asked the child what scared him about the "ground hoggy," he only answered, "Something scares him!" So, without going further into the fear, I started talking about Daddy's "peepee" and how big it was and that someday, when my son was big, he too would have a big one like that. I repeated these comments casually, a few more times. Within a week, the fear which had hung on for months, disappeared.

I have heard similar stories from other mothers. If the child can talk (and many don't at age two, when this fear emerges), the child can ask for protection. If he can't talk and simply refuses — without explanation — to go to the bathroom, there are toilet training problems and, as we know, there is a great deal of child abuse when this occurs. Even with a talking child, it is very easy to get impatient: "Now, there is no Indian in the bathroom. You get in there or you get a spanking!" Not only have we forced the child into a situation which terrifies him, but we have done this during a period related to toilet functioning. We have also proven to him that we are not willing to protect him, whether the fear is related to his father's nude body, to the flushing noise of the toilet, or to any other reason known only to him.

There is a grave danger that we may ignore fears simply because

191

they take on a shape which is common to all children at the particular time in which they emerge. The books say that five-year-olds are afraid of lions and tigers, so we figure that's normal. If the fears become too intense, however, something must be done.

Freud interpreted the fear of the wolf as the child's fear of the father. Of course, any Daddy, no matter how loving, is really quite terrifying and can easily become the symbol of a wild animal in the child's mind. This does not mean, however, that this is always the case. Most often, especially in our permissive way of rearing children, I have found that the symbol is the child's fear of his own anger. At that stage, he still thinks he is omnipotent and can destroy people if he gets angry. The feared symbol is far more often his fear that his own anger might run out of control and destroy the ones on whom he is dependent for survival.

A friend of mine had a new baby and since she did not want her four-year-old to feel neglected, she permitted the little girl to hit out at her and even to hit the baby. Almost immediately, the four-year-old became paranoid. When people came to the door, she would run, screaming, "They're going to kill me! They're going to kill me!" When the mother told a psychiatrist friend, he advised her not only to forbid the child to hit the baby but to tell her firmly, "I will not let you hurt the baby, and I will not let you hurt me, either!" Within days of the time that the mother set firm limits on the child's actions against the newborn, the fears disappeared completely.

There are hidden reasons for many fears. Whether the adult understands them or not, they are very real to the child. One toddler kept flushing the toilet and insisted that he had "flushed the moon down the toilet." It took a while for the family to realize that there were no severe Freudian implications there; the child had simply seen the bathroom light's reflection on the water in the toilet bowl. When he flushed the toilet, that image disappeared. (I can easily imagine a mother beating the daylights out of her little boy because he insists on flushing the toilet over and over again!)

As the child gets older, the fears are different. Sometimes they are quite rational. A karate teacher asked an unusually small for his age nine-year-old student why his punches were always aimed too high. "Because that's where the other guy usually is, way up there!" was the reply from the diminutive warrior. For a while, this same little fellow would get beaten up regularly, because he refused to defend himself. He had gotten it into his head that if he fought back, he would kill someone. It wasn't until he acquired more karate skills that he learned the gentle art of threatening the other guy with dire results and, since he now knew how to back up the threats, the others left him alone. The parents had been very wise not to laugh at the child's fears but to give him the skills he needed to protect himself.

There are no hard and fast rules on how to deal with fears. When my child was eight and ashamed that he was afraid of the dark, I explained to him that as he grew older, he would no longer have that fear. "It's inherited from our ancestors," I told him. "It was important that a child stay within the light of the fire, because if he ran about in the dark, some wild animal might eat him."

"Now you've really scared me!" exclaimed my son and hid his head beneath the covers. So much for amateur psychology! Nevertheless, fears at any age should be treated with respect, though not with too much attention or they might become an attention-getting device. If you make a child feel you are willing to listen to his feelings without punishing him or belittling him, he is more likely to come out and tell you (and, for that matter, allow himself to know) what the real cause for the fear might be.

The child who panics at school tests and so destroys his own chances for success may do so for many reasons. Some may be quite realistic. The pressures put on our children in school are a reflection of our very competitive existence.

The needs for the teachers to perform, for the schools to show high test scores, for the school boards to have excellent schools in comparison with the rest of the nation's, are all subtly passed on to our kids. More frequently, however, fear of tests may be related to quite another fear: The fear of success! If I succeed at this, I may succeed at something else. If that something else is related to anger and the child feels his anger may get out of control, he will subconsciously destroy his own chances of succeeding. This anger may be aimed at a smaller brother, at a father with whom he is competing, or at some intolerable situation at home. The situation is similar to that of the young karate student, who is afraid that in his anger he will do some real damage.

It is incredibly hard not to get impatient at a fearful child. In our society (or for that matter in most societies), courage is to be admired and fear ridiculed. If our child is fearful, it seems to reflect on us. Sometimes nurses and counselors at school are helpful. Parents are not always the best therapists of their own children, but often some of the techniques discussed in Chapter 8 are very successful. We are bombarded with horrible occurrences from our TV screens, and probably the only thing which makes it possible for children to go out into the world, which as far as they know, is peopled with TV villains and monsters, is that the heroes always win — and in a time span of 57 minutes.

The universality of children's fears are shown in the time table of the Gesell Institute, reprinted in Part VII of the Appendix.

Sexual Exporation

Reprinted from *Hi Mom! Hi Dad!* © 1977 by Lynn Johnston, with permission from Meadowbrook Press.

In 1950, Frederick Wertham wrote a book called "55 Bad Boys." It related his experiences with delinquent teenagers in the Chicago slums. We must take into consideration that the period during which he counseled these kids was a time before drugs had become the number one problem with children and the time before there had been any kind of sexual enlightenment in our culture. Sex information was not yet taught in the schools to any great extent, so the problems Wertham dealt with were somewhat different from the ones he might have had to deal with today. What Wertham found was that, in almost every case, these boys "acted out" because they had a terrible lack of self-esteem. The reason for this lack: They could not deal with their emerging sexual feelings.

Specifically, their guilt centered around the fact that they mastubated. If discovered at it, they had been beaten, shamed, or threatened with damnation or loss of reason. One even had been made to do penance on his knees for hours on end.

After a while, Wertham never even bothered to ask if the teenagers masturbated. If he had asked, they would have denied it. He saved valuable counseling time by simply asking them what they thought about when they were doing it. Just the discovery that they were not the only ones who did such a strange thing was tremendous. What a relief to find that there were others who struggled with the same feelings! Once they realized they were not "bad" boys, they no longer had to prove to anyone that they were. Once they had accepted themselves, Wertham helped them find a "hero" or someone whom the boys could emulate, and, without becoming dependent on him as a counselor, they were able to find goals and pursue their lives in non-destructive ways.

No matter how advanced we seem to have become in our sexual enlightenment, the topic of masturbation is still a very hidden one. It is seldom mentioned in polite society, and much abuse occurs when a child is discovered engaged in any kind of sexual exploration.

Masturbation tends to occur spontaneously around the age of five or six and then to diminish during the so-called latency period. It emerges again during the teen years to continue, in some cases, all through adulthood. I don't think parents still threaten their children with "cutting it off" if they touched the penis, or that little girls are still made to feel that they "lost it" because they touched themselves. Nevertheless, it makes parents feel uncomfortable because the children must be taught not to do it in public. Even if threats are not made, there is a silent prohibition, and the word "self-abuse" has stuck for a long time.

Today there are wonderful books on sex — written for teenagers — which try to dispel the old myths. Yet the tarnish and the guilt seem to linger on. A young man was asked not long ago why he felt so guilty about masturbating when no one had told him any of the old fairy tales or punished him for doing it. He answered, "Yes, but no one ever talked about it!" What it amounts to is that with all our wisdom and enlightenment, we have not really learned how to cope with the mystery of sex.

The intrigue with the mystery starts early. When the child is five years old, or a little older, chances are that we'll discover him with a friend, male or female, exchanging the secrets of their bodies. Even if we understand that this is a normal growing-up procedure, we must stop them because we don't want the child to be ostracized by the whole block. It would be hard for him to have to live down the reputation of being a corrupting influence on the neighborhood! "Go put your clothes back on, and we'll go wash the car!" or "bake some bread," or "go to the store," or whatever you manage to mumble at that point, is as good a ploy as any. The less fuss made, the better. Otherwise, it's like banning a book in Boston for containing pornographic material. It's the one thing which will sell millions of copies. If you can't keep the children busy and occupied so that there is no chance to fool around, it may become necessary to tell them that people don't let others see them naked until they are married. This is not quite truthful in this day and age, but at that stage it will do. It is important to add that in certain societies (or in nudist colonies) it is all right, but in our society, — "that means the people in our town and in the whole United States" — we keep our clothes on, just as we go to the bathroom by ourselves.

Unfortunately, our society is hopelessly caught up in a dichotomy about sex. Sexual words are used as swear words, but in marriage sex is supposed to be the culmination of love. Our children are permitted to see violence, but sexually explicit movies are out of bounds for them. Personally, I would rather have mine exposed to a little sex than to all that violence!

The way we relate to our children's sexual explorations depends on the attitudes with which we were brought up; this means not only with what our parents taught us, but also with our own misunderstandings: what we THOUGHT our parents taught us. Mrs. Elizabeth Alexander, that marvelous teacher who taught my parent-education class in Los Angeles, put it this way: If you feel that masturbation is very bad, and you look in the bedroom and find the child doing it, you may say nothing. But then, when he comes into the other room and spills his milk, you will hit him! If you feel strongly about such things, it is better to stop him and tell him so than to have the anger build inside of you and you take it out on the child in other ways.

Dr. Lawrence Cheldelin reports that if a younger child maturbates excessively, taking him on your lap twice a day and rocking him for 10 minutes will stop the practice within about three weeks. When teenage masturbation starts, chances are you won't know anything about it. Children have that instinctive secrecy about sexual matters. When I was single, I used to think that if I ever had any boys, I would teach them all about the techniques of making women happy. What a perfectly idiotic idea! There could be nothing more ridiculous than a boy doing on his first date exactly what his mother had told him to do!

Unfortunately, no matter how much children complain that their parents never told them about sex, this is really the one area in which they want to be on their own. Girls may be a little more open in that area, but on the whole, sex is the one step into selfhood which they must take themselves. Besides, almost any form of sex education given by the member-of-the-opposite-sex parent will have some seductive quality to it. This subliminal seduction can be just as emotionally devastating as actual incest.

If a child has been raised in all areas of his life to take the responsibility for his own actions, this attitude will hopefully carry over into his sex life. He does not want to hear from his parents about sexual things. Just as he was not willing to see that there was no Santa Claus, no matter how many signs pointed in that direction, he does not want Mom and Dad to know about such things. "Well, they must have done it at least once, for here I am!" is about as much as he will admit to himself.

A casual mention of sexual matters when both Mom and Dad are in the car on their way to the store, is probably as much as you can get him to accept. It puts such things as masturbation in the right perspective as to its relative importance when it is mentioned casually under such circumstances. It is a good idea to mention occasionally that if he has any questions which he does not wish to discuss with his parents, it's OK to check with the doctor or the school nurse. Find a book that has the facts of life in it (written with an attitude toward sex that you find you can live with) and give it to him. Then the child can use it as the urge strikes him, or he can leave it on the shelf unread, like some of the other books which you thought he might like and which he never opened.

Much abuse occurs when parents find "dirty books" and "dirty magazines" in the child's room. Most parents are becoming more lenient about this situation. The current trend is just to ignore the material and leave it in its hiding place.

Since I was aware that my son would go through such a phase, I carefully selected some very beautiful books and magazines which portrayed sex as something warm and honest and visually beautiful. Equally carefully, I kept them in somewhat out-of-the-way shelves and closets, hoping he would come across them. If he must read them secretly, he would at least get a healthy perspective on the mysterious activity.

Much to my chagrin, I don't have the faintest idea if he ever found any of those books. Some day, when he is much older and has children of his own, he will probably tell them about this and laugh at his ridiculous mother. Perhaps he will find the secret of knowing how to give children sexual knowledge without invading their privacy. Times and social demands change, and it is not fair for one generation to transmit its sexual hang-ups to the next one.

The Working Mother Syndrome

The psychological truths of yesterday, even though they are the foundations on which we can understand the lives of our children, change as our society changes. For better or worse, the family structure is changing. The father takes a more active part in raising the child and, therefore, becomes more than just the strange figure who comes home at night to take Mommy's attention away. In some instances, he becomes the main care-taker of the child, and the parental roles become almost reversed. The child today has to deal with an entirely different reality from the one that children dealt with in Freud's time.

What effects this change in care-taking will have, has not been evaluated yet. There is one syndrome, however, that I have observed frequently over the last 20 years and which I would like to bring up.

For lack of a better name — something mysterious and Greek, like Oedipus Conflict or Electra Complex — we might just call it the Working Mother Syndrome. With so many broken families, or families in which the mother works away from home, this new phenomenon presents a very real tragedy, because a tired, harassed mother is more likely to lose control and hurt a child. Once a mother understands what is happening, I think she can deal better with the problem.

Mother has been trying very hard to do a good job at work, in spite of getting no rest at home. Tired after the day's work, she can hardly wait to see the child for whom she is doing all this and yet, the moment she picks up the child at the baby sitter's, all hell breaks loose. The babysitter says, "Why, your child is marvelous, he's such a good boy." Daddy says, "He was marvelous, all day!" But let Mother come through the door, and the child regresses about two years — he whines, and demands, and cries over every little thing.

I have seen this from both sides. I have taken care of someone else's child, who has been amazingly mature, coping with everything that happened — far beyond what could be expected at his age level.

Reprinted from *Do They Ever Grow Up?* 1978 by Lynn Johnston, with permission from Meadowbrook Press.

The moment the mother enters the room, he starts finding fault with everything. He does not want the sweater put on. Or he does want the sweater on. He needs to have his shoes tied. He does not want to have his shoes tied. The whole world suddenly seems wrong to him.

In short, he has to find something to cry about. It is as if all the self-control he has mustered in order to survive without the mother all day is suddenly thrown to the winds. Here is Mommy, and now he can let go. He feels a mixture of relief at seeing her and a sense of security that allows him to behave like a baby again. I am sure a certain amount of anger because he resents that she has deserted him all day is involved here. And the mother bears the brunt of his confusion. It's as if the rest of the world gets to see her child at his best, and the mother gets to see him only at his worst.

Not only is she tired herself at this point, but she is made to feel that she, and only she, is a total failure at raising the child. After all, he's marvelous for everybody else! Later on, we may hear from the child, "Well, I never got along with my mother." Little does he realize that, at the moment he finally got to be with his mother, he was so torn by conflicting emotions that nothing she could do would have pleased him.

What can be done? To begin with, let's understand the situation. The conflict is not with the mother so much as with the situation. Since usually there is nothing you can do to change the situation, try to allow some of the emotions of the child to get sorted out.

Mother's are usually not allowed the "coming home cocktail," which used to be the right of the working male. But try to get something to eat just as you leave work, so your blood sugar is not low and you can take the coming conflict. Try to have a snack for the child, and don't try the "don't-eat-now-we'll-have-dinner-soon" routine. The child, in being away from you, has had as rough a time as you had at work.

You may have more than one child and you may have to drive the gang home. Stay in the car with them for a few minutes and let some of the steam blow off before you tackle the traffic and a bunch of rowdy kids at the same time.

Depending on the child's age, a cuddle is very important. He may not let you hug him right away, because he is angry that you left him. Remember: This is not a rejection; it's a sign of how much it cost him to be without you all day. Explain how much you missed him and how you wished you could have been there. Even if the child is too young to understand fully, he somehow gets the message. Sometimes, a long session of rocking him in your arms is in order, even if he is beyond the rocking age. Tell him how marvelous he was to have taken care of himself all day long. Once this sort of thing has been discussed with him fully, you may need to repeat it only occasionally. Most of the time, just a hug or being held while you ask him about his day will do. How often you have to repeat this sort of thing depends on the need of the child, and, most certainly, on your own need.

As the child gets older, there may also be the time to say, "I know you had a long day. So did I. Hold off with your shenanigans a little longer. I need a rest too!"

Louise Bates Ames says the greatest job of a child is to make himself independent of the mother, as she is the most important person in his life. It is out of an attempt to become independent from her that the most conflicts will arise. It is therefore a compliment if the child chooses to fight most with his mother. It's a hard-to-take compliment, but nevertheless, understanding the mechanism behind all of this will make the problem a little easier to bear.

Mealtime

The dining table is one of the places at which child abuse occurs with devastating regularity. The child who has perception and coordination problems is the most likely to get beaten. Somehow, parents keep thinking he spills the milk on purpose, when he simply has not learned to judge distances properly. Children who have a lack of space perception or whose eyes do not function properly are especially at risk. Most children achieve the ability to judge distances at close range by the time they are two years old. For some children this is difficult, especially when they are tired. And even if they are not beaten, they are called clumsy and careless and other names that hurt. In poor families, where a glass of milk is a precious thing, it is understandable that spilling milk is a major crime. If this kind of accident occurs more than seems normal it is a good idea to check out the child's vision and hand-eye coordination.

As a matter of fact, the very early years, when the child is still in a high chair, is a good time to help hand-eye coordination along. Place the finger foods (pieces of bread or fruit) all over the food tray, so he has to find and reach for them. Optometrist Dr. Larry Burr suggests that Cheerios all over the tray are great for teaching children to use fingers and eyes together and for helping them to judge distances. (Be sure, though, that the child is mature enough not to choke on those little things.)

Early feeding is a messy thing; it seems especially so to those mothers who had been raised to be painfully neat and clean. But eating time is a first experience in science for the child. Dump bread into the milk, and it turns soggy. Catsup feels squooshy between the fingers and makes lovely red patterns on the table. The small child has taste buds on the outside of his mouth; what food gets smeared there tastes just as delicious as what goes inside! The stimulation he gets around his mouth from those taste buds will help the brain to gain knowledge of the mouth area and be helpful in learning speech later.

There is this terrible fear that if you let the child eat messily, he will do so for the rest of his life. It is hard to realize that, once the child has messed around enough, he will start to eat properly. Believe it or not, he will stop dropping a messy spoon on the floor once he has rediscovered that the law of gravity is constant and that the spoon will invariably land on the floor and not on the ceiling!

Somehow, it's like tying shoelaces. When you no longer have to tie a child's shoelaces, because he learned to do it himself, you can no longer remember when and how the fantastic moment occurred. So it is with eating: When the child has reached a certain maturity, suddenly he seems to handle knife and fork by himself, and you

Reprinted from *Hi Mom! Hi Dad!* © 1977 by Lynn Johnston, with permission from Meadowbrook Press.

can eat at the same table without any major mishaps!

It used to be the big thing, and probably still is, that a child had to eat everything on his plate. Parents of all nations have their own little way of forcing children to eat their food: "Eat it, or the Russians will come and get it." "Just think of the poor starving Armenians!" In another period of time it might be: "Think of the poor starving Cambodians!"

Nobody thinks of the poor stuffed child who is sitting at the table right here. I hate to think of all the poor little rich children who were told to eat one more bite and promptly threw up. If a child is not allowed to trust the messages his own body sends him when he has had enough, how is he to trust any of his feelings? The child's entire self-awareness and sense of "I" is centered in his ability to judge what he needs to eat.

Some children present great feeding problems: They simply don't like anything. Nutritional deficiencies often affect the child's sense of taste. (See Chapters 5 and 10 on sensory and nutritional problems.) Children who will eat everything we put in front of them and who don't have input from their own senses as to when they've had enough are just as much in danger of not getting the proper nutrition. They must be taught gently to listen more to what their own senses tell them.

Now comes the paradox: First we say that the child must eat right or he will have all kinds of emotional and physical problems, and then we say that he must eat what he wants to eat. Perhaps we should simply ask him "How much do you want?" The secret, of course, is not to have anything unhealthful on the table. That of course, is being a bit unrealistic, because it is hard to keep grandmothers out of the house, not to mention kindly neighbors with their beautiful chocolate cakes.

When I went to school, we had been told that, if you give a child a choice of different foods, over a period of a week the child would choose the exact amount of each different kind that would provide him with what he needed. What they did not tell us was that the foods offered to the experimental group of children, did not include candy, ice cream, and C O O K I E S! The result of this lack of information was that by the time my son was six, he was a complete junk-food addict. The doctors I consulted because the child was so allergic and seemed hypoglycemic to me, told me that nutrition had nothing to do with his allergies. They assured me that children did not become hypoglycemic. No wonder I had just about ruined the child for life before he was even ready for school.

It's a hard trick to keep the junk food out of the house. It is even harder to keep the children away from the soda pop and candy machines in school. At least some of the schools are finally becoming aware of the impact on the children's behavior. In Oregon, this stuff is no longer allowed to be served before lunchtime, and in some of the California schools, only fruits or nuts are allowed in the vending machines!

As the child gets older, you can tell him that he, alone, is responsible for what he eats, and then make some kind of deal with him to stay away from junk food for three weeks. After that, he's on his own. Chances are that by the end of three weeks, he will feel so much better that from then on he will be quite careful about what he eats. You might even explain about hypoglycemia. Being able to tell your friends, "Sorry, I can't eat that cake, I have hypoglycemia," is becoming a sort of status symbol with the younger crowd.

It is a terrible weapon to hand to children that what they eat or not eat is of any concern to you or might upset you. Mealtime should be a joy, not a time when everyone vents all the anger they have stored up during the day.

If you can have a peaceful table like "The Waltons" seem to have at each meal, with all the dishes nice and hot at the table, and everybody carefully timed to be there at the same time — that's great! If you can't, don't worry. Remember: In "The Waltons" there are at least one or two prop men in charge of seeing that everything is ready on time. And even though all the children have read the script and memorized their lines, you have no idea how many "takes" it took to get the scene just right!

There is horrendous pressure at the dinner table to socialize the child. Children should be taught manners, not with any great deal of pressure, but with the understanding that if they eat elsewhere, they should be comfortable about knowing how to behave. Mealtime should be a fun time, when you can come and eat if you are hungry, or just sit and talk if you care to. Since we have refrigerators, mother need no longer be a slave to the family dinner hour. It is very frustrating to have worked hard to get a hot meal on the table and then to find that the kids won't eat! If everyone is anxious at the table, the food is not digested properly, anyway. If you have a child who has a tendency to be hypoglycemic, if you make him wait until dinner time to eat, his blood sugar will have gone down too low and he won't be any joy to be with. Keep nuts and fruits around the house, let the children eat what they want at the table, and make the situation as comfortable for yourself as possible. When the parents are relaxed at the table, the kids will want to join in the fun before long!

Bedtime Story

One other behavior which can drive a parent to the very edge of violence occurs at bedtime. Even the most normal of all children will, as with all other forms of behavior, go through a very predictable timetable of bedtime shenanigans. If you have a child who is no problem at night, this may not mean your methods are successful: You may just be lucky!

Some children simply are not good sleepers.

We are one of the few societies who enforce separation of the child at bedtime. Whether this is good or bad is a difficult question. There has been a new movement of a few young parents to permit all the children to sleep with the parents in one bed. Theoretically, this sounded good: The children were to have a sense of security and closeness. However, even though the parents moved to another room to have sexual relations, the results were catastrophic. One little boy became a pyromaniac at six. Apparently the physical warmth and the skin contact created more sexual stimulation than he could handle. Somewhere between complete closeness and complete separation lies an answer.

In America, an infant is expected to sleep through the night after a few months. Then, if the child is one of those who keeps waking up, he is permitted to cry for a few nights until he gives up and remains asleep through the night.

Sometimes this has been known to work even with children who have diffuse minimal brain damage, but I wouldn't count on it. Cats normally sleep a great deal; when they have an injury in the pons, they do not sleep. Now, if children have a brain injury that affects their sleeping, this same brain injury probably causes all kinds of other problems. When the parents are worn out from lack of sleep, their control is low, and anything can happen. The child will later be diagnosed as neurotic or delinquent because he was abused, but chances are the abuse occurred because the child was so difficult!

When you have a child who simply cannot fall asleep, it is not because he doesn't want to — he just can't. Children who sleep little tend to be very bright. It is not clear, whether one has anything to do with the other, but chances are they are brighter because there are more hours in the day for them to learn things. This does not make matters any easier for those who have to take care of the child.

A little detective work may sometimes find the solution to the problem, sometimes nothing works. Perhaps the chocolate milk at 5 o'clock was too stimulating. Did the doctor prescribe an antihistamine to put him to sleep the night before? Even something as mild as that can disturb the sleep rhythm, and you'll need that antihistamine again and again!

Is the child awake at night because the mother works, and night is the only time she's around? A psychologist said that when the mother is away during the day, the baby dreams of food at night, gets hungry, and cries. When mine was about 20 months old, I figured that he should be grown enough not to have a night bottle any more. I did work, and I needed my night's sleep very badly. But four o'clock in the morning, I heard my little fellow toss in his sleep and mumble, "Noonoo Soup. Beans!" and so I figured the psychologist must be right and continued with the night bottle. (Very bad for the teeth!) Children who wake up with nightmares (usually at three in the morning), often with their nose running like that of a drug addict who is having withdrawal symptoms, are probably hypoglycemic. Their blood sugar has just taken a nose dive, and the adrenalin is going to work to hike up the blood sugar before there is too little sugar to feed the brain. The result is an anxiety reaction. (See Chapter 4.) Only within recent years has it been recognized that children, too, can suffer from hypoglycemia. This could be inherited, could be caused by the wrong diet, or it could be caused by too much stress.

Dr. Broda O. Barnes sees a connection with low thyroid function and hypoglycemia, but probably the entire endocrine system is involved, and all measures that could help should be considered. There are some children who are so hypersensitive to noise that noises not audible to anyone else in the house can wake them up. Carl H. Delacato tells of a child who woke up every night at three, and remained wide awake. Since the little boy was very sensitive to sound, a team of friends was enlisted to patrol the neighborhood at three o'clock and, sure enough, a neighbor — two blocks away — would come home from his night work at that time and his garage door squeaked! The parents gave the neighbor a can of oil, and the child slept through the night.

Children who are very sensitive to noise can be helped by putting a white noise machine in their room. These gadgets provide a mild amount of neutral noise to cover many of the other sounds which might bother the child. Since these machines are rather expensive, a fish bowl with a bubbling oxygen pump will serve the same purpose; so might a radio tuned to a music station.

Perfectly healthy children can also have problems, especially at bedtime. A very gentle bedtime story can often prevent nightmares. Sometimes, leaving a door open will do the trick. Sometimes, nothing works. The separation anxiety can be very great between the ages of two and seven, and there seems to be an eternal demand for another kiss, another glass of water, a trip to the toilet. Believe it or not, this behavior will eventually change as the child gets older.

Some parents are very rigid: "After ten, solve your own problems!" is the rule of the evening. If that works, great. I found it easier to tuck the child in a blanket on the couch and let him go to sleep there. Each child is different, and what works for one does not for another.

Chapter 15

Postscript

Charles Dickens wrote in his opening to *A Tale of Two Cities*, "It was the best of times, it was the worst of times..." That is just as it is with all times. And so it is with ours. The one difference between the best and worst of times of Charles Dickens and of our times, is that today, whatever happens is dumped into our laps at least three times a day, with the morning news, with the six o'clock news, and with the late news.

As a result, I believe, we are all just a little bit insane. We hear that 50 people died in a fire; we grimace and go on eating breakfast. We hear of some sniper shooting innocent people from a church tower, and we go ahead and brush our teeth. We hear of some child being murdered in a bizarre case of sexual abuse, and we calmly leave the room to clean the kitchen. If we were sane, we would probably all sit in a corner, pull a blanket around us, and weep. As it is, we have become so immune to hearing about political and personal disasters about which we can do nothing anyhow, that we have become passive.

This book is a statement that there are things which can be done, and there are answers to be found for those who mean the most to us — our own children, the children of our friends, and the children who have become the responsibility of the community. Most of the research for this book took years to accumulate. Much has been available to people for years. And yet, while the material is available, I am constantly appalled by how much is still being ignored.

In some ways, this is very understandable, for the simple reason that each child is so very different yet at the same time so very very similar to the next. If we cannot always get all the answers from some expert who is supposedly the authority on child care, it is because, as Robert Oppenheimer said, "We are all ignorant, only on different subjects."

The time has come when all of the experts must stop going to workshops and conventions in their own fields — workshops in which they only hear what they should have long known or should have learned on their own from professional journals.

Psychologists should attend workshops on neurology, nutrition, and learning disabilities. Teachers should speak at meetings of neurologists and of social workers, at conferences for doctors and for nutritionists. The judges and all the members of the juvenile delinquency departments should be working with allergists and nutritionists, with developmental specialists and psychologists. Only then will the work of each truly affect the way we deal with our problem children.

The way things are at the moment, if we go for help to most of these experts, they see the child only for a short, short period of time. And the parent is the one who lives with him and works with him constantly. The parent is the expert on the child. The parent is the one who must continue to look for answers as to what can be done. No matter what age the child, from infancy to adulthood, the situation need not be hopeless.

By the time the book is edited, printed, distributed and found on the library shelves, new discoveries will have been made. That is good, and that is how it should be. The statement this book hopes to make is that there are answers and we must never cease to try to find them.

S E C T I O N   III

APPENDIX   I. - X.

Appendix

I. No Miracles — An End and a Beginning

Randy's grandparents brought Randy to see Florence Scott at the Oregon Hope and Help Center the morning after her phone call. A closer observation of the teenager showed him to have the signs usually seen in children with very diffuse brain damage. These children are almost always in trouble because to an untrained observer there are no visible handicaps.

There was an additional problem in Randy's case: He had been abused and his strange behavior was considered to be emotional (caused by the abuse), so nobody bothered to look for physical causes. To make matters worse, there was no contact with Randy's mother, who might have been able to furnish a history of the child's development.

One of Randy's most obvious problems — obvious to Florence Scott at least — was his hypersensitivity to touch. This kind of hypersensitivity is the result of a brain injury which distorts the signals coming into the brain from the tactile system, the nerve messages which come from the skin, the muscles and the nerve endings close to the bones. These messages were perceived by Randy so keenly that touch could actually be painful to him.

Florence Scott designed his therapy so its first aim was to make these senses — his proprioceptive senses — more normal. His grandparents took over the responsibility for this part of the program. Several times a day, starting with the lightest touch, they stroked his skin, brushed it and patted him. Eventually the intensity of the contact was allowed to become greater, and deep massage which increased the sensations coming from muscles and the nerve endings along his bones, was added to the routine.

The rest of the program was carried out at the Center, where volunteers moved Randy's arms and legs in the manner in which a baby would make his first movements across the floor. But Randy himself was responsible for another part of the program, and this presented another problem. Since Florence Scott had no medical records to help determine whether Randy's brain injury had happened after birth, during birth, or before birth, she designed a program which recapitulated any neurological development which he might have missed — even while still in the womb. These movements he would have to make himself. He was given a series of four fetal patterns (movements which an unborn baby makes in the womb). He was also to crawl on his belly, and to creep on hands and knees.

"Patterning" movements are not exercises as we commonly understand the exercise to be: to strengthen muscles or to improve a skill. They are designed to feed information into the brain in the same manner and sequence as this information is given to the brain as a child develops: through all the different senses, taste, smell, vision, hearing, and the myriad bits of information which come through the sense of touch.

In addition to the physical movements, Randy was to have carbon dioxide inhalation. This is achieved by having the child breathe into a paper bag for one minute and rebreathe his own air. The carbon dioxide in the rebreathed air is greater than that of fresh air and increases the carbon dioxide level of the blood. When this happens, chemical sensors in the body trigger changes which will deepen the child's breathing and open the carotid artery to allow more blood to the brain. Rather than lower the amount of oxygen going to the brain, this method has been found to increase the blood circulation and aids in the rapid growth of new connections which have to be made there.

At first it was so difficult to keep Randy's attention for more than a few seconds at a time that a volunteer was assigned to work exclusively with Randy and help him return to the task at hand. He was to repeat each movement 30 times, but in the beginning it was considered a triumph if he completed 5 at a time.

As Randy was able to do more, further exercises were added. These covered movements from the infant stage to cross pattern walking.

By September arrangements had been made for Randy to go to school part time. He would, however, go in before the other students came and leave when the others had gone off to lunch. He simply could not tolerate the crowding and pushing that is considered normal in a school situation.

He continued the program at the Oregon Hope and Help Center. By December, he was able to go to a regular class and join the others at lunch time without feeling attacked every time someone accidentally touched him. He was now doing a cross-pattern program and working toward becoming totally right-handed. Cross-pattern walk is the normal walk in which the left hand is forward at the same time the right foot is out front, and the right hand when the left foot is forward. Normally, children have become either right-handed or left-handed by the time they are 6 years old.

By March, Florence Scott had Randy eliminate the early fetal exercises, which he could do easily by now, but he was to continue with the others. By then he was going to school full time and taking on the entire responsibility for his neurological program.

By the following year, Randy was working at the local library, had joined the golf club, the Key Club, Students of America, and the bowling team . . . all this in addition to going to school full time.

All of this sounds very smooth and successful and simple. The truth is, progress was painfuly slow. Jessica Kline, the volunteer who was assigned to work with Randy, writes this:

"Florence asked me to supervise Randy because it was obvious after his first several days at the Center that he couldn't do the program adequately without supervision. My reaction, when Florence asked me, was anything but positive. The brain-injured I'd worked with up to that time were six years old, or younger. They had moderate or severe brain injuries. I didn't know what to do with a 14 year old boy with emotional problems and a mild brain injury which made him hyperactive and highly distractable. I wasn't sure I could get a 14 year old boy **WITHOUT** problems to do a neurological program. I couldn't possibly supervise this kid!

"On the other hand, how could I refuse to try? He needed the program, but he couldn't do it alone. Unsupervised, he was disrupting everyone else's therapy and I was the only person then available to work with him. So I told Florence I'd see what I could do. Between September 21st and March 31st, I worked with Randy about 100 hours and, in fact, worked well with him.

"I began by asking Randy to show me his program. Each day he was to do a series of 27 neurological self-patterns (about 30 repetitions of each pattern); be patterned 4 times; crawl 5 minutes; creep 15 minutes; and mask (the name for the carbon dioxide inhalation therapy). My goal was to have him mask 20 times a day. As I got to know Randy, I gradually began to direct him, and soon I was structuring his time at the Center very closely.

"After a couple of weeks I jotted down a list of the problems I saw with what Randy did at the Center. You couldn't say he had a short attention span, because he couldn't pay attention at all — to anything. He could control his movements (say while doing a pattern exercise) moderately well for a few seconds, but then his movements would get bigger and bigger, more and more out of control and out of rhythm, until he was thrashing with the goal of his movement virtually lost. He couldn't set or keep a regular rhythm in his patterns. He couldn't or didn't remember what pattern followed what. He 'overflowed' (was hyperactive) in every area . . . by moving too much, talking too loud, telling bad jokes, continually getting into somebody's way. He provoked attention . . . negative if positive wasn't readily available . . . in enormous quantities. He was hypersensitive to touch and sometimes reacted very defensively to people touching him. He reacted badly to criticism. He didn't know much about what was and what wasn't socially acceptable and frequently irritated or offended people.

"The volunteers who patterned at the Center went from one patient to another, beginning with whoever happened to be ready first that day. They expected Randy to be up on that table, ready to be patterned, exactly when his turn came in the rotation, no matter where he was in the process of doing the rest of his program. Some patients and volunteers (who were frequently relatives of the other patients) resented the amount of time Randy used the Center's crawling mat each day. They were irritated by his bad jokes, his disruptiveness and his sheer hyperactivity. Most volunteers and patients didn't understand that much of Randy's disruptive behavior came from brain injury and in fact, they didn't believe he was brain-injured at all. After all, he was so different from the rest of the Center's patients, most of whom had trouble walking, or talking, or both. They thought he was merely a rude, bratty kid, whose problem was 'poor raising'. . . specifically, lack of discipline. And Randy, who might interpret somebody's accidental bumping into him as an attack, had to be patterned by these people, whether they were mad at him or not. So a significant part of my job in working with Randy was keeping a workable peace between him and other people at the Center.

"Since I had no preconceived notion of how to work with a kid like Randy, my way of working with him developed directly and often intuitively out of the experience of working with him. I thought a great deal and experimented a lot. If something worked, I used it. What didn't work, I threw out. The major things were: I set reasonable goals to work toward with him (though, especially in the beginning, I seldom told him directly what the goals were).

"I did many things to focus his attention on the work at hand.

"Before we began each pattern, I reviewed the important points with him. ('Lead with your head. Keep your body straight. Nice smooth rhythm all the way to 30.')

"I set the rhythm for him for most of his patterns and counted aloud as he did the exercises. To discourage goofing off, I told him I'd only count the repetitions of each pattern that were good enough to help his brain.

"In many patterns I used hands-on guidance to get him moving correctly and to keep him in rhythm.

"During and after each pattern I pointed out what he'd done right. ('You kept your hands flat all the way through, that's real good.') I used enormous amounts of what I called 'positive teaching' — i.e., telling him what to do in advance whenever I could, in addition to what **NOT** to do. ('When Florence is talking to someone in the kitchen, get your drink of water in the bathroom. That way you won't disturb Florence or the other person.')

"I was very careful to correct his behavior in ways which didn't arouse defensiveness in him or hurt his self esteem.

"I tried to equip Randy with habits which would enable him to do the program better on his own when I was not there to supervise him. I don't know how well I succeeded in this.

"When we began, I structured what Randy did extremely closely. I told him what to do constantly (probably several times a minute). As he got better, he took more responsibility. At the point where he stopped his program to go to school full time, he still needed supervision, but much less.

214

"As I worked with Randy I could easily imagine why he had been an abused child, simply because it was so difficult to have lasting impact on his behavior. In the beginning, for example, I could tell him, 'Just plain crawl, don't try to find a new or different way to do it. Just crawl!' and ten seconds later he'd be busily and happily inventing 'variation on Crawling No. 167.' During a 5 minute crawling session I might have to 'bring him back to task' 20 times. Certainly 10 times would be a minimum. In other words, **AT LEAST** twice per minute I had to redirect his behavior.

"When working with Randy I used frequency (telling him what to do or not to do several times per minute, often repeating myself) and duration (telling him the same things week after week, after week.) I escalated the intensity by focusing his attention on me, speaking to him in a firm, potent voice, and giving him simple, brief commands. I escalated the level of command by guiding him physically. All these are techniques to get through to difficult-to-reach people, and they helped me get through to Randy and to change his behavior for the better.

"I was able to work well with Randy because I had a reasonably good understanding of his brain dysfunction and how it affected his behavior and his abilities. I was able and willing to learn from experience what worked in getting him to do things ... or not to do things. I believed he did 'the best he could with what he had,' so I was able to 'avoid taking his pathology personally.' These are the attitudes that make it possible for someone to work with a difficult child. They are hard to achieve when such a difficult child is one's own, especially when the mother is young and inexperienced and may feel the child's misbehavior is her fault. A mother of a child like Randy has to cope with him 24 hours a day. I had the advantage of being with him for limited amounts of time and, during that time, had few other responsibilities beyond teaching him. I also had emotional support, mainly from Florence, when the work with him was frustrating or discouraging. Even so, working with Randy took enormous amounts of energy. Each day, I 'psyched myself up' to work with him for about half an hour before I started our sessions. I spent about an hour relaxing and recovering my energy after each of these sessions. (Our sessions ran 1½ to 2½ hours.)

"We all understood how easy it would have been for a mother to be overwhelmed by the demands of a child like Randy, and to beat or to slap him, especially if she had no understanding of his problems and no chance to escape from the situation."

215

The child who emerged after ten months of this total developmental approach was quite different from the early Randy. He no longer performed the strange, autistic rituals which drew people's attention. He no longer rocked and made strange noises. He was able to tolerate touch. This was enormous progress. Before, every time someone came near Randy, he felt threatened, not because he had been abused, but because being touched was literally painful to him.

Randy stopped making the strange noises. Whether these noises had been used to help him locate himself in space, or to drown out noises in his own ears, was never established. But he ceased making them. The world had become a stable and fairly secure place for Randy, not because the world had changed, but because his senses no longer presented him with incomplete and inaccurate information.

There is no doubt that Randy was also helped by the teachers and counselors who were also working with him, but the greatest progress was made during the period that Randy worked at the Center. In fact, the one time Randy's father was contacted, he stated that Randy changed more during that period than he had during the entire rest of his young life.

Randy visited the Oregon Hope and Help Center the summer before this report was written. He was on vacation from the university he attended. Randy was still handsome, just as he had been five years before when he and his friend had wandered in unexpectedly. Only this time, Randy was quiet — quiet and friendly and very much the gentleman.

He didn't brag. Florence Scott did not find out until later (and then from his grandfather) that this boy, who could not tolerate going to school, had made the dean's list at his university.

II. How to Stimulate A Baby

Ideally, to stimulate a baby, you start with a wanted baby, whose mother had eaten good food for several years and was protected from strain during the pregnancy — because then you have a greater chance of having a healthy, relaxed baby. After the birth, you make sure the mother continues to get extra rest and nourishment, and you let nature take its course. Both men and women instinctively stroke their babies, touching them gently, first with their fingertips and then with the palm of the hand. They rock them and coo to

216

them. They talk to them in higher-than-normal pitched voices and sing to them. They play "This little piggy went to market," and the baby learns the perimeters of his body. They hold him high up in the air and they bounce him on their knees and play "Trott, trott, trott to Boston. Trott, trott, trott to Lynn. Trott, trott, trott to Salem, and we all fall — in!" letting the baby tip backward on the last line, and baby gets vestibular stimulation.

Even a two-week-old baby has a "conversation" with the mother. Baby sticks out his tongue; Mommy does the same. Baby purses his lips; so does Mommy. Mommy mirrors baby's face, and Baby imitates Mommy. A two-week old baby gazes longer at his mother than at a stranger before he turns his face away (18 seconds out of 30, as compared with 7 or 8 at a stranger). Even at two weeks, although the baby's head is turned and he seems no longer to be listening, his body moves in the rhythm of the conversation of the adult. This rhythm will later be incorporated into the child's speech.

If you want to have an idea of what the baby's auditory world is like, invest in a tape or record which teaches a foreign language (or borrow one from your public library). It should be a language completely strange to you, such as Chinese or Russian. You will notice you are so busy listening, that in sentences or long words, only the last few syllables or the last word will stick in your memory. And so it is for the baby. The last word still echoes in his ears, while he can't make sense of the first ones because the other words followed too closely. And so, to help him find his way in the welter of strange sounds that your conversation is to him, repeat the last words of your sentence: "Now we're going to take a bath . . . a bath!" "Timmy is going bye-bye in the car . . . bye-bye in the car!" Pretty soon he knows what bath means, and when you bring the diaper bag, he shouts happily: "Car . . . Car!" Most mothers do this automatically. It's not just being silly; it makes life easier for the baby.

It's as simple as that. If you want to get a little more scientific than that, here are a few suggestions.

During the first few weeks, when the baby is held up, his body tilted just a little forward, the baby will make reflexive stepping movements. Place a finger in his hand, and he will hold on tightly. He cannot let go yet, but he can almost suspend himself from your finger. Toes will make a grasping movement around a finger placed just underneath them. His legs will make attempts at crawling. All these skills will disappear during the coming months until the baby can do them voluntarily at a later time. If you give the newborn a chance to exercise these skills now, they will return stronger (and possibly sooner) at that later time.

Attach a mobile over the baby's crib. Not only does it give him something to focus on, but he learns that by kicking his legs he can make those pretty colors move!

When the baby is not being changed or bathed or fed or cuddled, allow him to stay on the floor. Arnold Gesell said that the floor is the gymnasium of the infant. Being there will allow him to roll, to swim on his belly, to crawl backwards and forwards, to creep, and so on. There will be no technique necessary to stimulate him.

Problems come when the baby does not react to the mother. Doctors hesitate to make negative diagnoses early, so it is best to go ahead and do what you can on your own. Find out what will make the baby react. Some infants may be so sensitive to sensations that they will tune you out completely. This hypersensitivity may well be due to an injury in the cerebellum and may slowly yield to much rocking and other kinds of vestibular stimulation. Even well babies thrive on this. You can turn him over, swing him gently, or just carry him with you as much as possible. It has been found that the movement made by picking up a child as you face him is the most calming. Dr. Ruth Rice found that stroking, massaging, and rocking the baby four times a day for a period of four months, resulted in greater weight gain and faster neurological development and the gain was retained even months later.

There are several books out on baby massage. Be careful about massaging down the back along the spinal cord; a baby might go into seizures from that. There is another technique in these books which needs challenging: They suggest that you make a circle with your thumb and forefinger and, starting at the infant's wrist, draw it up toward the torso. This sends very confusing messages to the brain. Whenever we flex a limb, as one set of muscles contracts, the other set has to relax.

Touching the skin lightly will relax the muscles underneath. Giving deep pressure will tend to make them contract. As you give first light, then fairly deep pressure, be sure to stimulate first only the muscles which lift, then the set of muscles which pull down. This holds true for the arms and the legs as well as for the fingers and feet.

At the infant stage, both sides of the baby should react equally. If one side is not doing as well as the other, stimulate the stronger side for about one minute, then the weaker one for about three. Take your cue from the baby's reactions. Check a good baby book so you do not become unduly concerned about skills which a baby is not expected to have until a later age. If these skills do not appear on schedule, you can facilitate things for your baby. If the baby makes no attempts at crawling, you can build a slide and place the baby at the top so gravity will make it easier for him to move. Watch him constantly or build an edge so he won't fall off. (Normal babies crawl backward first, so if he does not move forward, you might first try having him come down backward!) As the baby gets better at crawling down the board, keep lowering the top of the board to make the slant less steep. A bright toy at the bottom will make the journey down more enjoyable. Give the baby a long rest each time — it's hard work for him.

You will probably never be able to prove later that what you did for your baby is the reason you have such a marvelous child! If you do try this type of stimulation, at least you know you tried your best to help, and you cannot possibly hurt a child with these methods.

Take your cue from the baby. The premature baby tends to be hypersensitive and needs a great deal of vestibular stimulation because he missed so much gentle movement by not having been in the womb the full nine months. The rocking chair is your greatest help; rapid rocking seems to be more effective. Recordings of sounds from within the womb, which have the mother's heartbeat and other prenatal sounds, are available at most record stores. The child delivered by Caesarian section usually needs more touching, having missed the tactile stimulation which comes from the journey through the birth canal. This child tends to have a hard time knowing where his body ends and the rest of the world begins. Give deep massage and hold him tight, but be careful not to bruise him.

For all the ways in which babies are alike, there are also no two babies who are exactly alike. As the saying goes: Go by the baby, and not by the book!

III. Mini-lesson In Neurological Organization
(Or how to explain to a friend or neighbor why you are doing sensori-motor exercises with your learning-disabled child.)

As an experiment to show how the brain works, ask your friend or neighbor to put water on the stove for tea or coffee. What happens?

He picks up the water kettle, swishes it from side to side, decides if it needs more water and, if it does, adds some and puts it on the burner. Point out to him that the nerve endings in the hands told the muscles of the arms how much strength he had to use to lift the kettle. The change in weight in the kettle as he twisted it from side to side, and the noise of the water hitting the sides of the kettle told him how much water was in it. He never lifted the lid to check for the level of the water!

Suggest a second experiment: Ask him to turn himself around and around until he gets dizzy. (Be sure to have him do this where he cannot get hurt if he falls.) For a moment or two after turning, he will have to hold on to something to keep from falling. If you ask him what is happening, he will tell you the room is spinning.

Explain to him that the fluid inside the semicircular canals in his ears is still in motion because of inertia. As a result, the tiny hairs inside the canals are reacting to this movement in sending messages to the various parts of the brain. The reaction of the brain to these messages is to tell the eyes that the room must be moving, or the little hairs would not be agitated by the fluid. He needs to hold on, because the same information sent by the little hairs' reaction to the moving fluid is also telling his body to adjust to this moving room. He will then use the pressure — exerted by his hands in holding on — to tell himself the world is, after all, as it should be: steady, quiet and permanent.

The brain functions in a wholistic way, rather like a sophisticated computer — the "It's a bird... it's a plane... it's Superman!" sort of thing. Until all the information is in, we do not know what we are seeing.

Let's presume you are in the hospital with bandaged eyes. Your best friend brings you a bottle of cologne, but after she leaves, you knock it off the night table and it breaks. Once you are out of the hospital again and your eyes work fine, you go to the store to buy another bottle because you don't want your friend to know you broke her gift.

One problem: What was the name of the cologne? So you tell the saleslady the cologne came in a square bottle with a ball on top. The saleslady explains that this kind of bottle is made by a certain company, but there are 10 different kinds of scent in the same type of bottle. Now you have to sniff every single bottle made by the company until you come to the one whose smell suddenly makes you recall all the horrible memories of the hospital, and then you know you have found it. Once you have seen the name, you no longer have to go around sniffing every bottle; you just ask for it by name.

Now, let's presume a little further — that the damage to your eyes had been permanent and you never got your sight back. You might be able to find out what the name of the cologne was by sniffing it and having someone tell you the name on the bottle, but you would still not know the names of the other scents in the same-style bottles. You would be able to distinguish them only by smell and not by sight.

The child with a learning problem or an unexplained behavior problem usually has a similar difficulty with one or more of his senses. This could be because an injury to his brain interrupted the flow of information he needed to have stored in his brain. It could also be because there was never a chance to get the information, simply for lack of experience. Usually, the child uses all his other senses to make up for the lacking information and, unfortunately, covers up the lack so well that it is very hard to find out just what is wrong. It is often not necessary to find out exactly what happened. We can go about putting the missing information into the little computer which is his brain by proceeding along the following premise.

The brain at birth (and even before birth) is not, as was believed for a long time, a blank slate or, to use the computer comparison, a blank tape. From the moment of the child's birth, there is a tremendous amount of information already programmed into the brain. We can see this preprogramming when we observe the reflexes of the baby. There are about 20 of them at birth, most of which have a life saving intent. The withdrawal reflex makes the foot withdraw from a pinprick. When you touch the side of the baby's cheek, the rooting reflex makes the baby turn his head to find the nipple. These are simple reflexes.

Then there are more complex ones which affect an entire set of different muscles. One of these is the labyrinth reflex, which is triggered when gravity moves the fluid in the semicircular canals in the ear and which influences the entire position of the baby's body.

Turn the baby face down and the knees will pull up, the little fists will pull up to the shoulders, and the head tuck in. This prevents the baby from smothering. When you turn the baby on his back, you can see the asymmetric tonic reflex at work. The head turns to the side on which the arm is stretched out; the other hand is curled at the shoulder. This puts the baby in the best position to see his own hand, to learn what it feels like to move that hand on purpose and what muscles he has to use to move that hand. He learns that this thing which mother places in his hand, and which is smooth and hard if he puts it in his mouth, rattles when he shakes his hand. The rattle helps his eyes find his hand and, at the same time, he learns that if he moves the hand on purpose, the rattling noise continues! If he turns his head, the whole position of his body is reversed. He can now see with the other eye what the world looks like. The identical information goes into the other side of the brain.

1— Labyrinthine Prone Flexion Response

2— Labyrinthine Supine Extension Response

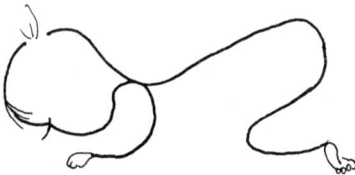

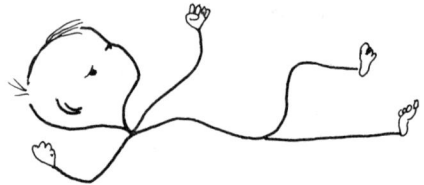

3— Asymmetric TNR Response (Child is on his back; head turned to the left)

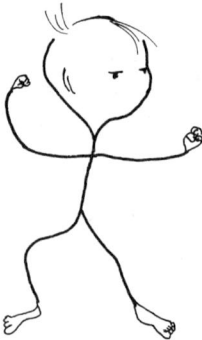

4— Head-extended Symmetric TNR Response

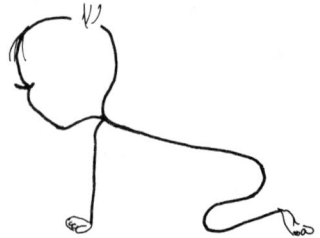

It does not matter what you call this process. Joseph Chilton Pearce calls it the formation of a matrix; Jean Piaget calls it a schema; and Carl H. Delacato calls it neurological organization. These reflexes put the child into a position to put all the information he needs — feel of the skin, pressure, taste, smell, vision, hearing

— into those parts of the brain where they link with the other sensory information. This information gives him the motor control he needs to move into the next developmental phase. It also gives him the ability to retrieve the information received through an alternate sense system; that is, he hears some sounds and knows mother is coming. (You can find the keys in your pocket without ever looking at them, even if you have never consciously learned what keys feel like.)

To repeat: Each developmental phase, triggered by reflexes which put the baby into the proper position for the necessary input, gives the brain sufficient information for the child to go on to the next stage of development.

Now, to get back to how the sensori-motor approach helps the child with a learning problem. Let's say Johnny can't read as well as he should. We have established that Johnny has had good teachers, and there seem to be no emotional reasons for this failure. Now we start looking for other possible reasons.

We ask Johnny to hop on one foot and find that he can't do it. We do not attempt to teach him to hop on one foot, we presume that because he does not have enough control over his body to balance it on one foot, we need teach him the control, not just the hopping. So we ask him to walk and find that his walk is uncoordinated and awkward. We do not then proceed to teach him to walk, but we presume he did not receive enough input to his nervous system from the prior development to give him enough information to walk properly. We then take him to creeping on hands and knees. We find that his toes stick up when he does so, that his hands turn out instead of pointing straight ahead, and that, basically, his creeping is uncoordinated. Even so, we do not teach him to creep, because again, we presume the prior development did not give him enough information to permit him to creep well. We then ask him to rock back and forth, and maybe to walk on his knees. He does both very well. At this point we give him a chance to rock and to walk on his knees for a while, and suddenly, when we next ask him to creep again, his creeping has become smooth and serialized!

Now we see his system has received enough input from the rocking movement to permit him to creep well. However, we also presume that, since he never crept properly before this, we had better give him a chance to catch up on the information he needs from the creeping to go on to walking more smoothly. Now we have him creep for about half an hour a day, for a period of about three or four weeks, until we are sure we are getting a nice smooth, constant performance which will send all the important information to his brain:

My hands are so far from each eye;

It takes so many moves to get me to the nearest corner;

If I move fast, I get there faster;

If I hear my mother's voice, it comes from the right, or the back, or the left, depending on how quickly each ear gets the sound waves, etc., etc.

After all this information is firmly stored in the network of the brain, we ask Johnny to walk and — hurray! — his walk has improved. And so it goes. As he walks, the eyes receive the information needed for distance viewing. They tell his body how to align itself with the help of the cues given by straight and horizontal lines so he can stand up straight and can even learn how to hop on one foot!

Now Johnny knows how to creep, how to walk and how to hop on one foot. He still does not know how to read and write. But now we can teach him quite easily how to read and write, because now he can judge the distance his hand needs to move across the paper to make a letter. He can judge whether the "b" goes to the right, or to the left, like a "d". His eyes have learned to follow a line from left to right and also from right to left, so he can find the next line on the page quickly and without losing his place. School is now no longer a nightmarish place for him, and learning becomes a challenge he can meet readily.

So very often we do not know why a child is not functioning well. Sometimes we have a clue because of his medical history. Decalcification of the teeth, especially if it is mirrored on both sides of the child's mouth, may indicate there had been a high fever at one time. Sometimes a child had reverted to an earlier behavior pattern after a sickness. These could be clues that a virus (or even the antibiotic used to fight it) destroyed some connections in his brain. Sometimes there is a history of a fall or even a blow to the head.

The cause does not matter. If we go about giving him the missing information in the sequence of normal development (and we may have to go back to crawling or even fetal movements!), we are likely to catch the problem, even though we may not have had a clear idea as to just what was wrong.

IV. Evaluating and Treating Sensory Problems

By permission from Carl H. Delacato

DEFINITIONS:

HYPER: A condition of any one of the sensory systems which allows too much of the sensory input to reach the brain.

HYPO: A sluggish sensory system which allows too little of the sensations to enter the brain.

WHITE NOISE: A sensory system which is so inefficient that its own operation creates an interference or "static" which is perceived by the brain as if it really existed.

TACTILITY: Feelings of temperature, pain, pressure and proprioception, i.e., feeling input from the muscles.

TACTILITY, HYPER: The child hates being touched, hates hot and cold, can tolerate only temperatures close to body temperature. Likes soft and furry toys and material. Likes to stroke himself with those. Hates rough clothes, especially woolens, and may fight putting them on. Can't tolerate pain. Tolerates only light, rhythmic stimulation he gives himself. Has tendency to feel warm to the touch and to perspire easily.

TACTILITY, HYPER; PROTECTION: Eliminate any rough or scratchy clothing. Any touching of the child should be extremely gentle. Protect him from pain as much as possible. Be especially gentle when bathing, drying, or cutting toe- and fingernails. Haircuts are difficult for this kind of child. Try to maintain even temperatures. Warn people not to touch or tickle him. (Do not warn other children. They are likely to take advantage of a ticklish child and do exactly what they are not supposed to do — tickle him.)

TACTILITY, HYPER; TREATMENT: See what the child does to himself that he seems to enjoy. If the child likes to stroke his cheek, he may permit you to do that. Once he begins to enjoy that, you may continue on to other forms of stroking. Gently stroke his head and neck; later, arms and legs. The first goal is to build in the child a tolerance for tactile stimulation coming from others.

TACTILITY, HYPO: This child tends to feel so little pain that he ignores bumps and spills which would have others crying. Such a child may be covered with bruises which he seems to ignore, and the mother may be suspected of child abuse. Such children often smile when they are spanked, and this can easily infuriate parents to the point where they will hit the child even harder and seriously injure him.

These are also the self-mutilating children, who pick at sores and scars until they bleed. They love wrestling and fighting and often provoke fights.

They love bear hugs, and hurl themselves at the people they love, something which is not apt to get them approval.

TACTILITY, HYPO; PROTECTION: This child needs as much tactile stimulation as possible. Provide bear hugs, tumbling and wrestling. His skin needs much attention. Alternate hot and cold water in his shower. Dry him with a rough towel and give deep massage. Be careful not to hurt him, because while he does not feel pain, he is still vulnerable.

TACTILITY, HYPO; TREATMENT: Massage him deeply; also pinch his skin, but not to the point of bruising! Increase the frequency with which you do the activities, stimulating the skin by increasing the duration and the variety of tactile inputs. Be especially aware of those areas which he seems to pick on most, and provide the most stimulation there. This can include the mouth and the face. Massage with a vibrator is very successful, since it reaches all the senses from the outside of the skin to the nerve endings attached to the bones. In giving massage, gently move the joints of the bones, starting with the fingers and moving up to the wrist, the elbow, and the shoulder. When finished, rub the areas with a rough towel. Mention each area as you are doing these things. Ask him what he is feeling and if he likes what you are doing.

TACTILITY, WHITE NOISE: These children scratch nonexistent itches on their bodies. Many times they will shiver as though some unseen object has touched them.

They seem to go along calmly for a period of time, and then suddenly display an outburst of tactility, almost as if there were a gradual buildup of tactility coming from within their bodies. These outbursts may take the form of hitting themselves or others, or there may be a sudden need to be touched by someone or to be held. Sometimes their skin seems to ripple or get goose bumps for no evident reason.

TACTILITY, WHITE NOISE PROTECTION: The child needs to learn to distinguish which sensations come from within and which from without. That way, he will not blame others for his discomfort and hit out at them. He needs much stimulation of all kinds from the outside: Tickling, rubbing and hugging, and must be told each time where the stimulation is coming from and who is doing it.

TACTILITY, WHITE NOISE TREATMENT: Teach the child the differences between different tactile inputs. Say each time: "Now I'm going to squeeze you, then I'm going to lift you up." When he begins to understand outside versus inside tactile information, invent as many ways of giving tactile stimulation as possible. Explain to him beforehand what they will be and say what they are while you are doing it. Vary the rhythm of the input so the child does not get bored and tune you out. Repetition is very important for that kind of child.

CAUTION: With the constant awareness of sexual abuse of children by educators and parents, be sure that any tactile stimulation is done either by the parents or in the presence of a second person!

VISION, HYPER: Hypervisual children can often read extremely well. Their visual recall is astounding. They may spend hours staring at a drop of water or the reflections of the sun in a glass of water. They love to look through pinholes and may use a single strand of hair as a sighting hair for more distant objects. The creating of extremely intricate designs is one of their favorite activities. They are fascinated by objects seen against the sky, such as airplanes, bridges, high buildings, or clouds.

Usually these children are afraid of the dark. They are frightened by sharp flashes and are uncomfortable at very bright places, such as the beaches in the summer. They love to look at spinning objects which are used for visual illusions, objects such as spinning tops, wheels on a train, and running fans. They are rarely fooled by visual illusions. They also generally do not like mirrors or their own reflections in the water.

VISION, HYPER; PROTECTION: Keep these children in subdued light, if possible. If they have to go outside, have them use sun glasses. Bright lights and shadows are hard on them. If they must go out, take them in the evening when the shadows are not as sharp. Eliminate mirrors, unshaded light bulbs and other flashing lights from their surroundings.

VISION, HYPER; TREATMENT: Discourage any visual activity which the child controls, such as twirling objects or manipulating reflections of the sun in a glass of water. Give him intricate tasks to do, such as completing puzzles and tracing. Teach reading, even if the child does not speak. Do not allow the child to spend too much time at any one task. Vary the kinds of projects you give him, and make them more complicated as the child learns from them.

VISION, HYPO: Rocking is the giveaway for hypovisual children. Most people can tell if they are sitting or standing up straight by aligning themselves with the vertical lines of the walls and the horizontal lines of the floor and ceiling. The hypovisual child needs the pull of gravity against his body to keep his balance. He is fascinated by bright lights. He is constantly trying to investigate the relationships of objects in space, as if he were not sure an object is the same when seen from another angle. He generally needs to touch most objects, since his eyes don't fully tell what they are. (Rodin became a sculptor rather than a painter, essentially because not until his late teens did anyone recognize that he could barely see.)

The hypovisual child is afraid of heights, stairs, dark tunnels, and often, of speed. His visual abilities cannot cope with speed and with depth. As a toddler he may want to sleep on the floor, because he is frightened by the height of his bed. Hypovisual children may walk back and forth across the place where one rug meets another of a different color. They are assuring themselves that the difference in hue does not also indicate a difference in height. They are intrigued by mirrors and shiny objects. Moving leaves and swaying trees fascinate them. They also throw objects, trying to determine distances, though they rarely throw heavy objects, unlike hypoauditory children, who do so to make noise.

VISION, WHITE NOISE: This child sees things that are not there. They are created from the inside, possibly by pressure on the visual nerve. He may be paying attention to specks of dust or little particles floating in the fluid of his eye. In extreme cases, there might be hallucinations created from lack of visual stimulation, such as those which astronauts experience during experimental sensory deprivation. He seems to stare right through you, because he is too occupied by his inner vision. He may tap or push his eyes to see flashes of light and light displays created by the brain.

VISION, WHITE NOISE; PROTECTION: Gain the child's attention by creating a visual interest outside his private display. Playing with a lighted penlight in a semidark room is most likely to gain access to his vision, because it activates one of the earliest reflexes. Manipulate this light and show him that you are doing so, but do not let him control it. Above all, do not try to force him to pay attention to you; let him come to you instead.

VISION, WHITE NOISE; TREATMENT: Use a brightly lit mirror to gain his attention. Have him move toward something outside of his inner vision. Vary the distance and the direction from which you are finding objects to lure him: His attention is turned off unless there is a frequent change in pace or distance. In extreme cases, the child sees a flicker around people, which makes them appear unstable and inconstant to the child and, therefore, very frightening. He may find this so discouraging that he is turned off by the world altogether.

Use a brightly lit full-length mirror, lit preferably with natural light. As he sees himself in the mirror, trace the outline of his body on the mirror with your finger. Point to different parts of his body. Have him point to parts of your body. Show him your motions and his motions in the mirror. Be sure everything is done smoothly. Try to discourage his habit of looking inward, and replace it with a visual world which is stimulating but not so complicated as to be discouraging. Repetition is very important.

TASTE, HYPER: The hypertaste child is a very picky eater. As a rule of thumb, hypertaste children tend to use the tip of their tongue for tasting. They are monitoring sweet and salty foods. They also tend to explore objects with the tongue. The tongue is also usually very sensitive to tactile input. As a result, these children will react violently to the texture of foods as well as to their taste. They detest bubbly water and may throw up if surprised by the texture of food.

TASTE, HYPER; PROTECTION: Give these children bland foods without spices. Never give them carbonated drinks because the carbonation tends to increase the taste effect of the drink. Make sure the bland foods are nutritious, because you will not be able to get much food into these children. When feeding them, introduce them to a food mixed with some familiar food which they will accept.

TASTE, HYPER; TREATMENT: Slowly introduce new foods. Take a small drop of some new bland food and put it on the roof of his mouth, right behind his front teeth. Always tell him the name of the food. When he learns to tolerate this experience with bland foods, start introducing some sweet and salty foods. (Remember to place only a small drop behind the upper teeth and then a drop on the tongue.) Tell him what taste it is. With patience you can work up to sour and bitter tastes, such as vinegar and mustard. Use sour and bitter last.

TASTE, HYPO: These children will eat anything and everything. They are dangerous to themselves, because they will drink such horrible-tasting things as gasoline and other poisonous substances they may come across. In less severe cases, they may simply eat too much.

TASTE, HYPO; PROTECTION: First of all, remove all dangerous substances from the house. This includes cleaning agents, strong soaps and, especially, detergents. Since he will eat anything you give him, make sure the food is nutritious and well-balanced.

TASTE, HYPO; TREATMENT: Since he has no taste discrimination, it must be taught. With this kind of child, it has been found that it is easiest to start with the back of the tongue. Give him bitter tastes in liquid form. Give only bitter tastes for a period of two weeks, then pass on to sour. Pickle juice is a good one. Put a drop on each side of the tongue, and let him see and smell the pickle jar. Tell him what it is. After another two weeks, introduce salt tastes on the tip of the tongue, then two weeks of sweet tastes. (For each application, a few drops will be enough.) After that, start bitter again, only this time, change the tastes every day. If by then he can identify the tastes, you can mix the applications each day. Always put the tastes in the areas indicated, because those are the areas where the taste buds are sensitive to that particular taste.

TASTE, WHITE NOISE: This child is constantly aware of the taste of his mouth. He tastes his own saliva, and constantly sucks his tongue or feels along his teeth. Children who normally do not do this may do so after a bout of illness, when they have been treated with an antibiotic, which has altered the flora of their mouth. These children are usually apathetic about food. They may have a thick tongue as a result of the sucking. Sometimes they regurgitate their food and retaste it.

TASTE, WHITE NOISE; PROTECTION: Discourage regurgitation and rechewing of food. Obviously you cannot control this in the child, but you can keep him so busy right after eating that he has no time to be interested in taste at that point. Try to get him to exercise his tongue. When you brush his teeth also brush his tongue, both top and sides, but be careful not to irritate it. Some children react well to a strong mouthwash, but do not let the child swallow the mouthwash.

TASTE, WHITE NOISE; TREATMENT: Take a piece of food representative of one of the four tastes: salt, sweet, sour and bitter. Place it in the space between his teeth and his cheek. Don't let him chew it. As it dissolves the taste will overpower the taste of the child's saliva. Find which tastes he tolerates best. Be sure to tell him what it is, and what you are doing. Start with the taste he likes most. Show him what it is, let him smell it, and then place it between teeth and cheek and allow it to melt in his mouth. This should be done from four to eight times daily. If he does not tolerate the bitter or sour tastes, use a food which has only a trace of sour or bitter, such as cooked fruit with lemon juice and chopped up bitter endive.

When he has learned to tolerate these tastes, start teaching him to differentiate between them, by giving them to him one after another and having him tell you what they are. With this kind of child start with the tip of the tongue and with sweet and salty. Tasting games are fun. Repetition is very important.

HEARING, HYPER: Children with auditory problems are terribly dependent on the noise level of their environment. The hyperauditory child has tremendously sensitive ears, so that the noise level acceptable to others often becomes unbearable to him.

When this happens, he simply turns off all the sounds coming from a source outside himself. This is not a conscious decision over which he has control. In extreme cases, he is totally deaf to the outside world and on hearing tests will test out as deaf. Airports, concerts, parties, or noisy traffic are threatening places for him. He will be prone to car sickness and will get dizzy playing spinning games which others might enjoy. He is easily identified by the pallor of his face, which seems to be gray, almost as if he were in shock.

WARNING: Don't be misled by the noises he makes himself. Those he can tolerate, because he can control their level.

HEARING, HYPER; PROTECTION: Be careful where he sleeps: Every little noise will wake him. If there is no place to provide quiet, turn on a radio which plays quiet, uninterrupted music. The musical background will mask the noises which normally will wake him up.

These children run away from sound and can easily become lost at noisy places when they seek a quiet place to hide. Be sure to conduct a quiet search, because noises may frighten them off.

If the noise level is too great for the child, he can be given special earplugs. These will cut down the noise so he can tolerate it. This should be done only for survival at the early stages of the treatment.

HEARING, HYPER; TREATMENT: Provide the child with a quiet environment, talk to him in a quiet voice. In extreme cases, he will relate better to whispers. Whisper at every opportunity. Games can easily be invented. When he begins to allow you to whisper into his ears, you have made progress. Provide vestibular stimulation. This means giving the semicircular canals in his ears a chance to experience many different kinds of movements. The gravitational pull of the fluid in these canals signals, through the movement of the fine hairs in the canals, how the body has to adjust to keep the child from falling. This is a sort of switching mechanism, which connects the eyes and the muscular reactions — in short, it controls not only hearing but the entire balancing system of the body. (In these children you may find a kind of rigidity in the way the head is held. It's as if shoulders and head have to be moved at the same time,

because the child might lose his balance if he moved his head separately.)
To stimulate this system, allow the child many gravitational experiences,
such as being turned over or rolled on the floor. Let him hang upside-down
and jump on a trampoline, turn him on a swivel chair, and stop the
movement of the chair at unexpected moments. (This form of stimulation
is indicated for the hypoauditory child as well.)

HEARING, HYPO: This child is the banger, the shouter, the noisemaker.
Not enough sound reaches his brain, so he seeks loud noises. He is attracted
to noises. He flushes the toilet, likes to run the vacuum cleaner, and moves
toward anything which makes noise. He likes to experiment with the echoes
of his voice in different acoustical areas. He especially loves areas such as
gyms and toilets with bare walls, which will echo sounds. He loves to listen
to loud lawn mowers and, especially, engines which make rhythmic noise.
He loves to slam doors and drawers. In fact, he may tear things apart for
the noise they make. He loves crowds, circuses, and loud games.

HEARING, HYPO; PROTECTION: The child should be allowed plenty
of noises, but singly, and not with a noisy background. Be sure to have
the ears checked to see that there is no physical obstruction which prevents
sound from entering. However, the label hypoauditory does not necessarily
mean the sound is not going in, but more probably means there is no
distinction being made among sounds. The obstruction may not be in the
ear but exist in the auditory cortex of the brain. This may have been caused
by an injury or may simply be lack of exposure to words. A city-raised adult,
walking through a jungle will not be able to interpret the sounds of the
jungle which a native child of six easily could. The hypoauditory child will
enjoy traffic noises but may be incapable of distinguishing the different
sounds and where they come from. As a result, he cannot protect himself
in traffic and get out of the way. He should, therefore, be watched carefully
in such situations. Since he does much sound exploring by banging and
making loud noises, he should be allowed a place where he can do so
without bothering anyone. He will love animals that bark and may even
tease them or abuse them to hear the barking sound, so he must be
supervised when playing with dogs, to protect both child and dog.

HEARING, HYPO; TREATMENT: Allow the child a microphone or a
walkie-talkie and show him how it works. Let him use it repetitively to
explore sound. Talk in a loud firm voice, but do not force the child to listen;
try to get his attention. Cassette tape recorders are wonderful, because the
child can hear a certain passage over and over again to learn to evaluate
the sounds. Probably the best way of knowing what this kind of child
experiences might be to buy a foreign-language record and try to learn
to speak a language from it. Teaching a foreign language to this kind of
child is a good way to stretch his ability to distinguish sounds.

HEARING, WHITE NOISE: The child with white noise in his hearing
is overwhelmed by the noises his own body makes. He can listen to the
pulse in his own throat, the static in his ears, or the rumbling of his stomach.
The white noise can also be the result of very little or no noise coming in

from the outside.

When we are in a quiet place, like a snowy forest, where all the noises are absorbed by the snow, we can hear a ringing in our ears. Astronauts, experimenting with totally soundfree surroundings, have also reported auditory hallucinations.

HEARING, WHITE NOISE; PROTECTION: Have the ears checked for sound obstruction or pressure. Do not permit the child to listen to his inner sounds. Keep at him constantly with sound, particularly speech. He must be kept busy doing all kinds of chores and activities to distract him from inner sounds. Cats make excellent pets, because the child listens to the cat's purring. To help him distinguish the inner sounds, encourage odd positions such as lying on the floor, standing on the head, rocking with his eyes closed.

HEARING, WHITE NOISE; TREATMENT: Teach him the difference between outer and inner sounds. Keep him away from a constant type of sound, such as a humming air conditioner or the sound of the ocean. Invent games with a stethoscope, so he can listen to his heartbeat and his pulse, and teach him what they are. Then gently talk into the stethoscope and make sure he sees that you are making the noise. Discourage the sounds he makes by himself, such as humming or tapping. Have him listen to outside noises. A great game is a sort of blind man's buff, in which the child, his eyes covered with a handkerchief, is given spoken clues to help him find a hidden prize. The more sound games you can invent, the better. Repetition is of great value.

SMELL, HYPER: The child who is hypersensitive to smells lives in a horrible world. In the extreme cases, these children throw up at the smell of their own feces. The hypersmell children who make it to school are overwhelmed by the onslaught of smells from all sides which the others never notice.

There is the residue of the pungent cleaning solutions used to keep the school disinfected, the smell of wet clothes on the hangers, the odor of coloring pens, the clothing of other children, and the ever-changing smell of the one adult, the teacher.

Especially during the winter, when the rooms are not well ventilated, just being there becomes difficult for the child.

SMELL, HYPER; PROTECTION: Once you are aware of how the child is affected by smells, try to keep your own body smells at a minimum. Wear cotton clothing which is less likely to accumulate body odors. The child is not fooled by perfumes, deodorants, or strong-smelling soaps. Chlorophyll tablets help eliminate body odors. Women should try to avoid close contact with the child during their menstrual periods, because their body odor changes at that time. Keep the rooms well ventilated, or seat the child near a window. Avoid cooking things like cabbage or fish which have a strong odor. If the child's attention is not captured by trying to overcome his repugnance to the odors, he can learn more easily. He is more likely to allow himself to make friends if the odor of the other children is not offensive to him. Be sure to explain to others how smells affect him, so they will

232

not be puzzled by his stand-offish behavior.

SMELL, HYPER; TREATMENT: Once the child's environment becomes less threatening, start giving him gentle and mild smells. From a distance of several feet tell him what the smell will be. Then slowly approach him and let him smell it at a closer distance. Do not put the smell right under his nose. It is better to start too far away and ask him at what point he can smell what you are offering. Repeat this one smell at a time.

Take him outside to a non-smell-polluted area and let him discuss what he can smell. Let him learn to distinguish people by their smell. You are teaching him to tolerate smells which he cannot control. As he learns to tolerate more smells, include more household smells. Slowly he will gain a more normal tolerance of the smell environment.

SMELL, HYPO: The hyposmell child seeks intense smells. He may have smeared feces as an infant. He may smell his hands and feet to get his body smell. He loves strong-smelling food and eats indiscriminately. Like the child with hypotaste, he may drink household cleaning fluid or other dangerous material. He loves bathrooms and his own smell. He may sniff people up close. The stronger the smell, the happier he is.

SMELL, HYPO; PROTECTION: Give the child as many smells as possible and as strong as possible. Introduce them right under his nose and play games with smells, having him discriminate between them. Slowly move the smells farther and farther away from him until he learns to discriminate a less intense smell.

SMELL, HYPO; TREATMENT: Slowly discourage his interest in smelling things up close. Get him to identify smells at longer distances. Teach him that smells come to him through the air and if he cannot smell them except at "nose distance," to all intents and purposes, they have no smell.

SMELL, WHITE NOISE: This child has a constant smell in his olfactory system and often monitors it by placing his hands over his mouth and blowing the air from the mouth into his nose. He sometimes sticks things up his nose to change the smell. Often he varies between going toward outside smells and running away from them. Sometimes he breathes very rapidly, apparently to try to clear the smell out of the nose. He becomes very upset when a cold stops up his nose.

SMELL, WHITE NOISE; PROTECTION: Keep the house as smell-free as possible. Use smell-free soaps, and do not dry-clean his clothes. The idea is to keep the child as free from smells as possible. He must learn to pay attention to smells which come from outside himself.

SMELL, WHITE NOISE; TREATMENT: Give the child a special "smell for the day": A perfume, kerosene, ammonia, or the like, and put it on his clothes. This smell will be stronger than what he can smell inside himself. The smells should be easily identified, and he must be told several times a day what smell he is wearing. After a few weeks, choose smells which are not quite so easy to distinguish. Show him different materials whose smells you want him to learn. Play smelling games. Slowly develop his discrimination by having him identify smells with his eyes closed. Play the games as often as possible.

WARNING: These suggestions are only very sketchy. For more information read "The Ultimate Stranger: The Autistic Child" by Carl H. Delacato.

Extreme cases are rarely seen in the classroom. The problem behavior resulting from the more subtle sensory distortions will have to be analyzed carefully because they are hard to detect. Look for unexplained reactions of the child.

Children may have more than one sensory problem. Some of them may be caused by an actual mild form of brain damage; others, especially "hyper" problems, may exist because the child, in overcompensating for the lack of input from one sensory channel, is orienting himself in the world through another sense.

All children who have sensory problems should be checked to see if their total neurological organization is normal. If a sensori-motor program is indicated, this may be delayed until the child's sensory channel has been normalized and he is more comfortable in the world. Usually a marked change can be noted within as little as three to four weeks.

The cause for a sensory problem may be other than neurological disorganization. Cerebral allergies can cause distortions. Hyperglycemia (too much sugar in the blood, as in diabetes) and hypoglycemia, as well, will create a change in sensitivity.

If the symptoms are constant, a desensitization program seems indicated. If they occur irregularly, it is wise to check for allergies. If they occur only during certain periods of the day, hypoglycemia may be the culprit.

Zinc deficiencies can cause taste distortions. Magnesium deficiency, or lack of B vitamins are both associated with severely heightened sensitivity and irritability.

Especially for sensory problems which are "hypo" (not enough information is received) and those which are "white noise" (sensations originate from within the child), that particular sensory organ must be checked for some abnormality. (An ear, for instance, may be infected or filled with fluid from an allergy. The tongue might show some allergic "geographic" patches.) Even though the receptor organ may seem normal, do not presume that no problem exists; its cause may well be in those areas of the cortex which connect this particular information with the rest of the brain, not in the receptor organ.

It is also important to remember that if a child could not pay attention because his senses were playing tricks on him, he missed a lot of information. Even after his problem has been eliminated, we cannot expect him to know as much as the other children. He has missed many years of normal learning and we must help him catch up.

The child's problem behavior is the symptom. The sensory problem may be the cause of the unexplained behavior, but the reason for the sensory problem will vary, and the child must be treated accordingly.

V. How To Test Your Child For Allergies

by Ray C. Wunderlich, Jr., M.D.

Your child can be allergic to anything, including himself. Most often, however, allergic reactions occur in response to foods, inhalants, or chemicals. The first step in diagnosis is to acquire a high index of suspicion. Children are allergic who wheeze, cough, sniff, and itch. But those who are tired and irritable may be equally allergic. Symptoms due to allergy include nearly any symptom which one could mention.

Test your child for allergies by looking at him. Signs of allergy include dark circles under the eyes, extra wrinkles around the eyes, puffiness of the eyelids, swelling at the sides of the nose, puffiness over the cheekbones, short upper lip, open mouth, pale skin in the absence of anemia, nose rubbing, noisy breathing, and rash on the tongue (geographic tongue).

Test your child for allergies by asking yourself these questions. Does your child wake up in the morning all stuffed up? Symptoms which are most prominent when the child first wakes up suggest that the bedroom may be the culprit. Your child could be allergic to dust mites which live in the bedding. Or: Blankets, books, fuzzy and stuffed toys, or shag rugs could be the offender.

Ask this question, too: "Does my child exhibit symptoms or signs to a greater degree when outdoors?" A yes answer strongly suggests pollens may be the offender. This is especially true when wind worsens the symptoms or when a visit to the seashore improves symptoms. (Sea breezes carry little or no pollen.) Children whose symptoms are heightened indoors are apt to be reacting to house dust or molds. Substances such as chemicals may, of course, be present in the outdoor environment (auto fumes, industrial effluents) or within the home (insecticides, hair sprays, cleaners, etc.).

Ask, too, Are my child's symptoms worse when it rains or whenever damp weather occurs? A yes answer is a good clue that mold allergy is present. Symptoms which clear when it rains indicate pollen allergy because rain clears pollen particles from the air.

Parents can ask their physician to order two blood tests which screen for the presence of allergy: the White Blood Count with a Differential Blood Count is one. When the total white blood cell count is low, the usual reason is allergy, usually food allergy. Also, when the report indicates a high percentage of eosinophils, allergy is suggested. (Parasites may also increase the eosinophil count). In general, when the eosinophil count is greater than 4%, allergy can be suspected.

The Immunoglobulin E Level (IgE) is the second blood indicator for allergy. Different laboratories have different testing methods, but if the laboratory reports elevations above what, by their tests, is considered normal range for a child that age, then an allergy to inhalants is suggested and the chances are very good that the child will respond well to allergic desensitization.

Treatments for allergy to pollens, dusts and molds can be highly successful. Avoidance can be accomplished by the use of air conditioning and electrostatic precipitating air filters. Desensitization (hyposensitization) can be accomplished by injections or by sub-lingual drops. For most persons, the use of vaccines without phenol is preferred: The results are usually good.

For foods, remember that most food allergy is of the type which is not readily apparent. Foods consumed every day and in the largest amounts are overwhelmingly implicated in the origin of symptoms due to food allergy. It is no accident that sugar, cow's milk, wheat, corn, yeast, eggs, chicken and beef are the commonest foods responsible for allergic disorders. These, indeed, are the foods which, in our culture, are eaten frequently and in large amounts. Therefore, when checking your child for allergies, ask this question: "What foods does my child eat on a regular basis and in large quantities?" The parent must, of course, recognize that toast is wheat, buns are likely to be wheat, pasta is wheat, spaghetti is wheat and crackers are wheat. Also that milk is milk, cheese is a milk product, cottage cheese is a milk product, and yogurt is a milk product — so is ice cream. Then, too, know that corn is present in many foods such as corn syrup, corn solids, corn starch, as well as cereals and the vegetable corn. Parents should be aware that indiscriminate elimination of foods from the diet can be a dangerous procedure. Serious malnutrition can be produced. Counseling from a nutrition-ally oriented physician should be sought.

Food allergy can be responsible for elevation or depression of the pulse rate. This fact can be used to advantage as a test for food allergy. First, identify the foods to be tested. Withdraw these foods from the diet for 5 days while supplying the child with foods which have theretofore been used infrequently. Then feed the child a large serving of the food to be tested and check his pulse rate before and after the test meal. Measure the pulse rate of the child for 1 minute before and after eating these foods. Measure the pulse every five minutes for 1 hour. To see what allergic responses occur by offering large amounts of one type of food after it has been taken out of the child's diet is technically known as "challenging." The following day another food can be tested, and so on. Watch for any adverse symptoms which are provoked and compare the pulse rates of the challenged foods with those of the infrequently eaten foods. Pulse rates which increase or decrease by more than 10 points and which are not explained by other factors (anxiety, movement, etc.) suggest that the food may be allergenic for that individual. Common symptoms observed on food challenges are runny nose, sneezing, itching, weakness, headache, depression, "hyper" behavior, palpitations, blurred vision and ringing in the ears.

Parents can test for chemical allergies by selective exposure of the child to suspected offenders. For example, to test for hypersensitivity to gas used in a cooking range, have the child live for several days in an environment which is free of gas. Then take the child into a home which contains a gas heating range. Notice the behavior and appearance of the child for any significant change. Commonly a gas-sensitive child will show behavior changes, perhaps will also develop dark circles under the eyes.

Formaldehyde, a common chemical today, can be checked by bringing the child into a store which stores and sells new carpets. Redness of the eyes, cough, wheeze, and altered behavior are common reactions. Other chemicals, such as exhaust fumes, magic markers, mimeograph sheets, paint, lacquers, etc. can similarly be tested by avoidance followed by exposure-challenge.

Allergy and allergy-like disorders are major conditions which impede the development of children and make them irritable and unhealthy. No program of health care for children is complete without a careful consideration of the role of allergy in the function of the individual child.

VI. Evaluating A Child's Neurological Organization

To see if a child will benefit from a program of neurological organization, the simplest way is to ask him to creep and to crawl. The following test chart was designed by John Unruh and is brought here with his permission.

To score: The child must do all of the subheadings of each number correctly to get one point. Add up points earned for crawling

— moving forward with the belly touching the floor like a six-month-old — and for creeping — moving forward on hands and knees like a nine-month-old. Perfect score for each should be 9.

If the results of the test show that improvement is needed, give practice in these areas and retest after two months to check the progress.

I have never seen a child who is a statistical mean. There are billions of cells in the brain, which makes it quite obvious that each child is an individual one. Parents who have a difficult child are often exhausted, they feel that they have tried everything already, and the thought of working with that child for another year on another program — one which also might not work — will seem overwhelming.

Start with giving yourself four weeks, actually three will do, but give yourself leeway. It won't cost a penny, and at least you will have tried! Before you start, make a list of the things your child does which bother you. (Sometimes it's something so subtle that it's hard to put your finger on it.) Then see what has changed by the end of the three weeks.

If the child is hyperactive, he might seem to go really wild during those first three weeks. See what happens during the fourth.

If the child talks too loudly, he might make even more noise at the start. See what happens after the first three weeks.

If the child is going to school, take a sample of his handwriting — randomly — from his schoolwork and then three weeks later, a new sample. Do not take something he wrote specifically for you. See if there are any changes. Is the writing smaller and the slant of the letters more even? This would be a sign that he is gaining more control.

After three weeks, what can he do in athletics that he could not do before?

You may see some changes after two weeks, changes so small that you won't be quite sure they are happening. At first they will come and go. But by the end of the month the new skills will be quite consistent.

CRAWLING

Top View

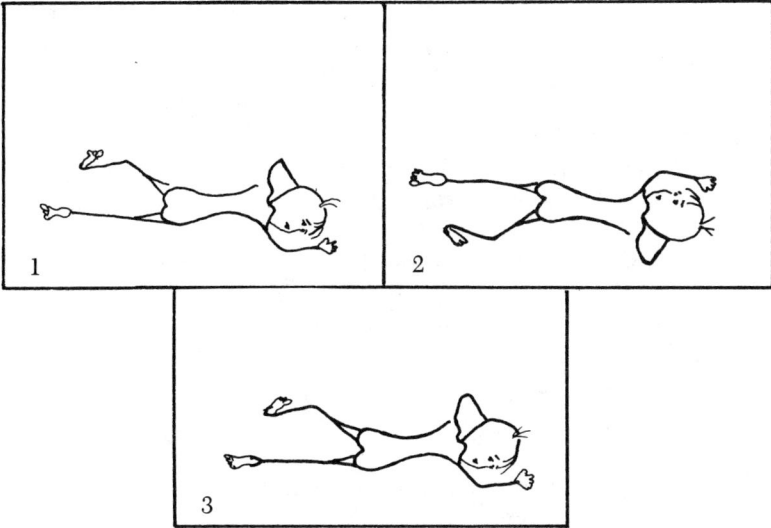

Side View

CRAWLING

1. Arms and legs in a cross pattern
    a. right hand and left leg work simultaneously
    b. left hand and right leg work simultaneously
2. Head in cross pattern
    a. head turns to up hand
    b. eyes focus on up hand
3. Coordination and serialization
    a. body from head to toe flat on the ground
    b. head, arm and legs work in unison
    c. body moves forward smoothly
4. Down arm position
    a. below the up arm
    b. must not aid forward movement
5. Up arm position
    a. 90 degree angle at the shoulder
    b. 90 degree angle at the elbow
6. Down leg
    a. extended line with the spine
    b. relaxed
    c. must not aid forward motion
7. Up leg
    a. 90 degree angle at the hip
    b. stay in contact with the floor
8. Hand position
    a. up arm
        (1) fingers pointing straight ahead
        (2) relaxed
    b. down arm
        (1) relaxed
9. Foot position
    a. up leg
        (1) big toe is tucked
        (2) forward movement is gained by this toe
    b. down leg
        (1) relaxed
        (2) instep rests against floor

Score_____ Working number_____

CREEPING

1. Arms and legs in a cross pattern.
    a. right hand and left leg work simultaneously
    b. left hand and right leg work simultaneously
2. Head in cross pattern
    a. head turns to up hand
    b. eyes focus on up hand
3. Coordination and serialization
    a. back stays straight
    b. head, arms and legs work in unison
    c. body moves forward smoothly
4. Down arm position
    a. below the up arm
    b. elbow is slightly flexed and in line with shoulder
5. Up arm position
    a. elbow is slightly flexed and in line with the shoulder
6. Rear leg
    a. behind the forward leg
    b. thighs in line with the hip
    c. lower leg dragging foot
7. Forward leg
    a. thigh in line with the hip lifting slightly when flexing hip
    b. lower leg dragging foot
    c. knee in line with the hip
8. Hand position
    a. fingers relaxed
    b. fingers and hand pointing straight ahead
9. Foot position
    a. relaxed
    b. instep drags along the floor

Score_____ Working number_____

CREEPING

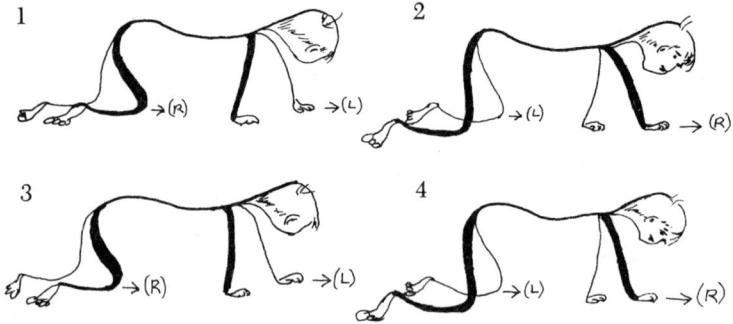

You cannot expect to see progress in reading for several months. What you will be evaluating there is the child's rate of progress. If before the program the child had improved his reading skill by only 6 months' progress in a 12-month period, and during the program improves 6 months in a 6-month period, he has achieved a reading improvement rate of a normal reader. Chances are that he will improve faster than that and eventually catch up with his classmates.

If you have success — in any area — within these first four weeks, you know that you're on the right track. You might then consider going to some professional center to get further help. If that is impossible, get some more books on the subject and continue on your own. Carl H. Delacato, Glenn Doman, Miriam Bender — all have made it possible for you to find the information you need.

The sessions can be lots of fun. If there is more than one child in the family, the other members are allowed to do the exercises only if they have been good — sort of as a treat. The child being programmed must know he has no choice. There's no reason, though, that exercises can't be turned into games. To crawl on his belly, he can pretend he's a soldier. Creeping around the house — through the living room into the kitchen and back out the other way — he can be Mario Andretti going into the third lap at the Indy 500 and stopping at a pit stop for a "fill up" of orange juice. If you have to count, as you will for some exercises, 60 is much faster if you count to 30 and then backward to a count-down of zero and "we have blast-off!" It all depends on the age of the child.

Remember, these exercises are quite hard. Be sure to put knee pads in the child's pants if there are no rugs, and if there are rugs he must wear pants. If a child gets rug burns on his knees, it will

SKILL DESCRIPTION	TIME
1) CRAWLING: on stomach; cross pattern; turn head severly	5
2) CREEPING: on knees; cross pattern; look at back of hand	5
3) SLOW WALK: cross pattern; look at forward foot; point with opp. hand	2
4) SKIP: cross pattern; swing arms	2
5) FIST: start closed fist; open slowly but steady; independent pressure on fist as opened	1
6) JUMP ROPE: work up to 250 jumps per session; don't bend knees much	2
7) PENCIL I: Pencil at reading distance; Head straight; follow pencil left and right with eyes; independent holder	1
8) PENCIL II: Pencil at reading distance; Head straight; follow pencil left and right with eyes; Mike holds pencil with right hand	1
9) PENCIL III: Pencil at reading distance; Head straight; follow pencil left and right with left eye covered; Mike holds pencil with right hand	1
10) PENCIL IV: Pencil at reading distance; Head straight; follow pencil left and right with right eye covered; Mike holds pencil with right hand	1
11) HOP: Hop on right foot; hold knees near even	1
12) CHAIR STEP: 18" step; Step up with right; Step down with left	1
13) WRITING ACTIVITY: Write with red lead on white paper; use glasses with red lens on left, no lens on right. Drawing O.K. sometimes.	10
14) READING ACTIVITY: Use glasses with black lens on left and no lens on right; 1. Do the getting ready together 2. Parent reads story pointing to each word 3. Mike reads story, parent points 4. Mike answers test questions 5. Parent grades test	3 Stories
15) LEISURE ACTIVITY: Use glasses with black lens on left and no lens on right. Any activity i.e. dinner; TV; games	30:00

243

hurt the next time and he won't want to creep.

If you are doing crawling in place, you may have to help the child move his head — at least at first. (Be sure not to cover his cheeks with your hand. When the cheeks touch the floor as he moves his head from side to side, they activate the rooting reflex and help him move his head.) Help him by touching the arms and legs as he has to move them. No sense yelling at him for something he simply does not know how to do: If he knew how to do it, there would be no need for you to do all this with him. Especially if you are not sure what you are doing, start at the developmental stage below the one at which the child tests out as having a problem.

If you are in a position where you cannot get help from people who have training in these methods, it is a good idea to have an optometrist check your child's vision before you start the program. Vision and hearing should have been checked if the child has a problem, but in this case, have him also check for hand-eye coordination. Then when you take the child for another test the following year, you will have a clear indication of whether or not you have made more progress than could normally be expected for that period.

On the previous page is a program for neurological organization as might be given by Delacato and Delacato Learning Consultants for a child who has trouble reading, but is otherwise well. The time allowed for each activity will vary with the needs of each child. Right-sided children are made more right handed; for left-handed children the left side is emphasized, but this is only after a preference has been established.

Total time, even with allowing for some occasional griping is less than two hours. The different developmental centers have slight variations.

VII. Tests for Vitamin C Spillage and Hypoglycemia

A simple test for vitamin C spillage is to take a 10% solution of silver nitrate (available at pharmacies) and add an equal amount of urine. One cc — about half a thimbleful — is sufficient. A precipitate is formed. If that is black it means that ascorbic acid is present, which means that the person has enough and is excreting the rest. If it is gray or silver or white, the body is absorbing whatever vitamin C it is getting. Results may vary during the day. Silver nitrate is poisonous, so it is probably not a good idea to have it in the house when there are small children.

C-STIX — to test for vitamin C spillage — are made by Ames Laboratory, which is a subsidy of Miles Laboratory, but I have searched in pharmacies both in small and in large cities, and they were not available. They could have been ordered, but only in large quantities.

Dr. Lendon H. Smith recommends giving the child vitamin C up to the amount that his stool becomes just a little soft, and then cutting back a little from that amount, as the easiest way to insure that the child receives enough.

NUTRITION - BEHAVIOR INVENTORY©

Name_____   Age _____

Male____ Female____   Date_____

THERE ARE 52 ITEMS IN THIS QUESTIONNAIRE. THERE ARE ONLY FOUR CHOICES FOR EACH QUESTION: NEVER, RARELY, OCCASIONALLY, OR USUALLY.   PICK THE ANSWER THAT IS CLOSEST TO HOW YOU FEEL OR ARE IN EACH SITUATION.   THERE ARE NO RIGHT OR WRONG ANSWERS. IF YOU HAVE ANY QUESTIONS,   ASK THE PERSON WHO IS GIVING   YOU THIS QUESTIONNAIRE.

TO SCORE THE QUESTIONNAIRE, ADD UP THE NUMBER OF RESPONSES CHECKED UNDER "RARELY", "OCCASIONALLY", OR "USUALLY." DO NOT ADD UP THE NUMBER OF RESPONSES UNDER "NEVER."

(FOR EXAMPLE, IF 5 RESPONSES WERE CHECKED UNDER THE RARELY COLUMN, THE TOTAL NUMBER OF RESPONSES FOR RARELY IS 5.)

FILL IN THE NUMBER OF RESPONSES FOR EACH COLUMN BELOW TO GET A TOTAL SCORE.

RARELY   ____x 1 = ____(a)
OCCASIONALLY ____x 2 = ____(b)
USUALLY   ____x 3 = ____(c)

(a) ____ + (b)____ + (c)____ = _____ TOTAL SCORE.

245

NEVER	RARELY	OCCASIONALLY	USUALLY		
				1	MY VISION GETS BLURRED OR DOUBLE.
				2	MY GUMS BLEED.
				3.	AFTER I FALL ASLEEP I WAKE UP AND THEN CAN NOT GET BACK TO SLEEP.
				4.	MY MUSCLES FEEL PAINFUL OR SORE.
				5.	I GET HEADACHES.
				6.	I HAVE ALLERGIES OR ASTHMA.
				7.	I GET CRAMPS IN MY LEGS.
				8.	I HAVE ITCHING OR CRAWLING SENSATIONS ON MY SKIN.
				9.	I SIGH OR YAWN DURING THE DAY.
				10.	MY STOMACH OR INTESTINES ARE UPSET.
				11.	IF I MISS A MEAL OR IT IS DELAYED, I NOTICE MY HEART BEAT FASTER.
				12.	I GET MAD OR FURIOUS FOR NO APPARENT REASON.
				13.	I EASILY GET BRUISES OR BLACK AND BLUE MARKS.
				14.	I HAVE NIGHTMARES OR BAD DREAMS.
				15.	I GET FAINT, DIZZY, WEAK SPELLS, OR COLD SWEATS.
				16.	IT IS HARD FOR ME TO CONCENTRATE.
				17.	I AM SLEEPY AFTER I EAT.
				18.	I NIBBLE BETWEEN MEALS WHEN I AM HUNGRY.
				19.	I GET JITTERY OR NERVOUS WHEN I AM HUNGRY.
				20.	I GET VERY TIRED OR EXHAUSTED.
				21.	I NO LONGER FEEL TIRED AFTER I EAT.
				22.	I GET HUNGRY OR FEEL FAINT IF I DO NOT EAT OFTEN.
				23.	I FEEL BETTER AFTER MY FIRST SNACK OR MEAL OF THE DAY.
				24.	I DRINK COFFEE OR TEA IN THE MORNING TO GET STARTED.
				25.	I OFTEN FORGET THINGS.

NEVER	RARELY	OCCASIONALLY	USUALLY	
				26. I EAT SWEET THINGS OR DRINK CAFFEINATED COFFEE, TEA OR COLA.
				27. I HAVE MORE THAN 3 CUPS OF COFFEE, TEA OR COLA A DAY.
				28. I ADD SUGAR TO MOST THINGS I EAT OR DRINK.
				29. I AM VERY RESTLESS.
				30. I FEEL VERY SLEEPY DURING THE DAY.
				31. I DRINK ALCOHOLIC BEVERAGES.
				32. I CAN NOT WORK UNDER PRESSURE.
				33. IT IS HARD TO DECIDE ON THINGS.
				34. I CRAVE SWEET FOODS, CANDIES OR DRINKS.
				35. I FEEL DEPRESSED.
				36. I CONSTANTLY WORRY ABOUT THINGS.
				37. I GET CONFUSED.
				38. I HAVE TROUBLE MAKING DECISIONS.
				39. AT TIMES I FEEL LIKE I AM HAVING A NERVOUS BREAKDOWN.
				40. I GET DEPRESSED OR FEEL THE BLUES OVER NOTHING.
				41. I GET IRRITATED.
				42. I GET IMPATIENT.
				43. I BLOW LITTLE THINGS OUT OF PROPORTION AND EASILY LOSE MY TEMPER.
				44. I GET FEARFUL.
				45. I FEEL VERY NERVOUS.
				46. I EAT WHEN I AM NERVOUS.
				47. I AM HIGHLY EMOTIONAL.
				48. I WANT TO KILL MYSELF.
				49. I CRY FOR NO APPARENT REASON.
				50. I GET DROWSY.
Totals				

51. WHAT TWO FOODS DO YOU LIKE OR CRAVE THE MOST?
A._____ B._____

52. DO YOU SMOKE CIGARETTES? YES____ NO_____

247

Hypoglycemia

On Alexander Schauss' Nutrition Behavior Inventory, every fifth question beginning with question number five deals with those most common symptoms of hypoglycemia (i.e., 10, 15, 20, etc.). If the score is above 20 among these ten questions, presumptive evidence exists that a blood sugar imbalance exists. It may also indicate, along with any score of 30 or over on the whole test, a problem of carbohydrate intolerance and/or adrenal insufficiency. A five to six hour glucose tolerance test (GTT) would be highly indicated if a blood sugar disorder is suspected. Not only will the GTT confirm the problem, but it will help to identify the type of hypoglycemia needing treatment.

This test, along with the hair analysis, blood samples, urine analysis, and other provocative tests, can give the physician the most accurate picture of a person's metabolic activity. In this way, a specific type of treatment can be prescribed. (Reprinted by permission from the author, from "Orthomolecular Treatment of Criminal Offenders," by Alexander Schauss, 1978, Michael Lesser, M.D., 2340 Parker Street, Berkeley, CA 94704)

VIII. Tables of Predictable Behavior

The following lists are reprinted here with permission from Louise Bates Ames, who was kind enough to suggest I use whatever was needed. Unfortunately, this would have meant printing the entire book. Lists are available in her "Gesell Institute's Child from One to Six" on everything from eating behavior to dream occurrences. These few tables then, are shown largely to emphasize just how predictable difficult behavior has proven to be. Behavioral stages have changed little over the last 50 years during which research has been carried on at the Gesell Institute.

When difficult behavior occurs, it does so because of states of disequilibrium that are the result of the child's equally predictable growth spurts. Louise Bates Ames does not advocate allowing the child to run wild, but states that knowing that certain kinds of behavior are to be expected, will help the parents to be more relaxed about guiding the child toward more mature ways of coping.

Different Fears at Different Ages

The children frightened Davey on Halloween night and he's been jumpy ever since. A baby-sitter threatened Joe with the "bogey-man" and he's suddenly refused to sleep without his light on. An unfamiliar dog bit Betsey, and now she's afraid of dogs.

Into any child's life can come frightening and unhappy incidents which set up special fears, and you as parents naturally do your best to protect your children from such specially frightening incidents.

But you cannot protect them from all fears. As children grow up, they seem to need to go through a series of fears which come in and then later drop out. Each child differs somewhat, but, in general, each age brings its own characteristic fears. A much abbreviated summary of some of the most common fears which are likely to develop in almost any child, from age to age, is as follows:

2 years: Many fears, chiefly auditory: trains, trucks, thunder, flushing of toilet, vacuum cleaner.

Visual fears: dark colors, large objects, trains, hats.

Spatial: toy or crib moved from usual place, moving to a new house, fear of going down the drain.

Personal: Mother's departure, or separation from her at bedtime. Rain and wind.

Animals—especially wild animals.

2 ½ years: Many fears, especially spatial: fear of movement or of having objects moved.

Any different orientation, as someone entering house by a different door.

Large objects—as trucks—approaching.

3 years: Visual fears predominate: old or wrinkled people, masks, "bogeymen."

The dark.

Animals.

Policemen, burglars.

Mother or Father going out at night.

4 years: Auditory fears again, especially fire engines.

The dark.

Wild animals.

Mother leaving, especially going out at night.

5 years: Not a fearful age. More visual fears than others.

Less fear of animals, bad people, bogeymen.

Concrete, down-to-earth fears: bodily harm, falling, dogs.

The dark.

That Mother will not return home.

6 years: Very fearful. Especially auditory fears: doorbell, telephone, static, ugly voice tones, flushing of toilet, insect and bird noises.

Fear of the supernatural: ghosts, witches.

Fear that someone is hiding under the bed.

Spatial: fear of being lost, fear of the woods.

Fear of the elements: fire, water, thunder, lightning.

Fear of sleeping alone in a room or of being the only one on a floor of the house.

Fear that Mother will not be home when child arrives home, or that something will happen to her or that she may die.

Afraid of being hit by others.

Brave about big hurts but fears splinters, little cuts, blood, nose drops.

7 years: Many fears, especially visual: the dark, attics, cellars. Interprets shadows as ghosts and witches.

Fears war, spies, burglars, people hiding in closet or under bed.

Fears now stimulated by reading, radio, cinema.

Worries about things: not being liked, being late to school.

8 to 9 years: Fewer fears and less worrying. No longer fears the water; less fear of the dark. Good evaluation, and fears are reasonable: about personal inability and failure, especially school failure.

10 years: Many fears, though fewer than in the ages which immediately follow. Animals, especially snakes and wild animals, are the things most feared. The dark is feared by a few. Also high places, fires and criminals, or "killers" or burglars.

A few are beginning spontaneously to mention things they are *not* afraid of: chiefly the dark, dogs, and being left alone.

Sex Play

The child's interest in sex may be embarrassing, but it usually is not particularly devastating to you so long as it remains in the realm of pure theory. Questions about babies and the relations of the two sexes to each other may embarrass, but they usually do not really disturb you.

When that interest takes the form of actual sex activity, however, your reaction may be less calm and much more emotional. There is probably nothing which disturbs the mothers of young children more than to discover them taking part, with other children, in sex play—or to hear of their activities along this line from other, indignant, mothers.

A knowledge of the customary stages of sex play which we have found to take place in perfectly normal, well-brought-up children during the first ten years of life may help you to meet neighborhood sex-play situations calmly and without too much horrified surprise:

2½ years: Child shows interest in different postures of boys and girls when urinating and is interested in physical differences between the sexes.

3 years: Verbally expresses interest in physical differences between sexes and in different postures of urinating. Girls attempt to urinate standing up.

4 years: Extremely conscious of the navel. Under social stress may grasp genitals and may need to urinate.
May play the game of "show." Also verbal play about eliminating.
Calling of names related to elimination.
Interest in other people's bathrooms; may demand privacy for self but be extremely interested in the bathroom activity of others.

5 years: Familiar with but not too interested in physical differences between sexes.

Less sex play and game of "show." More modest and less likely to expose self.
Less bathroom play and less interest in unfamiliar bathrooms.

251

6 years:	Marked awareness of and interest in differences between sexes in body structure. Questioning. Mutual investigation by both sexes reveals practical answers to questions about sex differences. Mild sex play or exhibitionism in play or in school toilets. Game of "show." May also play "hospital" and take rectal temperatures. Giggling, calling names, or remarks involving words dealing with elimination functions. Some children are subjected to sex play by older children. Or girls are bothered by older men.
7 years:	Less interest in sex. Some mutual exploration, experimentation, and sex play, but less than earlier.
8 years:	Interest in sex rather high, though sex exploration and play is less common than at 6. Interest in peeping, smutty jokes, provocative giggling; children whisper, write, or spell elimination or sex words.
9 years:	May talk about sex information with friends of same sex. Interest in details of own organs and functions; seek out pictures in books. Sex swearing, sex poems, beginning.
10 years:	Considerable interest in "smutty" jokes.

It is very important to keep in mind that usually none of the children who take part at any of these ages in recurrent neighborhood sex play are to "blame." Sex play often just naturally occurs if several children are left together unsupervised and with nothing better to do. Giving them more supervision, or providing ideas for other activities, will often prevent such behavior, or at least keep it within certain confines.

IX. Introduction to the Brain

The following pages were composed by Mildred Robeck, professor of Education at the University of Oregon, for a symposium held at the University of Oregon on July 15-19, 1980. They are reprinted here by permission. They are also available in the publication "The Brain: Recent Research and its Education Implications," published by the University of Oregon, 1982.

The Neuron

The neuron is the basic unit of the brain, which contains a communication network of perhaps 15 billion individual neurons. Types of nerve cells differ in appearance according to their location and function, but they share a common organization.

1. Structure of Neurons

   1.1 The cell body is surrounded by a membrane which is capable of generating nerve impulses. Contained within the membrane is the nucleus which encloses a complete DNA component (the genetic code) and the biochemical organelles for supporting the life functions of the cell (Figure 1a).

   1.2 The axon is a long fiber which leads away from the cell body and carries coded signals to other cells in the brain or nervous system. Axons tend to end in branches which make contact with other cell bodies (Figure 1b).

   1.3 Dendrites tend to form clusters of fine extensions around the cell body, where they receive incoming messages from other dendrites, axons, or cell bodies. These impulses are cumulative and may either excite or inhibit the firing of the receiver.

   1.4 Synaptic knobs are the terminal button-shaped projections at the ends of dendrites or axon branches. These buttons, containing vesicles of chemical transmitters, discharge their contents when a neuron fires, to bridge the synaptic gap and transmit the electrochemical message (Figure 1c).

2. Myelination

   In development, neural pathways become more efficient with the growth of a fatty sheath around the axon (Figure 2a).

   The myelin sheath is formed as Schwann cells or glia (oligodendroglia) wrap themselves around an axon. Gaps remain at intervals between the individual loops where an exchange of ions takes place when a cell fires. The exchange of ions (changes in millivolts of electron potential) speeding down the axon constitute the message along a neural pathway (Figure 2b).

   2.2 The location and thickness of the myelin sheath has been studied to determine the important periods of brain development and to compare myelination of different systems with behavior (Figure 3).

3. Growth of Neural Systems

   Nearly all nerve cell bodies are developed and in place at birth.
   (An exception are the neurons of the cerebellum.)

   3.1 Elaboration occurs through the growth of new connections.
       Adult cerebral nerve cells interconnect with 1,000 to 10,000
       other cell bodies.

   3.2 Sensorimotor period, from birth to about 24 months, is
       characterized by rapid elaboration of sensory reception and
       association areas of the cortex (Figure 4).

Brain Organization

Some research on the human brain has been accomplished by mapping the
major areas and how they are organized into what A. R. Luria, a
Russian neurosurgeon, called "the working brain." This outline
suggests different ways of looking at brain organization, based on the
interests of the explorers: (1) anatomy, as probed from the outer
cortex inward; (2) language areas, as mapped in clinical research; and
(3) brain development, as traced from primitive beginnings to newer
and more complex structures.

1. Anatomy of the Cerebrum

   The cerebrum is the enlarged upper organ of the CNS, most recently
   evolved, most elaborated, and largest of the brain structures. It
   consists of two nearly identical hemispheres. The cerebral
   hemispheres are bilateral, appearing nearly symmetrical, but
   having specialized functions. White matter is the fibrous
   internal structure of the cerebral hemispheres. These densely
   packed fibers are classified by function (Figure 5).

   1.1 Conduction fibers transmit impulses electrochemically
       between nerve cells.

       Association fibers transmit impulses within a hemisphere --
       usually connecting adjacent areas (gyri). Projection fibers
       connect lower centers with cerebral centers. Commissural
       fibers connect the two hemispheres. The corpus callosum is
       a broad band of commissural fibers connecting the two
       hemispheres. The anterior commissure also transmits across
       hemispheres. Sectioning both structures prevents direct
       communication between hemispheres (Figure 6).

   1.2 The cortex of the cerebral hemispheres consists of gray,
       outer layers of the cerebrum. These layers are highly
       convoluted and complexly organized. Gray matter is colored
       by neural cell bodies (which are tightly layered in the
       cortex) and their synaptic connections.

   1.3 The lobes are major bulges in the surfaces of the cortical
       structure. Each hemisphere is divided into four lobes by
       fissures or grooves called sulci. A central sulcus, the
       fissure of Rolando, divides each hemisphere into anterior
       (upper or fore) and posterior (near) regions. The frontal
       lobes, regions in front of the fissure of Rolando, contain
       major centers for regulation of motor activity, motor
       association, and purposful activity. Regions located behind
       the fissure of Rolando contain major centers for primary sen-
       sory association and multimodal sensory integration. The
       parietal lobe, located immediately behind the central sulcus,

254

is the reception area for body senses. The temporal lobes, located behind and above the ears, receive and associate auditory sensory information. The occipital lobes, located on both sides at the back of the cerebrum, receive and process visual sensory information. Generally a cortical sensory area is identified as primary (receiving), secondary (association), and tertiary (integration). A ridge on the surface of the cerebrum is called a gyrus. Major gyri are mapped by function.

1.4 Lateral organization is complex in humans because left-right is neither completely charted nor completely consistent in individuals. The typical organization described here applies to genetically right-handed persons. Lateral asymmetry means that each hemisphere is dominant for certain functions. The left hemisphere is primary mediator for verbal functions (understanding and producing speech and to a lesser degree reading and expressive writing). The left hemisphere also controls motor activities on the contralateral or right side of the body. The right hemisphere is typically dominant for spatial and other transformations that do not lend themselves to verbal processing.

2. Language Areas of the Cortex

The areas of the cortex which are specialized for speech and language become committed early in childhood to particular locations in the left ·hemisphere (in nearly all right-handed persons). Three areas are known, but their function and location vary somewhat in different individuals (Figure 7).

2.1 The primary speech area is the largest and the earliest identified of the regions specialized for language (Figure 2). Wernicke's area, located just behind the left auditory reception area, is specialized in the comprehension of language. The angular gyrus is located immediately behind Wernicke's area and is thought to integrate visual and auditory information. Corresponding areas in the right hemisphere are specialized in nonverbal mediation such as music and complex visual patterns.

2.2 The secondary speech area, called Broca's area after its discoverer, is located in the left frontal lobe where it is involved in the production of speech and langugage. The arcuate fasciculus is a bundle of nerve fibers which connect Wernicke's and Broca's areas.

2.3 A tertiary speech area is located high on the motor cortex. Its specific function is not known.

3. Development of Brain Structures

The central nervous system (CNS) consists of the brain and the spinal column. They form from a fold, the neural groove, in the outer layer of germ cells (Figure 8).

3.1 In a three-week fetus the forebrain appears as a bulge at the upper end of the neural tube. By eight weeks the forebrain has differentiated into primitive cerebral hemispheres (telencephalon) and a diencephalon (thalamic region).

255

3.2 The <u>midbrain</u> is located behind or below the forebrain. This area forms the <u>misencephalon</u> and approximates the location of the midbrain in adults. The rhombic formation or <u>rhomben-cephalon</u> is the fourth major structure to appear at this stage.

3.3 The <u>hindbrain</u>, or <u>myelencephalon</u>, is the lowest of five major formations. The myelencephalon leading from the brain stem is known as the medulla in the adult brain. The medulla is the receiving area for the constant flow of sensory information and forms the beginning of an <u>ascending reticular formation</u> (Figure 3).

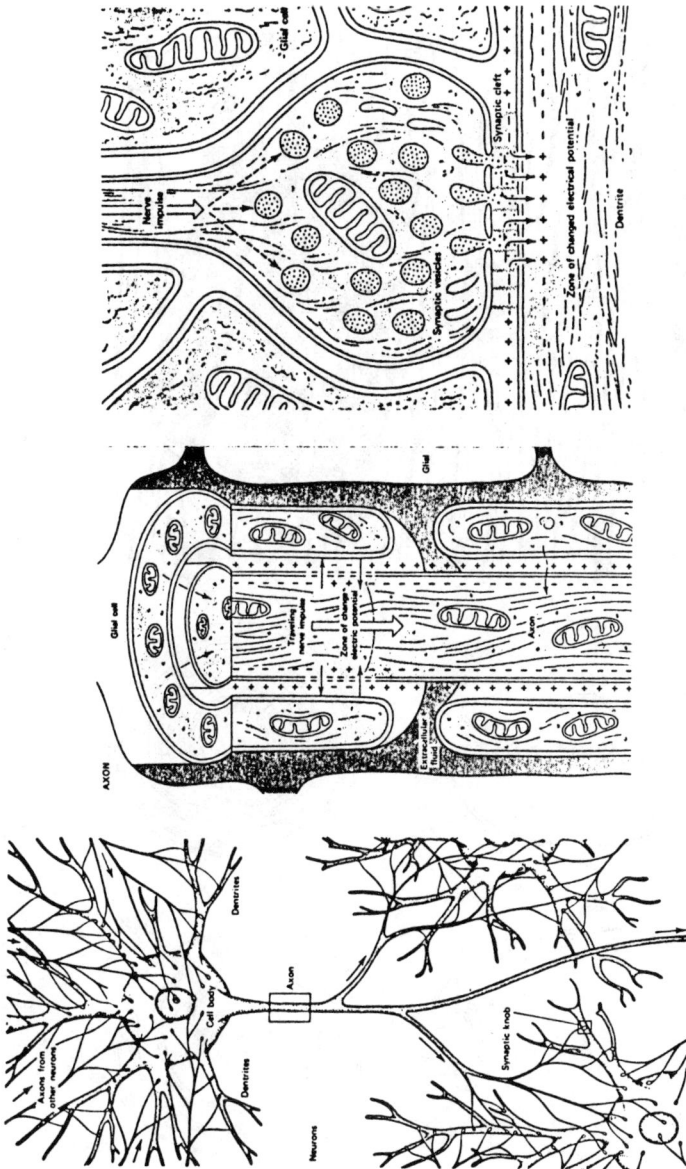

Figure 1: Structure and Function of Neurons -- Neural connections (left);
Transmission of impulses through axon (middle); synaptic bridge (right).

257

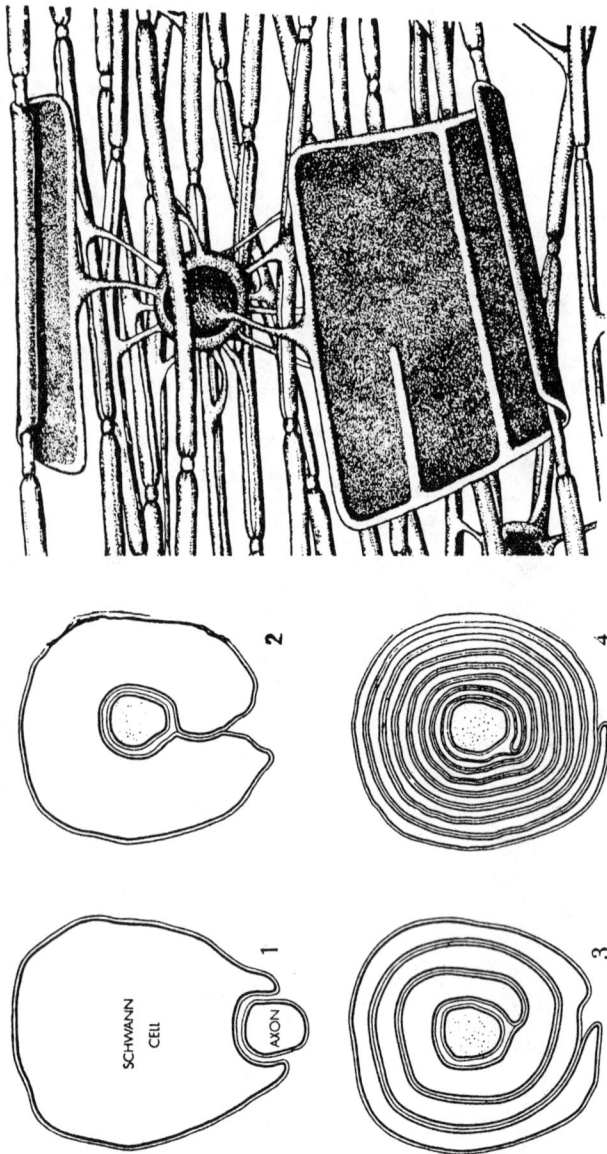

Figure 2: Myelination -- Growth of Schwann cells (left); Sheathing by oligodendroglia in the brain (right).

258

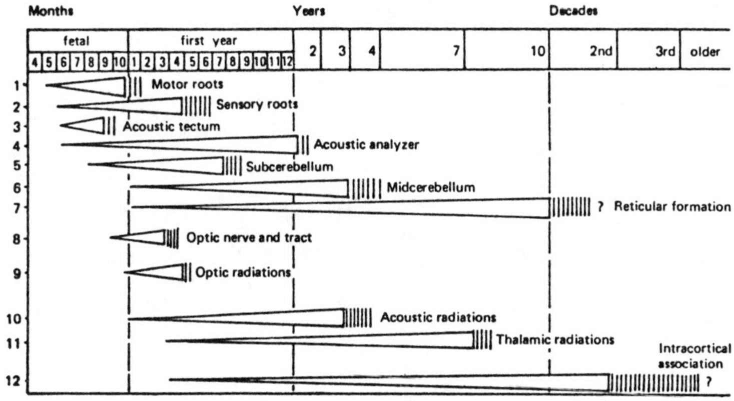

Figure 3: Periods of Intensive Myelination in Different Neural Systems --
From before birth to beyond the third decade of life.

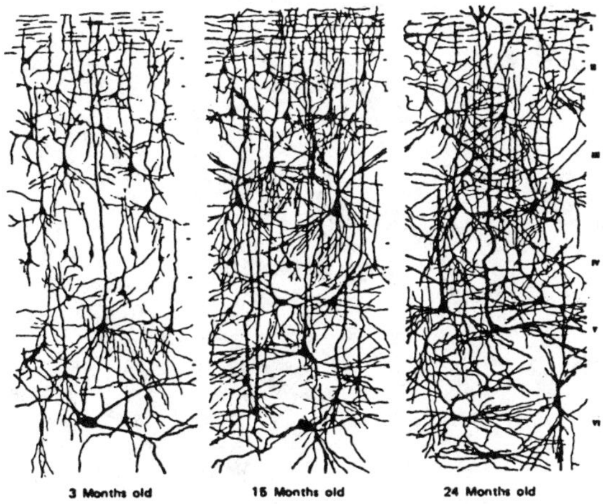

Figure 4: Dendrite Growth in the Visual Cortex of Infants.

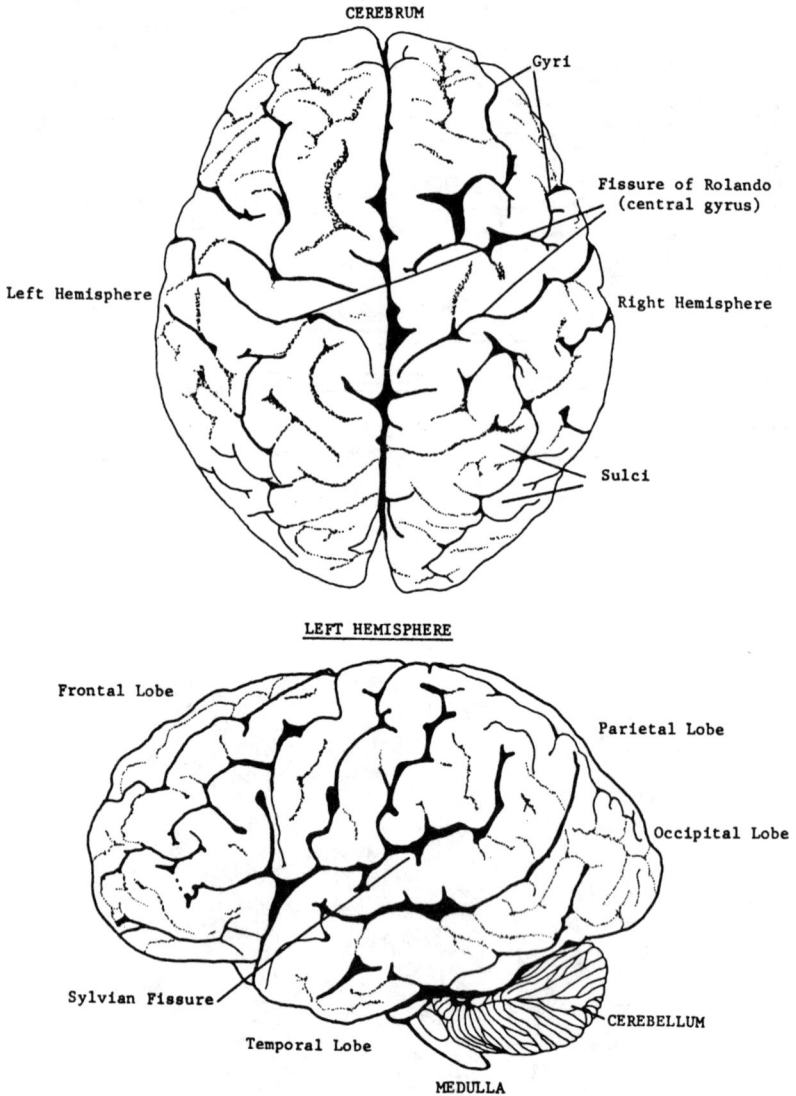

Mildred Robeck

CEREBRUM

Gyri

Fissure of Rolando
(central gyrus)

Left Hemisphere

Right Hemisphere

Sulci

LEFT HEMISPHERE

Frontal Lobe

Parietal Lobe

Occipital Lobe

Sylvian Fissure

CEREBELLUM

Temporal Lobe

MEDULLA

Figure 5: Outer Features of Human Brain -- Right and left
hemispheres (from above); left view of the cerebrum and cerebellum.

260

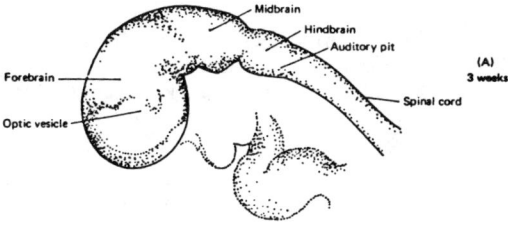

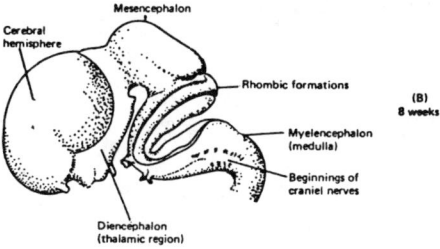

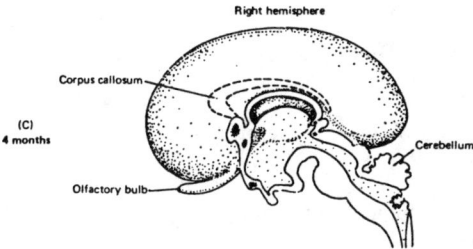

7 months

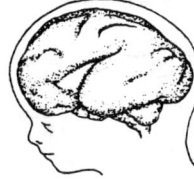

8 months

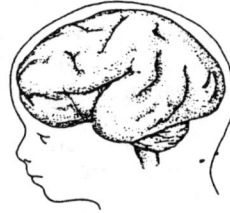

9 months

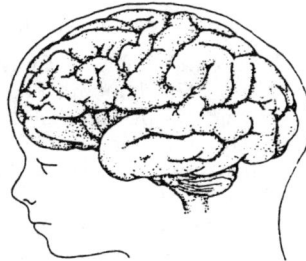

Brain Development --
Early prenatal stages (left);
Third trimester (right).

X. Partial List of Organizations who use Total Child Approach

The following centers are certified by the American Academy for Human Development, which is an organization of therapists who are trained in a developmental and nutritional approach. All centers work in cooperation with the child's doctor.

Children's Therapeutics Program
715 Lake Street
Oak Park, IL 60301
Developmental Center for Handicapped Children
3201 Marshall Street
Dayton, OH 45429
Fitchburg Center for Brain Injured, Inc.
159 Richardson Road
Fitchburg, ME 01420
Help for Brain Injured Children
981 North Euclid
La Habra, CA 90631
Institute for Reading Development
Good Counsel Hill
Mankato, MN 56601
Patterning Center for the Brain Injured
21 East Harding Road
Springfield, OH 45504
Rehabilitation Center for Neurological Development
850 South Main Street
Piqua, Ohio, 45356
San Diego Academy for Neurological Development
3900 Cleveland Avenue
San Diego, CA 92103

The following centers are under the direct guidance of Carl H. Delacato:

Delacato and Delacato Consultants in Learning
Suite 107, Plymouth Plaza
Plymouth Meeting, PA 19462
Delacato and Delacato Center for Neurological Rehabilitation
The Autistic Unit
32 S. Morton
Morton, PA 19670
Delacato TIKVA Project
Pua Street, –9
Haifa, Israel
Delacato Kibbutz Project
c/o Mrs. Jennie Sasson
Rehabilitation Clinic of the Federation of Kibbutz Movements
57, Arlozoroff Street
Ramat-Gan, Israel

Asociacion para Ayuda Lesionados Cerebrales
    Bruch 150, 3º 1ª
    Barcelona, 37, Spain
Frau Waltraud Hunze
    Director, Delacato Project
    Buschdorfer Str., 8
    5300 Bonn 1, West Germany
Associazione Italiana Delacato
    Ufficio Amministrativo
    Via Pescara n. 1
    64026 Roseto degli Abruzzi
Centro Delacato degli Abruzzi
    Via Pescara n. 7
    64026 Roseto degli Abruzzi
    Direttore: Dr. Mariateresa Ruggeri
    Direttore Medico: Dr. Angelo Cioci
Centro C.H. Delacato
    Via Don Bosco 9/E
    80141 Napoli
    Direttore: Sig. Lidia Mercurio
    Direttore Medico: Dr. Antonio Guizzaro
Centro di Riabilitazione
    Cooperativa Intervento
    Via Felisati 62/F
    30171 Mestre-Venezia
    Direttore: Dr. Carla Dal Maso
    Direttore Medico: Dr. Maurizio Trentini

Independent centers with a similar holistic approach are:

Mary F. Ochs Learning Center
    3591 Templeton Rd. N.E.
    Warren, OH 44481
Hope Education Center
    295 Junction Avenue
    Livermore, California
Oregon Hope and Help
    P. O. Box 406
    152 Arthur Street
    Woodburn, OR 97071
Mountain West Clinic for Neurotherapy
    1392 Notre-Dame, Apt. 2
    St. Cesaire, Comte d'Iberville
    Quebec, Canada J0L 1T0

The relative position on this list is no indication of relative merit. Only
    the parent can judge the value of any therapy given to the child by
    any of these centers.

263

Bibliography

Able-Peterson, *Children of the Evening*, G.P. Putnam's Sons, New York, 1981

Abrahamson, E.M. & A.W. Pezet, *Body, Mind and Sugar*. HR & W. New York, 1951

Adams, Karen. *No More Secrets*. Impact Publishers. Chicago, IL, 1981

Allen, Charlotte Vale. *Daddy's Girl*. Wyndam Books. New York, 1980

Adams, M.S. and Neel, J.V. *Children of Incest*, Pediatrics, 1967, vol. 40:55-62

Ames, Louise Bates. *Gesell Institute's Child from One to Six*. Harper Row. New York, 1979

Ames, Louise Bates. *The One Year Old*. Delacorte, New York, 1982

Ames, Louise Bates. *Is Your Child in the Wrong Grade?* Doubleday, Garden City, New York, 1967

Ames, Louise Bates. *Don't Push Your Preschooler!* Harper Row, New York, 1981

Ames, Louise Bates and Frances Ilg. *Your Four Year Old: Wild and Wonderful*. Dell, New York, 1980

Ames, Louise Bates. *Your Five Year Old: Sunny and Serene*. Dell, New York, 1981

Arehart-Treichel. *The Pituitary's Powerful Protein*. Science News, vol.114 no. 2, p. 374-375. November 25, 1978.

Armstrong, Louise. *Kiss Daddy Goodnight:* Speak-out on Incest. Hawthorne Books. New York, 1978

Ashby, W. Ross. *Design for a Brain*. Science Paperbacks. Chapman, London, 1960

Ashkenazi, Azaria, et al. *Immunological Reaction of Psychotic Patients to Fractions of Gluten*. Am. J. Psychiatry, vol. 136, no. 10, Oct. 1979. pp. 1306-1309.

Atkins, Robert. *Nutrition Breakthrough*. Cancer Control Soc. Los Angeles, CA 1979

Ayres, A. Jean. *Sensory Integration and the Child*. Western Psychological Services. Los Angeles, CA. 1979.

Barnes, Broda Otto. *Hypothyroidism: The Unexpected Illness*. Crowell. New York, 1976

Barosky, E. I. *Abuse and Neglect of Handicapped Children by Professionals and Parents*. J. Peditr. Psychology, vol. 1, no. 2, June, 1976. pp. 44-46.

Barsch, Ray. *Perceptual Motor Curriculum*. Special Child Publications. Novato, CA 1976

Baruch, Dorothy. *New Ways in Discipline*. McGraw. New York, 1949

Baruk, Henri. Patients are People Like Us: Half a Century in Neuropsychology. Morrow. New York, 1978

Bender, B. *Self-Chosen Victims: Scapegoating Behavior, Sequential to Battering*. Child Welfare, vol. 55, no. 6, June, 1976. pp. 417-422.

Bender, Miriam L. *The Bender Purdue Tonic Reflex Test and Training Manual*. Academic Therapy Publication. Novato, CA 1976

Bennet, Ivy. *Deliquent and Neurotic Children*. Basic Books. New York, 1960

Bergman, Abraham B., et al, eds. *Sudden Infant Death Syndrome*. Univ. of Washington Press. Seattle and London, 1970

Betz, Barbara. *Neurophysiologic Aspects of Behavior*. Am. J. Psychiatry. 136 (10) Oct. 1979. p. 1253-1256.

Boatman, Bonnie and Borkan, Eugene L. *Treatment of Child Victims of Incest*. Am. J. Family Therapy, vol. 9, no. 4, Winter, 1981. p. 43-48.

Brady, Katherine. *Father's Days*. Seaview Books. New York, 1979

Brant T.; Tisza V. *The Sexually Misused Child*. Am. J. Orthopsychiat. 1977. p. 80-90.

Breslauer,Ann, et al. *A Visual Training Program*. Academic Therapy. Spring, 1976, p. 321-334.

Breslauer, Ann and Shaddock, Lee. *Rationale for Developmental Evaluation and Placement*. Colorado School (pamphlet). March 18, 1981, p. 1-6.

Brown, Barbara B. *Supermind*. Harper Row. New York, 1980

Butler, Sandra. *Conspiracy of Silence: The Trauma of Incest*. New Glide. San Francisco, 1978

Calderone, Mary S. and Eric W. Johnson. *The Family Book About Sexuality*. Harper Row. New York, 1981

Calloway, Dr. Doris H. and Carpenter, Kathleen O. *Nutrition and Health*. CBS Publishing Co. New York, 1981

Carrol, Bernard J. *Dexamethesone Suppression Test*. Arch. Gen. Psychiatry. Jan., 1981.

Cater, John I. and Phyllis M. Easton. *Separation and Other Stress in Child Abuse*. Lancet, May 3, 1980.

Cohen, Neville S. *Out of Sight into Vision*. Simon & Schuster. New York, 1977

Crow, Gary. *Children at Risk*. Schocken. New York, 1978

D'Ambrosio, Richard. *Leonora*. McGraw-Hill Book Company. New York, 1978

Daniels, Alejandro J., et al. *Human Genes for S-adenosylhomocysteine Hydrolase and Adenosine D*. Science, vol. 126, May 14, 1982.

DHEW Publication. *Selected Reading on Mother-Infant Bonding*. Supt. Documents. U.S. Govt. Printing Office. Washington, D.C., 1979

Deci, Edward L. *Psychology of Self-Determination*. Lexington Books. D.C. Heath & Co. Toronto, 1980

Delacato, Carl. *Diagnosis and Treatment of Speech and Reading Problems*. Thomas. Springfield, IL, 1963

Delacato, Carl. *A New Start for the Child with Reading Problems*. David McKay, New York, 1981

Delacato, Carl. *The Ultimate Stranger: The Autistic Child*. 1974

Deppe, Richard R. and Judith L. Sherman, with Sydelle Engel. *The High Risk Child: A Guide for Concerned Parents*. McMillan. New York, 1981

Deutsch, Diana. *A Musical Pitch for Left Handers*. Science. Feb. 3, 1978.

Dobson, Dr. James. *The Strong Willed Child*. Tyndale House Publishers, Inc. Wheaton, IL, 1978

Doman, Glenn. *How to Teach Your Baby to Read*. Doubleday. Garden City, N.Y., 1975

Doman, Glenn. *What to Do about your Brain Injured Child*. Doubleday. Garden City, N.Y., 1974

Eagle, Robert. *Eating and Allergy*. Doubleday. Garden City, N.Y., 1981

Edmunds, Francis L. Rudolf Steiner Education: *The Waldorf Impulse*. Rudolf Steiner Press. London, 1962

Elmer, Elizabeth. *Children in Jeopardy*. University of Pittsburg Press. Pittsburg, PA. 1967.

Feingold, Ben F. *Why Your Child is Hyperactive*. Random. New York, 1974

Fine, Reuben. *The Psychoanalytic Vision*. MacMillan. New York, 1980

Fisher, Seymour and Rhoda L. Fisher. *What We Really Know about Child Rearing*. Basic Books. New York, 1976

Forward, Susan and Craig Buck. *Betrayal of Innocence: Incest and its Devastation*. Penguin. New York, 1979

Fox, Robin. *The Red Lamp of Incest*. Dutton. New York, 1980

Fredericks, Carlton. *Low Blood Sugar & You*. Cancer Control Society. Los Angeles, CA 1979

Galaburda, Albert M. *Dyslexia: A Flaw in the Brain's Blueprints*. Science News, Nov. 3, 1979, p. 311.

Galton, Lawrence. *Why Johnny Can't Learn: A Surprising Answer*. Parade. December 10, 1978, p. 25.

Galton, Lawrence. *You May Not Need a Psychiatrist*. Simon & Schuster. New York, 1980

Gebhard, Paul H., John H. Gagnon, Wardell B. Pomeroy, et al. *Sex Offenders*. Harper Row. New York. 1965.

Gelles, Richard J. *Family Violence*. Sage Publications. Beverly Hills, CA 1979

Geschwind, Norman, *Lefthandedness Association with Immune Disease, Migraine and Developmental Learning Disorders*. Proceedings, National Acad. of Science Institute. Vol. 16:5097-100, August, 1979

Gesell, Arnold, Frances Ilg, Louise Bates Ames, Glenna Bulli. *The Child from Five to Ten*. Harper Bros. New York, 1946

Gesell, Arnold, et al. *Infant and Child in the Culture of Today*. Harper Row. New York, 1974 (revised ed.)

Gibbs, Jewelle Taylor. *Depression and Suicidal Behavior among Delinquent Females*. J. Youth and Adolescence. vol. 10, no. 2, 1981.

Gil, David G.*Violence Against Children*. Harvard Press. Cambridge, MA, 1970

Gil, David G. *Child Abuse and Violence*. AMS Press. New York, 1979

Gilling, Dick and Robin Brightwell, *The Human Brain*, Facts on file Pub., New York, 1982

Gold, Svea. *Learning Disabilities: What Librarians Need to Know*. American Libraries. Nov. 1980. pp. 616-619.

Goodwin, Joan; Simms, Mary and Bergman, Robert. *Hysterical Seizures: A Sequal to Incest*. American Journal Orthopsychiatry. 49 (4), October, 1979, p. 698 ff.

Green, Arthur H. *Self-destructive Behavior in Battered Children*. Am. J. Psychiatry, vol. 135, no. 5, Oct. 1978. pp. 579-582

Greenberg, J. *Genetic Link to Depression:* Experts Claim Immunity." Science News, Jan. 12, 1981. p. 356.

Greenberg, Joel. *What Happens to MBD Children*. Report from the Annual Meeting of the American Psy. Science News, May 20, 1978

Greenberg, Joel. *Stifling Hyperactive Children*. Science News, vol. 115, May 26, 1979.

Greenstein, Tole N. *Vision and Learning Disabilities*. American Optometric Association. St. Louis, MO, 1976

Greenberg, Joel. *Sudden Infant Death*. Science News, vol. 113, no. 15. April, 1978.

Gross, Meir. *Incestuous Rape: A Cause for Hysterical Seizures in Four Adolescents*. American Journal Orthopsychiat. Feb. 1979.

Harrison, Michelle. *A Woman in Residence*. Random House, Inc. New York, 1982

Harsanyi, Zsolt and Richard Hutton. *Genetic Prophecy: Beyond the Double Helix*. Rawson Wade Publ. New York, 1981

Held, Richard, et al. Readings from Scientific American: *Perception*. W.H. Freeman and Co. San Francisco, CA 1972

Herbert, Wray. *The Evolution of Child Abuse*. Science News, vol. 122. July 10, 1981, p. 24 — 26.

Herjanic, Barbara and Ronald P. Wilbois. *Sexual Abuse of Children*. Journal American Medical Assoc. Jan. 23, 1978. vol. 239, p. 331-333.

Herman, Judith Lewis. *Father-Daughter Incest*. Harvard Univ. Press. Cambridge, MA and London, 1981

Hirsch, Miriam F. *Women and Violence*. Van Nostrand Reinhold Co. New York, 1981

Holden, Constance. *The Criminal Mind: A New Look at an Old Puzzle*. Science, vol. 199. Feb. 3, 1978. pp. 579-587.

Hunter, Rosemary S. and Kilstron, Nancy. *Breaking the Cycle in Abusive Families*. Am. J. Psychiatry, vol. 136, no. 10, Oct., 1979. p. 1320.

Ilg, Frances L., Louise Bates Ames and Sidney M. Baker. *Child Behavior*. Rev. Ed. Harper & Row. New York, 1975

Ingles, Ruth. *Sins of the Fathers*. Saint Martin's Press. New York, 1978

International Institute of Yoga. *Freedom from Stress: A Wholistic Approach*. Science and Philosophy Publish. 1980

Janov, Arthur. *The Feeling Child*. Touchstone Book, Simon & Schuster. New York, 1973

Janus, Sam. *The Death of Innocence*. William Morrow & Co. New York, 1981

Jaynes, Julian. *The Origin of Consciousness in the Breakdown of the Bicamara*. Houghton/Miflin. New York, 1977

Jones, Sandy. *To Love a Baby*. Houghton/Miflin. Boston, 1981

Justice, Blair and Rita Blair. *The Abusing Family*. Human Sciences Press. New York. 1976.

Kalokerinos, Archie, *Every Second Child*, Keats Publishing, (Thomas Nelson, Australia, 1974), 1981

Kandel, Eric R. and James H. Schwartz, *Principles of Neural Science*, Elsevier North Holland, Inc., New York, Amsterdam, Oxford, 1981

Kegan, Robert. *The Evolving Self*. Harvard Univ. Press. Cambridge, MA and London, 1882

Kempe, C. Henry and Rae Helfer. *The Battered Child*, 3d Rev. University of Chicago Press. Chicago, IL. 1974.

Kent, Ernest W. *The Brains of Men and Machines*. Byte/McGraw Hill. New York, 1980

Kimble, Daniel P. *Psychology as a Biological Science*. Goodyear Publ. Co. Pacific Palisades, CA 1973

Klaus, Marshall H. and John H. Kennell, *Bonding: The Beginnings of Parent-Infant Attachment*, A Plume Book, New American Library, New York, 1983

Knoblock, Hilda and Benjamin Pasamanick. *Gesell and Amatruda's Developmental Diagnosis*. Harper & Row. Hagerstown, MD 1974 (3d ed.)

Kratoville, Betty Lou, ed. *Youth in Trouble*. Academic Therapy Publications. Novato, CA, 1974

Krucoff, Carol. *Style of Walking May Invite Assault*. Washington Post/Eugene Register-Guard, Dec. 17, 1980.

Kunin, Richard A. *Mega-Nutrition*. Cancer Control Soc. Los Angeles, CA, 1980

Kuntzleman, Charles T. *Maximum Personal Energy*. Rodale Press. Emmaus, PA. 1981.

Langmeier L. and L. Matejcek. *Psychological Deprivation in Childhood*, 3d Ed.. John Wiley & Sons. New York. 1975.

Latimer, Dean and Jeff Goldberg. *Flowers in the Blood: The Story of Opium*. Franklin Watts. New York. 1981.

Levinson, Harold N. *A Solution to the Riddle of Dyslexia*. Springer Verlag. New York, Heidelberg, Berlin. 1980.

Leventhal, J. M. *Risk Factors for Child Abuse*. Pediatrics, vol. 68, no. 5, Nov., 1981. pp. 684-690.

Lewis, M. and L. A. Rosenblum. *The Effect of the Infant on its Caretaker*. J. B. Lippincott. Philadelphia, PA. 1974.

Mack, Allison. *Toilet Learning*. Little. Boston. 1978.

Mandell, Marshall and Lynne W. Scanlon. *Dr. Mandell's Five Day Allergy Relief System*. T. Y. Crowell. N. Y. 1979.

Marsh, Thomas O. *Roots of Crime:* A Biophysical Approach to Crime Prevention. Nellen Publishing Co. P.O. Box 18, Newton, NJ. 1981.

Martin, Harold P. *The Abused Child: A Multidisciplinary Approach*. Ballinger. Cambridge, Mass. 1976.

Marcus, Maria. *A Taste for Pain*. St. Martin's Press. N.Y. 1981.

McGaughm, James L. *Adrenalin: A Secret Agent in Memory*. Psychology Today, Dec. 1980. p. 132.

McGury, Ellen T. *Adlerian Approach to Intervention in Incestuous Families*. Individual Psychology Reporter, Publication of the Americas Institute of Adlerian Studies. Vol. 3, No. 1, Fall, 1984, p.1

McKean, Kevin. *Beaming New Light on the Brain*. Discover. Dec. 1981. pp.30-33.

Meeting in Atlanta of the Soc. for Neuroscience. *Paths Through the Brain Blood Barrier*. Science News.

Mental Retardation News. *Results of Sensorimotor Training Study*. Mental Retardation News, vol. 22, no. 3, p. 3f. June, 1973.

Michaels, Marguerite. *Why So Many Young People Die in Our Jails*. Parade, May 23, 1982, pp. 4-7.

Miller, Jonathan, *The Body in Question*, Random House, New York, 1978

Miller, Julie Ann. *Vision's Brain*. Science News. vol.144, no.22, p. 372f.

Napear, Peggy. *Brainchild, a Mother's Diary*. Harper Row. New York.

Neale, John M.; Gerald Davison and Kenneth P. Price. *Contemporary Readings in Psychopathology*. John Wiley and Sons. New York, London, Sidney, Toronto. 1974.

Nelson, Marie Coleman and Jean Ikenberry, Eds. *Psychosexual Imperatives: Their Role in Identity Formation.* Human Sciences Press. New York, London. 1979.

Novitski, Edward. *Human Genetics.* 2d e., Macmillan Publ., New York, 1982

Nuernberger, Phil. *Freedom from Stress:* A Wholistic Approach. Himalayan International Instit. Honesdale, PA. 1981.

O'Conner, S; Vietze, P. M., et al. *Reduced Incidence of Parenting Inadequacy Following Rooming In.* Pediatrics, vol. 66, no. 2, August, 1980. pp. 176-182.

Offer, Daniel; Richard C. Marhohn; Eric Ostrov. Psychological World of the Juvenile Delinquent. Basic Books. New York. 1981.

Oregon Children's Services Division. Child Abuse in Oregon. Oregon Protective Services. Salem, OR. 1979.

Pearce, Joseph Chilton. The Magical Child: Rediscovering Nature's Plan for our Child. E.P. Dutton. New York. 1977.

Pelletier, Kenneth R. Holistic Medicine: From Stress to Optimum Health. Delacorte Press. New York. 1979.

Pfeiffer, Carl C. Mental and Elemental Nutrients. Keats. New Canaan, CT. 1976.

Philpott, William and Dwight K. Kalita. Brain Allergies: The Psychonutrient Connection. Keats Publishing. New Canaan, CT.

Piaget, Jean. The Child and Reality: Problems of Genetic Psychology. Beekman Pubs. Woodstock, N.Y. 1973.

Pietsch, Paul. Shufflebrain. Houghton Mifflin. Boston. 1981. Pirro, Ugo. Mio Figlio non sa Leggere (My Son Cannot Read). Rizzoli. Milano, Italy. 1981.

Ramos, Nancy P., Ed. Delinquent Youth and Learning Disabilities. Academic Therapy Publication. San Rafael, CA. 1978.

Rapp, Doris J. Allergies and the Hyperactive Child. Cornerstone Library. New York. 1979.

Rist, Kate. *Incest: Theoretical and Clinical Views.* American Journal Orthopsychiat. 49 (4) October 1979, p. 680 ff.

Rist, Mary. *Incest: Theoretical and Clinical Views.* Am. J. Orthopsychiatry. March, 1979.

Rosenblatt, Seymour and Reynolds, Dodson. Beyond Valium. G. P. Putnam's Sons. New York. 1981.

Rush, Florence. The Best Kept Secret: Sexual Abuse of Children. Prentice Hall. Englewood Cliffs, N.J. 1980.

Sagan, Carl. The Dragons of Eden. Random House. New York. 1977.

Sanford, Linda Tschirhart. The Silent Children. Anchor Press. Garden City, N.Y. 1980.

Schauss, Alexander. Diet, Crime and Delinquency. Parker House. Berkeley, CA. 1981.

Schauss, Alexander G. Orthomolecular Treatment of Criminal Offenders. Michael X. Lesser. Berkeley, CA. 1978.

Schauss, Alexander G. and Simon Cifford. *A Critical Analysis of the Diets of Chronic Juvenile Offenders.* Orthomolecular Psychiatry, vol. 8, no. 3, 1979. pp. 149-157.

Schlesser, M. ; Winokur, G.; Sherman, B.M. "Hypothalamic Pituitary Adrenal Axis Activity in Depressed Illness. Arch. Gen. Psychiatry, vol. 37, p.737-743. July, 1980.

Schoettle, Ulruch C. *Treatment of the Child Pornography Patient.* Am. J. Psychiatry. Sept., 1980. p. 9.

Schulterbrandt, Joy G. and Allen Raskin. Depression in Childhood: Diagnosis, Treatment & Conceptual Mo. Raven Press. New York. 1977.

Science News. *The Machinery of Depression.* Science News, vol. 118, 1982, p. 86.

Science News. "Iron Studies that Fool." Science News. vol. 119, April 19

Science News. "Serotonin: A Natural Anti-depressant." Science News. April 10, 1982. p. 251.

Science News. *Genetic Depression and Viral Schizophrenia.* Science News. vol. 114, no. 15, Oct. 7, 197??. p. 244.

Science News. *Autism, an Intensive Approach.* Science News, vol. 118, p. 184.

Science News. *ncest and 'Vulnerable' Children.* Science News. vol. 116, Oct. 13, 1979.

Science News. *A 'Plastic' Cure for the Mind's Eye.* Science News, vol. 113, no. 15. Apr. 15, 1975. p. 228-229.

Science News. *Tracking the Chemistry of Depression.* Science News, Apr. 19, 1980. p. 247, 250.

Science News. "Lighting the Brain's Visual Path." Science News, vol. 14, p. 324f. November 11, 1978.

Science News. *Vitamin B6 Helps Autistic Children.* Science News. May 13, 1978.

Scientific American. The Nature and Nurture of Behavior: Developmental Psychobiol. W. H. Freeman. San Francisco. 1973.

Scientific American. Recent Progress in Perception. W. H. Freeman and Co. San Francisco. 1976.

Scientific American. Perception: Mechanism and Models. W. H. Freeman. San Francisco. 1971.

Simonds, John F. and Kashani, David. *Drug Abuse and Criminal Behavior in Delinquent Boys Committed.* Am. J. Psychiatry. 136 (11) Nov. 1979. p. 1444-1446.

Smith, Lendon H. Improving the Behavior Chemistry of your Child. Prentice Hall. Engelwood Cliffs, N.J. 1976.

Smith, Lendon H. Feed Your Kids Right. McGraw Hill. New York. 1979.

Smith, Lendon H. The Encyclopedia of Baby and Child Care, Rev. Ed. Prentice Hall. Englewood Cliffs, N.J. 1981.

Smith, Lendon H. Foods for Healthy Kids. McGraw. N.Y. 1981.

Smith, Michelle and Lawrence Pazder. Michelle Remembers. Congdon & Lattes, Inc. New York. 1982.

Stark, Elizabeth. *The Unspeakable Family Secret.* Psychology Today, May, 1984, p. 42

Steele, Brandt F. Working with Abusive Parents. U.S. Dept. H.E.W. Ctr on Child. Washington, D.C. 1978.

Steinmetz, Suzanne K. and Murray Strauss. Violence in the Family. Harper and Row. New York. 1974.

Stone, Irwin. The Healing Factor: 'Vitamin C' Against Disease. Grosset and Dunlap. New York. 1972.

Swan, Raymond. *The Child as Active Participant in Sexual Abuse*, vol. 13, no. 1, Spring, 1985, Clinical Social Work Journal, p.62-77

Swanson, Lisa M. S. and Mary K. Biaggio. *Therapeutic Perspectives on Father-Daughter Incest. Amer. J. Psychiatry, vol. 142:6, June, 1985, p.667

Tannock, Rosemary. *Doman-Delacato Method for Treating Brain Injured Children*. Physiotherapy, Canada, vol. 28, no. 4, Oct. 1976.

Tarnolpol, Lester and Muriel Tarnopol. *Comparative Reading and Learning Difficulties*. Lexington Books. Lexington, Mass. 1981.

Tileli, John A.; Turek, Diane; Jaffe, Arthur C. *Sexual Abuse of Children*. New England Journal of Medicine. Feb. 7, 1980, p. 319-323.

Tobias, Ronald. *They Shoot to Kill*. Paladin Press. Boulder, Colorado. 1981.

Trotter, R.J. *Fathers and Daughters: The Broken Bond*. Psychology Today, March, 1985, p. 10 Yearbook, 1897. New York State Reformatory, Elmira, New York, 1898

U.S. Dept. H.E.W. *1978 Annual Review of Child Abuse and Neglect.*Natl. Center on Child Abuse & , Washington, D.C. 1979.

U.S. Dept. H.E.W. National Center on Child Abuse and Neglect. *Child Abuse and Developmental Disabilities*. Government Printing Office. Washington, D.C. Nov., 1979.

U.S. Dept. of H.E.W. *Child Abuse and Developmental Disabilities*. DHEW Publication –79-3022, Feb., 1980. p. 45.

U.S. Dept. Health and Human Services. *Sexual Abuse of Children*. Supt. of Documents, U.S. Govt. Washington, D.C., November, 1981.

University of Oregon College of Education. *The Brain: Recent Research and its Educational Implications*. Univ. of Ore. College of Educa, Eugene, Oregon, 1982.

Vellutino, Frank R. Dyslexia: Theory and Research. MIT Press. Cambridge, Mass. 1979.

Verny, Thomas. *The Secret Life of the Unborn Child*. Summit Books. New York. 1980.

Von Hilsheimer, George. *Allergy, Toxins and the Learning Disabled Child*. Academic Therapy Pubs. Novato, CA. 1974.

Von Hilsheimer, George. *Understanding Young People in Trouble*. Acropolis. Washington, D.C. 1974.

Von Ruden Rodgers, Dorothy. *On Being and Becoming*. New Creation Publications, 24 School St., Randolf, Vermont.

Weiss, Bernard and Victor G. Laies. *Behavioral Toxology*. Plenum Press. New York and London. 1975

Wilson, John Rowan. *The Mind*. Time Life Books. Alexandria, Virginia. 1980.

Winick, Myron. *Nutrition and Brain Development*. Natural History, December, 1980, p. 6f.

Wooden, Kenneth. Weeping in the Playtime of Others. McGraw Hill. New York. 1976.

Wunderlich, Ray C. and Dwight J. Kalita Ph.D., *Candida Albicans.*Keats Publishing Company, 27 Pine Street, New Canaan, CT 06840, 1984

Wunderlich, Ray C., *Nourishing Your Child,* Keats Publishing Company, New Canaan, CT, 1984

Wunderlich, Ray C. Allergy, Brains and Children Coping. Johnny Reads. St. Petersburg, FL. 1973.

Wunderlich, Ray C. *Successful Treatment of Allergy in a Twelve Year Old Girl*. Academic Therapy, vol. 13, no. 5, May, 1978. pp. 511-514.

Wunderlich, Ray C. Kids, Brains and Learning. Johnny Reads. St. Petersburg, FL. 1970.

1897 Yearbook. New York State Reformatory. Elmira, New York. 1898

1898 Yearbook. New York State Reformatory. Elmira, New York. 1898

Biographies

In 1979, Svea J. Gold (MLS) produced a series of television shows for the Eugene Public Library under the auspices of the Department of Health and Welfare. This series provided parents with information that might keep them from abusing their children. This book in a sense is the continuation of that series, using the skill and knowledge of these consultants — authors in their own right — to help solve the problem of the seemingly increasing incidence of child abuse. They have provided specific ideas in their field of expertise, checked the area of their concern for errors, and have contributed some sections:

Louise Bates Ames (Ph.D)...whose research into the normal phases of child development and books on child rearing have changed the entire concept of child raising for all future generations...is one of the directors of the Gesell Institute for Human Development.

Carl H. Delacato (Dr.Ed.)...who with Glenn Doman has pioneered new forms of therapy for brain-injured children, has also been responsible for major breakthroughs in curing dyslexia and in the treatment of autistic children...he is the director of Delacato and Delacato Consultants in Learning and the Robert Doman and Carl Delacato Autistic Unit in Morton, PA.

Alexander G. Schauss (M.A.)...an internationally known criminologist, has opened the doors to understanding and treating criminal offenders by looking at the biochemical causes that influence behavior...is the director of the American Institute for Biosocial Research in Tacoma, Washington.

Florence Scott (R.N.)...formerly director of the out-patient clinic at the Institutes for the Achievement of Human Potential in Philadelphia, and who has been credited by Glenn Doman with being instrumental in developing the Doman-Delacato Developmental Profile...is the director of "Oregon Hope and Help" in Woodburn, Oregon.

Dr. Lendon H. Smith (M.D.)...Pediatrician, nutritionist and comedian par excellence, has written several best sellers, including "Feed Your Kids Right," and "Feed Yourself Right"... He practices in Portland, Oregon.

Dr. Ray C. Wunderlich, Jr. (M.D.)...who has been deeply involved in making teachers and doctors aware of a wholistic approach to curing childhood problems...is the author among other books of "Allergies, Brains and Children Learning" and more recently "Candida Albicans" and "Nutrition and your child." He specializes in preventive pediatrics in St. Petersburg, Florida.

Index

— N O T E S —

— N O T E S —

—NOTES—

— N O T E S —

— N O T E S —

—NOTES—